Policy, Leadership, and Student Achievement

Implications for Urban Communities

A volume in
The Achievement Gap, Research, Practice, and Policy
C. Kent McGuire and Vivian W. Ikpa, *Series Editors*

Policy, Leadership, and Student Achievement

Implications for Urban Communities

Edited by

C. Kent McGuire
Temple University

Vivian W. Ikpa
Temple University

INFORMATION AGE PUBLISHING, INC.
Charlotte, NC • www.infoagepub.com

Library of Congress Cataloging-in-Publication Data

Policy, leadership, and student achievement : implications for urban
communities / edited by C. Kent McGuire, Vivian W. Ikpa.
    p. cm. – (The achievement gap, research, practice, and policy)
  Includes bibliographical references.
  ISBN 978-1-59311-973-7 (pbk.) – ISBN 978-1-59311-974-4 (hardcover)
1. Education, Urban–United States. 2. School improvement
programs–United States. 3. Academic achievement–United States. I.
McGuire, C. Kent. II. Ikpa, Vivian W.
  LC5131.P65 2008
  370.9173'2–dc22

                                      2008027248

Printed in the United States of America

CONTENTS

■ P A R T 1 ■

URBAN CHALLENGES:
LEADERSHIP STRUCTURES AND GOVERNANCE

■ P A R T 2 ■

THE HIGHER EDUCATION CONTEXT
AND STUDENT PERFORMANCE

■ P A R T   3 ■

SPECIAL POPULATIONS AND STUDENT ACHIEVEMENT

■ P A R T   4 ■

EDUCATION POLICY, REFORM, AND STUDENT PERFORMANCE

■ P A R T   5 ■
THE K–12 URBAN CONTEXT:
IMPROVING STUDENT ACHIEVEMENT

SERIES EDITORS' INTRODUCTION AND SUMMARY

C. Kent McGuire and Vivian Ikpa

This is the first book in the series examining student achievement. The chapters in this book reflect the scholarly papers presented at the July 2006 Education Policy, Leadership Summer Institute (EPLSI) by K–16 educators, researchers, community advocates, and policymakers who work in urban communities. The Institute serves as a place where individuals interested in scholarly discussions and research directly related to: (1) how data can be utilized to inform policy; (2) examining the urban school context from the perspectives of the polity, school leaders; students; and other related internal and external actors; and (3) identifying strategies for improving student academic achievement can gather. During this week-long Institute, participants examined the structural problems and policy tensions affecting urban communities and student achievement. The Institute's theme, Meeting the Challenges of Urban Schools is reflected throughout this book. Specifically, this edition explores the interrelated aspects of policy, practice and research and how they affect academic achievement.

The five sections in this book examine different challenges facing urban schools and their impact on student performance.

Policy, Leadership, and Student Achievement, pages ix–xvii
Copyright © 2008 by Information Age Publishing

PART 1
URBAN CHALLENGES: LEADERSHIP STRUCTURES
AND GOVERNANCE

In Chapter 1, *Meeting the Challenges of Urban Communities: Funding School Districts*, McGuire contends that policymakers and educators are confronted with financial challenges that affect measures of economic well being and the life chances of urban children. In an effort to improve student achievement, those in leadership and decision making positions must constantly address the structural complexities and challenges enveloping an increasingly diverse society. He notes that there are structural features in funding systems that severely affect one's ability to meet students' needs. The author notes that adequacy as related to the allocation and distribution of resources is a public value that society embraces; however, the disparities in funding poor and more affluent school districts continue to present a challenge to those who must negotiate the decaying infrastructures pervading urban cities and schools. McGuire also claims that inadequate financial support serves to increase the social, economic, and academic achievement gaps between urban and non-urban schools. He asserts that in order to secure funding, those individuals in leadership positions in urban districts must be able to understand and negotiate the dynamics of an increasingly conservative political economy as they develop relationships with potential donors. He concludes that those who govern urban schools may need to consider the benefits of developing broader based corporate—local school district partnerships in addressing funding gaps.

In Chapter 2, *Which School Leadership Structures Generate Successes in Restructured Districts,* Hoff asserts that many urban school systems have been empowered by their states. When this occurs, a leadership structure is developed to run the school district. He contends that no single model has created a successful urban school district. This chapter defines the problems with empowerment, what constitutes success in an urban school setting, and discusses the existing state takeover models and the stakeholders that affect the success of schools. Hoff examines the failure of school districts in terms of financial support, student achievement, graduation rates, and infrastructure. The author believes that urban communities have unique needs as reflected in the diverse demographics and sociopolitical underpinnings. Hoff discusses who has power and control as related to public education and discusses who should be in charge. He addresses his concerns from the perspectives of various interest groups, parents, state legislatures, governors, mayors, school boards, and for-profit schools. He concluded that all of these external and internal actors will play a role in the success or failure of state takeovers.

In Chapter 3, *A Research-Based Profession Is Needed to Meet the Challenge of Urban Schools,* Gates argues that in an era of accountability and high-stakes testing, the words of President Kennedy, "A rising tide lifts all boats," would seem to have particular appeal. Originally used to address economic matters, the aphorism in an educational context suggests that universal educational reform will benefit all students. This would seem to be the logic upon which No Child Left Behind is predicated. While such a conclusion is appealing, it should be noted that the axiom is based upon the assumption that all boats are seaworthy. Considering the disparity of student achievement acknowledged along ethnic lines, it would appear that in reality, not all students may benefit equally. Gates believes it is doubtful that there is a simple panacea to ameliorate this significant and complex problem; however, an educational profession that is driven by research may offer effective solutions. The author offers suggestions and instructional strategies that have been proven successful in improving academic performance in K–12 settings. As Gates notes, educators in leadership positions should utilize research findings more extensively to inform policy and improve student achievement

PART 2
THE HIGHER EDUCATION CONTEXT
AND ACADEMIC PERFORMANCE

In Chapter 4, *Professional Identity Formation: Socialization and mentoring of Pre-Service Teachers in Urban Communities,* Obi challenges colleges and universities to reconsider how teachers are trained to teach in urban communities. She argues that emotional support and acceptance by members of learning communities; mentors and students alike, are crucial to the intern's self-development and fulfillment of self-acceptance. This chapter examines how interns involved in field experience, in their initial teacher preparation, acquire knowledge of the teaching profession, and its impact on professional identity formation. Data collected from interns attending an urban university were qualitatively analyzed. The intern's identity encompasses a sense of mastery of knowledge, skills and disposition of the profession; it implies a genuine readiness to face the global challenges of teaching. This study explores identity elements and experiences surrounding the interns' perceptions of acceptance into the profession of teaching. The findings from her study yielded information that will be beneficial in the education of our teachers, particularly those who are being prepared to work in urban schools. She believes that there should be clear articulation by the colleges and the public schools as to the requirements for the experience. She further argues that exposing pre-service teachers to ethnic minorities, cultural diversity, diverse learners, and urban communities is essential to forming a realistic and healthy professional identity.

Campbell shares the results from a qualitative study of Caribbean students' experiences and perspectives on adjusting to life and negotiating urban communities. In Chapter 5, *Caribbean Students' Adjustment to College: Implications for Higher Education Policy,* the author argues that colleges and universities need to develop and implement policies that are culturally responsive in serving the academic needs of students. As he notes, the goal of academic institutions should be to provide nurturing environments. He asserts that with more and more international students attending higher education institutions in the United States, colleges and universities should identify innovative programs that will address the needs of an ever-changing student population. This study focused on the Caribbean population as one of the international groups that make up a significant percentage of international students. The investigation-analyzed students' points of view that gave voice and allowed them to share their experiences and views on issues around their college adjustment. Moreover, the chapter examines the university's commitment to being culturally responsive in an era where diversity and acceptance are on the agenda of every institution. The results of the study provided insights and a better awareness of Caribbean students' college experiences as told by the students themselves. Students' experiences can provide new understanding for those in higher education and may help influence policy.

In Chapter 6, *Addressing the Needs of Hispanic Students in K–16 Settings,* Perez contends that since Hispanics are one of the nation's fastest-growing populations, demographic changes in schools and the general population should concern all policymakers. She believes that Hispanic students are not obtaining the intellectual knowledge, expertise, and language proficiency needed to secure the social and economic benefits that are associated with a college degree. The author asserts that in order to understand the issues that prevent educational success, a review of factors that prevent educational success such as academic difficulty, language, and finance should be examined. Additionally, she asserts that information regarding the new approaches to teaching should be devised and implemented. Based on the literature, research revealed that efforts to understand Hispanic students' cultural values could be used to develop programs that promote retention and success of minority students in schools and higher education.

PART 3
SPECIAL POPULATIONS AND STUDENT ACHIEVEMENT

In Chapter 7, *Meeting the Academic Needs of Urban Populations: Homeless Families and Students,* Matthews argues that urban communities are suffering because of a lack of funding of the Education Assistance Act and the No Child Left Behind Act. She contends that both of these regulatory policies lack the structure and implementation needed to address the needs of homeless populations. The author further states that as the number of homeless families increases, the allocation of funding from the federal government continues to shrink. She views this as a structural issue facing urban communities and one that it is not being addressed by policymakers. As a result, she believes that students in urban communities are not gaining access to a quality education. The author goes on to explore the policy context and the policy tensions associated with various interest groups.

In Chapter 8, *Wordsworth Academy: Adapting Educational Reform to the Private Alternative Setting,* Cadenhead asserts that educational reform must include every type of school. He contends that schools must be given the autonomy to develop and implement practices that are research based. He uses Wordsworth Academy Alternate School to support his views. The author agrees with Gates that schools need to use research models more extensively in making policy decisions. Cadenhead further states that if meeting the needs of the student population is the real goal, then reform will be best accomplished by success at the level of the individual school. The author offers a research-based guided tour through the various reform eras. He uses his rich leadership experiences in urban communities to conceptualize the educational reform policy context.

In Chapter 9, *Student Achievement and School Reform in an Urban School District,* Ikpa gives context to the race/ethnic achievement gap by examining resistance to school integration and the application of the doctrine of "separate but equal" to public schooling. The author argues that one of the earliest challenges to segregated schooling and the achievement gap can be traced to an African American community in 18th century Boston, Massachusetts and notes that after the American Revolution, the city of Boston developed the first urban school district in the nation. She describes current trends in the mathematics and science achievement gaps between European American and African American students in an urban school district.

In Chapter 10, *African Americans and Student Achievement: Assessing the P.A.T.H.S. Program,* Bowen-Lipscomb investigated the effects of participating in the P.A.T.H.S. (Providing Alternative Thinking Strategies) program on the academic achievement of third grade at-risk students in The Harrisburg, Pennsylvania City School District, an empowered school district. The purpose of this study was to ascertain whether there was an effect on the sampled 208 third grade at-risk urban students standardized academic test scores in reading and mathematics from their participation and exposure to the PATHS curriculum. Findings revealed that there was no significant evidence of the PATHS program having an effect on the standardized reading test scores of 3rd grade at-risk students. Thus, the findings did not find evidence of the effectiveness of the PATHS program on students reading and math test scores. Bowen-Lipscomb argues that this study provides the school district with some real opportunities for positive change in terms of school district policy initiatives, programs, projects, and research studies.

PART 4
EDUCATION POLICY, REFORM,
AND STUDENT PERFORMANCE

Supplemental Educational Services in Pennsylvania: Policy Perspectives, Effects and Challenges at the Local, State and Federal Level are discussed in Chapter 11. Pinckney examines the implementation and success of the Supplemental Educational Services (SES) provision of the No Child Left Behind Act of 2001 (NCLB) in Pennsylvania. After a discussion of theoretical frameworks, inherent policy tensions and policy effects, a discussion of Pennsylvania's implementation of the federal policy and its results is presented. The author's review of federal education policy is included and contrasted with current levels of involvement and policy approaches. Recommendations for needed changes to the NCLB-SES policy are also reviewed and considered. Pinckney examines the implementation and externalities associated with the SES provision of the No Child Left Behind Act of 2001 (NCLB) in Pennsylvania. Pinckney believes that the SES provision of the NCLB Act has had some benefits in the state of Pennsylvania, resulting from efforts of local and state level policymakers, administrator, and educators.

Johnson, identifies another challenge to urban communities in Chapter 12, *Alternative Certification: Does it Lend Itself as a Form of Viable Policy As a Factor in Teacher Preparation and Certification?* She suggests that in the United States, opposition to alternative teacher certification has ranged from teacher unions to associations representing college and university teacher educators. However, even in the light of being belittled and sometimes praised, by 1993 forty-one states instituted alternative certification programs for individuals who hold degrees and want to teach. The purpose of this chapter is to examine aspects of education policy involving traditional certification, and comparing those aspects to how present policies in regard to alternative teacher certification influenced different aspects of teacher education pertaining to the overall teacher certification process. Johnson discusses a conceptual framework of change components and elements relating to how information that concerns policy can be transferred and delivered. The change components and elements discussed in this chapter assisted in showing how information about policy can be interpreted, and how individuals perceive the influences of policy concerning teacher education and practice as they relate to the overall teacher preparation and certification process. The author further examines how alternative certification evolved, and why policymakers saw a need for such a certification. As Johnson notes, the terms alternative certification, alternate routes (paths), and alternative programs are used interchangeably. All of these terms imply a different way of obtaining a teacher certification other than the traditional way.

In Chapter 13, *Deconstructing Special and Gifted Education Policy and Practice: A Paradigm of Ethical Leadership in Residentially Segregated Schools and Communities,* Williams contends that the success of gifted and special education programs appear radically different as they are implemented for students who live in low income, urban areas as compared to middle-class to affluent suburban public school contexts. The success or failures of these gifted and special education programs experienced by administrators and supervisors who oversee them can be linked to the social-cultural environment. Furthermore, he asserts that contemporary education research on school reform and school choice has found that residentially segregated communities have a negative effect on school reform and various student programs. As a result, on a national level, low income, ethnically and linguistically diverse students are underrepresented in gifted programs and African Americans are overrepresented in special education programs. He believes that one way to address these issues is through developing a critical sociocultural lens for school leaders and administrators who oversee these programs. This chapter examines the impact that residentially segregated communities have on their schools gifted and special education programs and their students. The author states that failure on the part of administrators and school leaders to identify and address the critical needs and concerns of their school-community further widens the achievement gap and increases levels of inequity. Suggestions for closing the achievement gap that exist among identified students within these programs are proposed at the administrative level through the application of a critical lens that employs ethical leadership coupled with theories of social justice.

PART 5
THE URBAN CONTEXT: IMPROVING STUDENT ACHIEVEMENT

In Chapter 14, *Five Years: From Despair to Hope,* Anticoli discusses how the for-profit educational management organization, Edison Schools, Inc., partnered with the Philadelphia School District to improve student achievement. The author notes that Edison, Inc, became the management partner for 20 public schools in the school district of Philadelphia in August 2002. As he reports, this was part of a larger reform project initiated by Pennsylvania Governor, Tom Ridge. The author presents data from an urban school within the district indicating that student performance improved significantly in reading and mathematic for African Americans and Latinos under the Edison group.

In Chapter 15, *Building Capacity and Raising Awareness: Implementing NCLB and its impact on World Languages,* Torres suggests that a comprehensive foreign language experience is needed in public schools. He notes that many school districts begin foreign language instruction at the high school or middle school level; however, it should be implemented earlier. The author proposes a capacity building policy that will give all students access to foreign language courses. He also believes that under current policies, teachers and school leaders are feeling frustrated and that capacity building strategies must be in place across the system in order to address the confusion some educators experience. He argues that this is especially true when we begin to develop programs in order to meet the intended policy's goal, while unintentionally abandoning programs that students genuinely enjoy. The author states that participation in ELES provides students the academic and economic skills needed for success and this empowers both children and urban communities.

In Chapter 16, *Motivating Students Through Meaningful Assessment,* Zaring, notes that high stakes testing has led to the labeling of many urban students. She contends that one way of improving a student's level of motivation is to create a report card that accurately reports student achievement. She believes that students are frustrated with typical grading procedures and report cards because each teacher has a distinct way of determining grades. Thus, similar grades represent different levels of student achievement. Typical report cards provide students and parents only with percentage grades, thus reporting a very limited picture of student performance. The author states that a single number, calculated by combining several aspects of classroom performance such as homework completion, attendance, classroom participation, and project and test grades, does not accurately report a student's progress. She believes that it is difficult, for anyone to qualify levels of student motivation. Overtime, revising report cards to allow for a more meaningful measure of student performance will improve achievement.

In Chapter 17, *Universal Pre-Kindergarten as a Basis of Urban Educational Reform,* Kratzer contends that pre kindergarten programs have been successful in meeting the needs of African American, Hispanic and low-income children. He believes that such programs are essential to reducing the achievement gap. Kratzer argues that urban education would be better served by a governmentally mandated program offering universal pre-kindergarten in urban environments ("urbanversal"), addressing the achievement gap of low-income and minority learners in these settings. According to the author, this long-term plan for urban reform will require an in-depth examination of the current political climate, American ideology, and evaluation of our public values. He claims that Americans look for short-term solutions to long-term problems and that we need immediate, measurable results to justify creating and/or re-authorizing any policy.

ACKNOWLEDGMENTS

The authors express sincere gratitude to those who contributed to this book.

PART 1

URBAN CHALLENGES:
LEADERSHIP STRUCTURES AND GOVERNANCE

CHAPTER 1

MEETING THE CHALLENGES OF URBAN COMMUNITIES

Funding School Districts

C. Kent McGuire

Urban school districts serve large numbers of children living at or below the poverty level. These schools, like many other social institutions located in urban communities are overburdened and severely underfunded. Many individuals in these distressed districts, characterized by overcrowded classrooms, outdated resources, and limited funding, face day-to-day challenges that force them to develop and implement creative survival techniques. In an effort to improve student achievement, those in leadership and decision making positions must constantly address the complexities and challenges enveloping increasingly diverse and global urban communities. There are also structural features in funding systems that severely affect one's ability to meet students' needs. Policymakers and educators are confronted with financial challenges that affect measures of economic well being and limit life chances of urban children. Unfortunately, politicians, community leaders and other stakeholders are frequently engaged in political battles that give rise to disjointed decisions that do little to eradicate these structural

Policy, Leadership, and Student Achievement, pages 3–15
Copyright © 2008 by Information Age Publishing

obstacles. Those who govern financially bankrupt urban districts constantly complain about inadequate financial support (rightly so).

Adequacy as related to the allocation and distribution of resources is a public value that society embraces; however, the disparities in funding poor and more affluent school districts continue to present challenges to those who must negotiate the decaying infrastructures pervading urban cities and schools. Although school districts receive revenue from local funding sources, the state, as well as federal aid, funding is frequently inadequate in terms of building the capacity to meet the needs of students. Most local governments depend on property taxes and to a lesser extent income and sales taxes to generate revenue. However, public dissatisfaction with proposed tax increases often limits the power of elected officials to increase property taxes. As Mayraj Fahim (2005) noted:

> The fiscal challenges of American cities are structural. This is because local sources alone are insufficient and local government is further being burdened by unfounded mandates—that is, orders imposed by higher levels of government do not match with the financial support needed to implement such orders. (p. 1)

Inadequate funding serves to increase the social, economic, and academic achievement gaps between urban and non-urban schools. In a survey of 328 United States Cities, the National League of Cities (2003) found that spending exceeded revenue increases for the 2002–03 fiscal year by 3.1% when compared to the previous year. The study also indicated that the *expenditures—revenue gap* was directly related to rising employee health care costs, increasing pension costs, decreases in sales, income and tourist tax revenues. Additionally, many believe that reduced state funding, and increased spending for public safety and homeland security contributed to this widening financial gap. The respondents also state that the following factors prevented them from addressing the needs of the city: health care costs for city employees (63%) costs associated with employee pension plans (30%); decrease in state aid (29%); a weak economy local economy (25%); and infrastructure demands (25%) (Pagano, 2003).

DEMOGRAPHIC SHIFTS

Demographic shifts and global forces continue to affect the development and implementation of market-driven education policies and practices. Data from the National Center for Education Statistics (2007) indicated that in 2005, minority groups comprised 33% of the nation's population. Findings also revealed that as a percentage of the total population, Hispanics represent 14%, Blacks, 12%, Asians/Pacific Islanders 4%, and American Indians/Alaskan Natives, 1%. It has been predicted that if these demographic shifts continue, by 2020 minority groups will make up 39% of the total U.S. population (NCES, 2007). These changing trends have profound implications for education policymakers, and school governance.

The NCES Common Core of Data (2007), indicated that changes in the racial-ethnic population may be directly related to broader shifts in the general population that are directly impacted by immigration and fertility rates (p. 26). Minorities represented 34% of the total school age children in 1993, 39% in 2000, and 41.3% in 2003 (Figures 1.1–1.3) Between 1993 and 2003, the enrollment for Hispanic students increased by 6% while Asian and Pacific Islanders increased by 1%. The enrollment for Blacks and Native Americans remained constant during this same period.

A closer look at the central cities (see Figure 1.3) shows that in 2003 65% of all minorities were enrolled in urban schools. These urban areas had the largest increase in enrollment, 9 percentage points. On the other hand, only 21% of all minority students were enrolled in rural schools in 2003. Additionally, the percentage of minorities increased by 4 percentage points during the same period. Enrollment patterns also indicated that between 1993 and 2003, minority enrollment increased 5 percentage points in urban fringe areas and 8 percentage points in towns.

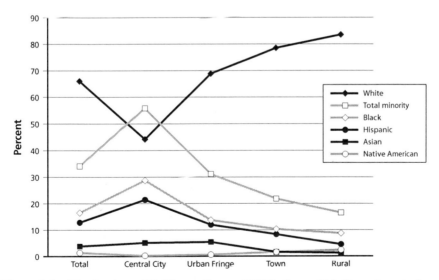

Figure 1.1 Distribution of K–12 enrollment (1993). *Source:* U.S. Department of Education, National Center for Education Statistics, The NCES Common Core of Data (CCD), "Public Elementary/Secondary School Universe Survey," 1993–94, 2000–01 and 2003–04.

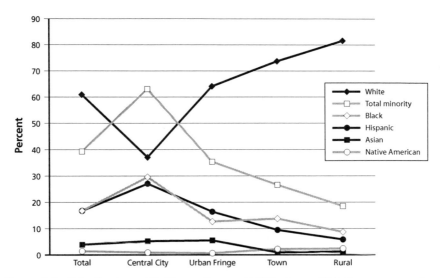

Figure 1.2 Distribution of K–12 enrollment (2000). *Source:* U.S. Department of Education, National Center for Education Statistics, The NCES Common Core of Data (CCD), "Public Elementary/Secondary School Universe Survey," 1993–94, 2000–01 and 2003–04.

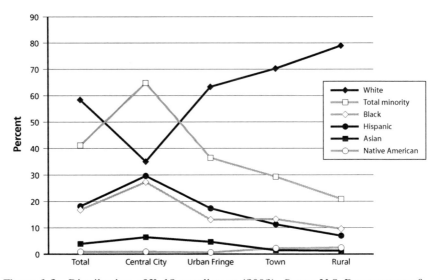

Figure 1.3 Distribution of K–12 enrollment (2003). *Source:* U.S. Department of Education, National Center for Education Statistics, The NCES Common Core of Data (CCD), "Public Elementary/Secondary School Universe Survey," 1993–94, 2000–01 and 2003–04.

A closer analysis of the primary grade level indicated that in 2004, minority groups comprised 42% of the total public school population in grades pre kindergarten through second (NCES, 2007). Further analysis of data also suggested that African American and Hispanic children are more likely to attend high poverty schools than their European American counterparts. As we examine achievement, it becomes apparent that the academic performance of special populations in urban communities is not being adequately addressed. Findings from the 2005 National Assessment of Educational Progress revealed that fourth and eighth grade Asian/Pacific Islanders and European American students scored statistically significantly higher percentages on reading achievement tests than their African American and Hispanic peers. Results also indicated that Asian American/Pacific Islander students out performed all other groups in mathematics. It is also interesting to note that in 2003, a significantly higher percentage of African American students in the elementary and secondary grade levels were expelled from school than their Hispanic, European American, Native American, and Asian/Pacific Islander counterparts. Data from the National Center for Education Statistics (2007) indicated that:

> Black, Hispanics, and American Indian/Alaskan Native American students are more likely to be eligible for free and reduced price lunch programs (frequently used as a measure of income level) than their White and Asian/Pacific Islander peers. Black and Hispanic students were also the most likely to attend high poverty schools, while Asian/Pacific Islander students were the most likely to attend low poverty schools. (p. 23)

It is also significant to note that:

- 31% of all students in the United States are concentrated in 1.5% of urban schools with total per person revenues that are only 89% of the average total pupil revenue.
- Underfunding of urban schools is affected by funding. Formulas, including low weights for compensatory education, bilingual or English as a second language programs.
- Urban schools enroll higher rates of immigrants and diverse students, including ethnic, racial, linguistic, and religious populations.
- Urban school enrollments are made up of 25% or more students who are low income.
- Urban students are likely to have higher rates of mobility, absenteeism, and poor health. They are also less likely to have health cover-

age, which decreases attendance and reduces funding based on attendance-based formula (p. 30).

CHILDREN LIVING IN POVERTY IN PHILADELPHIA

Data from the United States Census indicated that childhood poverty increased significantly between 1999 and 2004. The Poverty, Work and Opportunity Task Force (2007), chaired by Los Angeles Mayor Antonio R. Villaraigosa, was formed in January 2006 to respond to the structural conditions that give rise to the high poverty rates in the United States. Although extreme poverty envelopes the urban landscapes, we must be reminded:

> Poverty in America is not a racial or a regional issue. Thirty percent of all those identified as poor by federal statistics are white, 27 percent are African American, 21 percent are foreign-born Latinos and 8 percent are US-born Latinos. It is more important to debunk the popular misconception that somehow only urban centers are subject to "poverty." The rural areas are actually the most poor in the nation, as Fresno (CA) Mayor Alan Autry said, by pointing out that the San Joaquin Valley in California has the highest concentration of poverty in the nation. (Swann & Dyuduk, 2006, p. 1)

Findings from a 19-city Mayors Hunger and Homelessness Survey (2007) conducted by of the U.S. Conference of Mayors, found that high housing costs and the lack of affordable housing were linked to homelessness in households with children and hunger. The major findings from the survey indicated that the following structural problems are linked to increased poverty levels:

- The primary causes of hunger are poverty, unemployment, and high housing costs.
- The hunger crisis is fueled by the recent trends in foreclosures, the increased cost of living in general, and increased cost of food.
- The most common cause of homelessness among households with children is the lack of affordable housing.
- Among households with children, other common causes of homelessness are poverty and domestic violence. Among single individuals, the most common causes are mental illness and substance abuse.
- During the last year, members of households with children made up 23% of persons using emergency shelter and transitional housing programs in survey cities, while single individuals made up 76%. Only 1% of persons in these programs were unaccompanied youth. (p. 4)

Analysis of data also indicated that approximately 111,683 children in the city of Philadelphia were at or below the poverty level (Report Card, 2007). Additionally, it was reported that:

the percentage of children in Philadelphia living in poverty increased from 25.4% in 1999 to 30.3% in 2004. Nationally, childhood poverty has increased at a slower rate, from 16.6% in 1999 to 17.3% in 2004; during the 2006–2007 school year, 74% of Philadelphia public school students were eligible for free or reduced lunch programs; and in 2006, 3,989 were homeless and spent at least one night in a city shelter at some point during the year. (Report Card, 2007, p. 242)

There are more than 365,000 school age children in the city of Philadelphia (Table 1.1) and 114,927 White, 194,455 Black, 17,338, Asian, 54,714, Hispanic, and 10,093 represent two or more races. Family structure is directly related to economic stability and life chances for many of the city's children. This becomes apparent when one considers that more than 72,000 of these children reside in single parent households headed by females. Additionally, 16,578 grandparents are responsible for raising their grandchildren (Report Card 2007).

The city of Philadelphia is also severely affected by structural problems that must be addressed within in the parameters of limited funding. The percentage of children in need of healthcare continues to increase and in 2006, more than 25,000 children were without health insurance (Report Card, 2007). As shown in Figure 1.4, in 1997, there were approximately 216,778 children enrolled in the Philadelphia Medical Assistance Program. The number of children enrolled began to increase in 1999 and this trend continued into 2006.

TABLE 1.1 Philadelphia School Age Population

Age	Race				
	White	Black	Asian	Hispanic	2 or More Races
Under 5	34,202	54,888	5,785	17,659	4,873
5–9	29,089	48,109	4,053	16,809	2,595
10–14	31,576	55,337	4,797	11,857	1,489
15–17	20,060	36,121	2,703	8,389	1,136
Total Under 18	114,927	194,455	17,338	54,714	10,093

Source of data: Report Card 2007: The Well-Being of Children and Youth in Philadelphia.

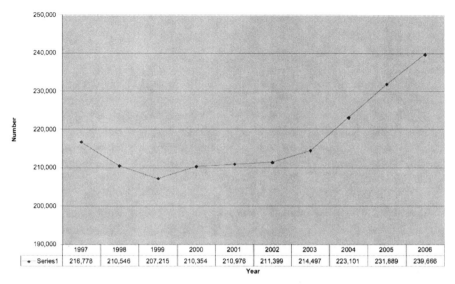

Figure 1.4 Philadelphia children receiving medical assistance. *Source of data:* Report Card 2007: The Well-Being of Children and Youth in Philadelphia.

ADEQUACY VERSUS EXCELLENCE

Urban children are capable of achieving academic excellence; however, many often need additional educational assistance and special programs. Unfortunately, many of these programs are quite expensive and additional financial support is needed.

Although research on the relationship between school finance and student achievement is mixed, Chubb and Hanushek (1990) reviewed 377 finance studies examining the relationship between spending and academic achievement. The researchers reported, that there was no strong systemic relationship between school expenditures and student performance. However, Hedges, Laine, and Greewald (1994) reanalyzed the same data and reported that a $500.00 increase in average spending per student would increase achievement by 0.7 standard deviation and this was found to be statistically significant. As the authors noted:

> When disparities in school funding exist on top of disparities in family income, it becomes clearer why there are such profound gaps in achievement between students from poorer backgrounds and those from wealthier homes. (p. 12)

The 2007 reauthorization of the *No Child Left Behind Act* is an attempt by the federal government to decrease the social and academic achievement gap between minority and nonminority students by employing corporate principles to school governance. No Child Left Behind stipulates that all race/ethnic groups, students with disabilities, limited English Proficient, and the economically disadvantaged meet the state of Pennsylvania's Adequate Yearly Progress (AYP) goals. The following gains were noted between 2002 and 2006.

> In mathematics, Hispanic students narrowed the achievement gap by 1.3 percentage points. In reading and mathematics for 2006, the percentage of Hispanic students scoring advanced or proficient was significantly below their White counterparts (28.7 percentage gap in reading and 23.7 percentage gap in mathematics).

> The achievement gap between Black and White students decreased by 4.5 percentage points and the gap in mathematics narrowed by 1.9 percentage points. The percentage of Black students scoring advanced or proficient was significantly below that of white students (24.3 percentage gap points in reading and 26.6 in mathematics. (Accountability Review Council, 2007, p. 16)

The emphasis on accountability, productivity, and efficiency is noteworthy; however, adequacy has not been given sufficient attention by policymakers. Urban school districts are finding it difficult to *"do more with less"* as related to funding.

Equity is a public value that should philosophically ground policy and practice in urban districts. In July 2002, 86 of the 322 schools in the Philadelphia School District were identified as low achieving. At this time, the district became part of a state takeover. A *Diverse Provider Experiment* was proposed and implemented by the district. A third of the district's low achieving schools were governed by for profit Educational Management Organizations (EMOs): Edison Schools, Victory schools and Chancellor Beacon Academies. Temple University, the University of Pennsylvania, Foundations, Inc., and Universal Companies were the nonprofit organizations responsible for managing 15 of these low achieving schools. The 21 restructured schools were also managed by the Philadelphia School District. Sixteen schools were referred to as the "Sweet Sixteen" because they were showing improvement in narrowing the achievement gap. These schools received extra funding from the state, but were not required to implement program interventions. Additionally, four of these schools were transitional charters and were managed by the Philadelphia School District (Table 1.2). These 86 schools received $37.5 million in state aid during the 2002–2003 academic year and in 2004–2005, and received an additional $30.9 million for the 2004–2005 school year.

> While the district-restructured schools and the Sweet 16 schools received $550.00 per pupil in extra aid. Foundations Inc., and Universal Companies,

two non-profit EMOs, received an additional $667 and $656 on per-pupil basis, respectively. For the for-profit EMOs, Edison received an extra $881, Victory Schools Inc., got an additional $857, and Chancellor Beacon Academies Inc., received an extra $650 respectively. Edison Schools received 65% more in extra funds than the Restructured Schools on a per pupil basis. (Accountability Review Council, 2007 p. 22)

Although, the schools managed by the district of Philadelphia made a significant improvement (45%) in increasing the percentage of schools making Adequate Yearly Progress from 2002–2006, Philadelphia charter schools showed the most significant increase, 55% (Table 1.3). The EMO schools increased less than all other groups, from 13% in 2003 to 26% in 2006. Given the investment in terms of increased state aid to the 86 schools, the 56-percentage points difference between EMOs and the state's AYP results, may be indicative of conflicts among public values. That is, excellence, equity and efficiency are not balanced. Analysis of results from the TerraNova in reading, language, mathematics, and science from 2002 –2005 indicated that the schools managed by the Philadelphia School District and Charters performed better than those managed by EMOs (Accountability Review Council, 2007).

TABLE 1.2 Philadelphia School Governance

Number of schools	Percentage of total schools	Manager	Governance
190	59	District	Philadelphia School District
46	14.3	Charter	Outside School District Management

86	26.7	Educational Management Organizations (EMO)	30 schools
			  For Profit EMOs
			  (Edison Schools, Victory Schools,
			  Chancellor Beacon Academies)
			15 schools
			  Non Profit organizations
			  (Temple University, University of
			  Pennsylvania, Foundations, Inc,
			  and Universal Companies

21	6.5	District	Philadelphia District Office of Restructured Schools
16	5.0	District	Philadelphia School District
4	1.2	Transitional Charters	Philadelphia School District

Source of data: Accountability Review Council: Report to the School Reform Commission— The Status of 2005–2006 Academic Performance in the School District of Philadelphia.

TABLE 1.3   Percent of Philadelphia Schools that Met AYP 2002–2006

Management type	2002	2003	2004	2005	2006	Change 2002–06
District managed	9%	24%	63%	53%	54%	45%
EMO managed	N/A	13%	48%	33%	26%	13%
District total	9%	22%	60%	49%	49%	40%
Charters	12%	11%	51%	46%	67%	55%
Philadelphia total	9%	21%	59%	49%	52%	43%
State of Pennsylvania	N/A	63%	86%	81%	82%	19%

Source: Accountability Review Council: Report to the School Reform Commission—The Status of 2005–2006 Academic Performance in the School District of Philadelphia (2007)

ADDRESSING THE FUNDING GAP

The decline in revenue reserves in urban centers can be directly linked to declining sales tax, income tax, and tourism tax revenues. Additionally, budget deficits have led to reductions in state support to local governments and officials are forced to deal with increased expenditures in wages, health care, and pensions. These demands have forced downsizing of the workforce, reduced budgets, limited capital investment, and depleted reserves (Panago, 2003). School districts receive funding from three sources: local, state, and federal aid; however, the 1980s gave birth to an era of New Federalism, which continues to thrive in 2008. This "do more with less" era is characterized by decreases in federal aid to education and an increase in corporate interest and influence. During the Regan and Bush I Administrations, federal funding of urban programs was reduced by almost 70% (Fahim, 2005).

The degree to which state aid has substituted for the void created by the loss of federal support has varied. Some states barely increased support while others initially increased support and then reduced it because of concerns over balancing their own budgets. As a result, cities are expected to do more with less (Fahim, 2005, p. 3).

It is obvious that many cities are not adequately funded and that there is a need to address issues surrounding underfunded urban schools. As Odden, Goetz, and Picus, (2007) noted, nontraditional resources can account for over half of the funding for schools in urban districts. Those who govern urban schools may need to consider the benefits of developing broader based *corporate—local school district partnerships* in addressing funding gaps. In order to secure funding, urban school district leaders must be able to understand and negotiate the dynamics of an increasingly conservative political economy as they develop relationships with potential donors.

Chief Executive Officers from the business sector have become key players in education reform initiatives. These individuals have joined forces with civic leaders, governmental officials and formed national task forces and commissions to address the fiscal challenges pervading the nation's urban schools. In 2007, corporate driven partnerships with urban school districts continue to exist. As was the case in the early 1980s, and 1990s, corporate media campaigns are frequently used to show support for public education and selected school reform initiatives that reflect the interest of business organizations. During the last two decades, two distinctive forms of corporate influence and dominance grew rapidly. These two modes of corporate involvement, business roundtables and business education partnerships, were typically organized to allow the business community access to the public education and the decision making process. According to McGuire (1990),

> These two modes of business engagement can be identified by their popular titles: business round tables and business education partnerships. Business roundtables (sometimes called task forces, leadership groups, forums or commissions) are typically organized for the purpose of bringing business community interests to bear on education programs and policy decisions. (p. 108)

The public schools cannot exist in isolation from various interests groups. These institutions must build coalitions as they attempt to marshall the needed resources to build capacity in urban districts. The corporate sector has a strong economic interest in public schooling. Traditionally, high school students have been primary sources of low and medium skilled workers; therefore, it is in the best interest of the corporate structure to play a key role in determining needed skills for the work force. It is the contention of many chief executive officers that if schools do a better job training and indoctrinating students to the corporate work culture, their training and retraining costs would be lower. In response to outside social forces and economic competition from abroad, businesses continue to develop collaborative relationships with career and vocational educational programs. In this time of rapidly changing markets and production technology, self interested business leaders may be ready to make large investments in building the capacity of schools to prepare workers for successful entry into the work force. While corporate interest in entry level job preparation is easy to understand, these entities also have a vested interest in overall community satisfaction which local school performance and academic achievement. Community confidence in the public school system is an important factor in the recruitment of highly skilled managerial and professional workers.

Businesses located in urban communities where schools have a reputation for poor performance may have difficulty persuading education-conscious workers to bring their families to live in the area. In sum, strategic economic interests encourage corporations to become concerned with how well urban schools (1) prepare individuals for the workforce; (2) contribute to a diverse, global culture that promotes productivity, efficiency and organizational innovation; and (3) assist in attracting high quality managerial and professional employees to their region.

REFERENCES

Accountability Review Council: Report to the School Reform Commission the Status of 2005–2006 Academic Performance in the School District of Philadelphia. (2007). Philadelphia: Author.

Chubb J., & Hanushek, E. (1990). Reforming educational reform. In H. Aron (Ed.), *Setting national priorities* (pp. 213–247). Washington, DC: The Brookings Institution.

Fahim, M. (2005). *Additional revenue sources are hard to find as US cities face increased responsibilities.* http://www.citymayors.com/finance/finance_uscities_2.html

Hedges, L. V., Laine, R. D., & Greenwald, R. (1994), Does money matter? A meta analysis of studies of the effects of differential school inputs on student outcomes. *Educational Researcher 23*(3), 5–14.

McGuire, C. K. (1990). Business involvement in the 1990s. In D. Mitchell & M. Goertz (Eds.), *Education politics for the new century.* Philadelphia: The Falmer Press.

National Center for Education Statistics, The NCES Common Core of Data (CCD). (2007). Public *Elementary/Secondary School Universe Survey.* US Department of Education, 1993–94, 2000–01 and 2003–04.

National League of Cities 19th Annual Survey. (2003). Washington, DC.

Odden, A., Goetz, M., & Picus, L. (2007, March 14). *Paying for school finance adequacy with the national average per pupil expenditures.* Seattle: University of Washington, Working Paper 2.

Pagano, M. (2003). *Cities fiscal challenges continue to worsen in 2003.* Washington, DC: Research Briefs, National League of Cities.

Report Card—The well-being of children and youth in Philadelphia. (2007). Philadelphia, PA: Philadelphia Safe and Sound.

Swann, C., & Dyuduk, Y. (2006). *Task force on poverty, work, and opportunity open to new approaches to old problem.* Washington, DC: The U.S. Conference of Mayors.

U.S. Conference of Mayors Status Report on Hunger and Homeless Survey. (2007). Washington, DC: Author.

CHAPTER 2

TAKING OVER

Which School Leadership Structures Generate Success in Restructured Districts?

Mark Hoff

Multiple school systems in the United States have consistently failed over an extended period. This failure takes many forms: financial, student achievement, graduation rates, and infrastructure. A particular focus of the No Child Left Behind Act of 2001 (NCLB) is student achievement. As a reauthorization of the Elementary and Secondary Education Act, NCLB directs states to modify Local Education Agencies (LEA) when they fail to make achievement targets (Hammer, 2005). The most drastic modification of an LEA is its abolishment or radical reconstitution. This occurs during a state takeover. Once a state has taken direct control of a school district, it must determine the best path for success. Agents of the state make these decisions, picking the best structure to affect the right types of change necessary to turn around a struggling school system. In restructuring failing urban school districts, what leadership structure is best suited to achieve success?

Policy, Leadership, and Student Achievement, pages 17–27
Copyright © 2008 by Information Age Publishing
All rights of reproduction in any form reserved.

POLICY CULTURE

The concept of a state-takeover of an individual school district is relatively new. Various forms of LEA have run schools in America for centuries.
Traditionally, through school boards, local residents have defined and met
the needs of their students using broad guidelines from state government
(Sewall, 1996). The concept of a state-run school is the antithesis of the
"small town America" myth that many Americans embrace. Urban communities have always come into conflict with this myth. The needs of large
urban communities, with broad socioeconomic underpinnings, are unique.
Hunter and Brown (as cited in Hammer, 2005) wrote that state school takeovers in the twentieth century started because of desegregation, a primarily
urban issue. Desegregation was largely a result of the *Brown* ruling by the
Supreme Court. The interaction between federal courts and state governments occur because of our constitutional system. Though education is reserved for the states by the federal constitution, it also falls into the federal
purview. A combination of congressional powers and citizen protections increases the role of the federal government in local education (Ryan, 2004).
As of 2002, 24 states had passed laws allowing the state to take over a school
district because of academic failures (Ziebarth, 2002). Federal court decisions and concern by state governments over the practice or performance
of specific school districts from 1980 to 2004 led to the state takeover of 54
school districts (Ziebarth in Hammer, 2005).

The success of these takeovers is unknown at this time. In some urban
centers organizational change has occurred, an organized curriculum and
investment of resources have yielded limited higher test scores (Cuban &
Usden, 2003). Yet, higher test scores are not the best gauge for success in
urban schools (Kohn, 2006). Many unknowns exist when it comes to state
takeovers. The research yields many failures and few successes.

States must make a choice between the agents and structures at its dis-
posal. Generally, when a state empowers an LEA, it uses its own department
of education, a board of control, a mayor, or some combination of these
agents to reconstitute ailing school districts. With poorly defined missions,
underlying social problems, negotiated resources, and historical legacies
these agents struggle to fix decades of issues. When a state reconstitutes a
school district, it promises its constituents that it will be successful. A choice
must be made of who should lead the reconstitution process. The past 20
years yield clues to, but no guarantees of, the best agent or agents to reconstitute a school district.

DETERMINING SUCCESS

One of the greatest challenges a state faces in creating a successful urban school district is determining what constitutes success. In an empowered school district a foundation must be built that allows success to occur. For a single school to evolve into a successful entity four core components must exist: meeting several NCLB adequate yearly progress criteria, providing a safe and maintained environment, fostering good communication between school and community, and the existence of team spirit (Gross, 1998). A state takeover of a school district must aim at developing these four qualities throughout the school district (S.J. Gross, personal communication, April 17, 2007). By developing these qualities a foundation will be built that allows schools to go beyond being sufficient. When empowerment occurs, sufficiency equals the most basic definition of success. The state must create an apparatus that facilitates the development of a solid foundation so that greater successes can occur once local control has been restored. To do this they must honestly and actively include local and state level stakeholders.

PUBLIC VIEWS

In taking over a school district, the state tries to create a better environment for students, teachers, administrators, community members, and taxpayers. In today's nomenclature, a better environment means closing the achievement gaps and raising the academic results of all students. This is the first component of the foundation that the state tries to fix. Fuhrman (2004), and many others, outlined the goals of NCLB and lamented the effect that they have on various aspects of the United States education system. From the perspective of parents, showing academic gains are the clearest signs of success that the state can have. Therefore, when reconstituted districts report results, they focus on their test gains, even if much of the system, at least from the inside, appears to be dysfunctional (Bartholomew, 2006). The public has been conditioned to accept numerical gains as true signs of success. Assessment scores provide a measurement of success while narrowly defining what success is in an urban school system.

In a hierarchical system, the state should define success and its agents should work toward the goals developed to achieve success. Increasingly, in urban settings, states are turning toward mayoral control of large urban school systems (Cuban & Usden, 2003). For the public, this provides a singular entity to praise or vilify for the changes that occur during a state takeover. It emphatically answers the question for all stakeholders of "who is in charge." In reality, the state is still in charge (Sloane, 2006). However, the state yields its authority to the mayor, even allowing in some cases for the mayor to be in a position to bargain with the state (Steiner, 2005). This type of leadership can be a winner for an ailing school system.

Boards of control can also be winners, but even limited success is much more difficult. Without that singular, the"buck stops here" ability, boards of control can suffer many ailments of their own. These ailments come from the same qualities that can make them more effective at balancing the needs of the community. In truth, a board of control is only as strong as the people on the board. If the board is composed of people who have differing opinions and represent factions that cannot find compromise, the project will fail. Rhim (as cited in Steiner, 2005) declared that the size and composition of the board that took over the Chester-Upland School District in Pennsylvania suffered this fate. The Chester-Upland board was composed of three members: one state official and two community leaders. They could not overcome their disagreements and failed to achieve their goals.

This failure does not have to occur. Boards of control, if composed of community members who were empowered by the state with resources, would have an excellent opportunity to build the civic capacity that Stone, Henig, Jones, and Pierannunzi (2001), feel is necessary to reform urban school systems. True community leaders have the unique ability to interact with local stakeholders. Parents, students, and small business owners can have actual contact with board of control members. Unlike a system driven by a mayor, these people are more accessible. Like regular school boards, these boards of control, composed of many community leaders who are appointed by the state, can incorporate local concerns with state mandates. Unlike local school boards, these boards derive their budgetary authority and administrative flexibility from the state, meaning that they can have a greater effect on the entire educational experience.

In whatever path the state chooses, mayoral control, a board of control, or some hybrid model of the two, a balance must be struck between the issues of excellence, equity, choice, and adequacy. The state must provide the resources to create an adequate educational environment. Furthermore, a culture of excellence must be fostered within the school and the community. All stakeholders should have ownership in the process that goes well beyond simply being told what to do by a few stakeholders. This provides a framework for people to have choice within their environments. The decisions made within an urban system must be equitable as determined by the objectives defined by the state.

For a state to empower a school district, the situation must be dire. It most likely means that at least part of the educational, and societal, system is dysfunctional. A balance must be struck between telling people what to do and doing what the local people want to do. The local citizens must realize that they are receiving funding beyond what they can contribute to the system, and the state must realize that if the local stakeholders do not "buy" into the process it will ultimately fail. It is with all of this in mind that the state must choose between mayoral control, a board of control, or a hybrid model.

INTEREST GROUPS

In determining the best-fit takeover for an urban area, state officials must examine many components. The first priority should be meeting the needs of the students. Again, what those needs are is up for great interpretation and is often determined by the goals and objectives of the various stakeholders. Examples of effective local stakeholder involvement occurred in the 1980s when the business community in Pittsburgh helped the struggling school district with reforms and in the 1990s when Boston politicians united to make changes in their fledgling system (Portz, 2000). To make the right choice in control, state officials must have a firm grasp of the needs, desires, and political realities of the stakeholders within the urban environment, the state, and the federal governments.

Students

Students are vital components to the empowerment process and their input should be sought out by policymakers (Kleiner, 1990). Unfortunately, regardless of the type of structure chosen, students are the least likely to have an impact on the decision. They do; however, have a vital role in the outcome of the process. Their eager participation in, or their disdain for, implemented strategies within the schools will define whether a program is ultimately deemed a success or failure.

Parents

Parents want the best possible outcomes for their children. In urban communities, they can provide the support that can make reform possible (Stone et al., 2001). Their voices can push the establishment. As an organized group, they have the power to sway an election, making them a constituency for mayors of empowered school districts. Parents can add to the educational process by becoming active in the classroom but they need to work with specially trained teachers who want their involvement (Gultz,

1999). Engaging parents in the schooling of their children is essential for state takeovers to be successful.

State Legislature

Composed of elected officials, state legislatures typically pass laws that make it possible for state legislators to be reelected (Sloane, 2006). Therefore, they want to make the empowerment work, but must keep their constituency in mind when making decisions. A balance must be struck when it comes to resource distribution, personal decisions, and delegation of state authority. The state legislature has the authority to determine its level of involvement in the process. With the ability to override a governor's veto or modify the rules that govern the state department of education, it ultimately rests with the state legislature to decide what type of state takeover occurs.

Governor

With the ability to concentrate media coverage and political contribution, the governor has the ability to control the political agenda. This is the same phenomenon, to a lesser degree, that has defined the Office of President of the United States in recent years (Ricci, 1993). This advantage provides a governor with the opportunity to be the primary negotiator in setting up a state takeover. An example of this occurred in Philadelphia; the takeover of the School District of Philadelphia was engineered in this fashion by Governor Tom Ridge (Whittle, 2005). Education reform is a golden issue for governors. The results of reform will largely be unknown by the time the governor leaves office. This allows a governor to claim to be a reforming governor without having to demonstrate lasting results. The choice of what type of takeover structure to embrace will be decided, in part, by the governor. The office of governor, in its current form, provides a perfect platform to be the negotiator between the state legislature and the LEA.

Mayor

With an inherent local connection, mayors of urban centers must be a part of the school empowerment process. When they are removed from the process, they can undermine the boards of control that the state puts into place. This is precisely what happened with the Detroit City Schools in the late 1980s and 1990s (Hula, Jelier, & Schauer, 1997). Mayors have the ability to bring business and local community leaders into the reform process. Their attention to education can bring the pressure and resources that systems need to assist in the transformation process. In a structured system, the mayor can serve as the negotiator for the local school district with the state.

Regardless of involvement, a mayor will be pressured by the success or failure of the school system. If it improves without mayoral involvement, other political actors will gain capital within the city, potentially weakening the mayor. If it fails without mayoral involvement, the public may cite the mayor for allowing it to fail because of a lack of involvement. Mayors who become involved with school reform will enjoy the benefits of success or they may be faulted if failure occurs. On the other hand, if a system has perpetually failed, at least the mayor can go to voters and show that an attempt at reform was made. Whether formally involved or not, mayors of cities that have empowered school districts will be involved in the process; the risks are just too high for them to ignore what other political actors are doing in their cities.

Current School Board

As the duly elected officials of the ailing school district, school board members have an obligation to the community. They may choose to try to be a part of the empowerment process or yield to a board of control. School boards can serve as a path to greater community involvement. They can also work as a community check on the board of control or mayor. School boards can lose all of their authority or become a place of refuge for parental complaints over changing schools.

Current School Administration and Teachers

When a school district is reconstituted, a state has the ability to change the staffing of local schools (Hammer, 2005). This creates a situation where most teachers and administrators would want to avoid a school takeover. Once the school takeover occurs, these individuals must find a place within the system and decide whether they will cooperate with the new leaders of the district. If teachers and school administrators choose not to cooperate, they will most likely lose their jobs.

For-Profit Schools

When a state takeover occurs and the process of reconstitution begins, for-profit schools are one choice that states can make. Returning to the

Philadelphia example, of the 86 schools that were targeted for specialized services in the School District of Philadelphia, 30 of these schools were reconstituted by for-profit companies (Research for Action, 2005). The long-term success of these companies is unknown. Chris Whittle (2005), founder of Edison Inc., believes that for-profit schools can play a critical role in reforming underperforming school in urban settings. The focus on creating better schools for children, with the incentive of profit, may provide impetus to help historically failing schools. These entities might have to deal with concerned stakeholders who may fear that they are not spending significant resources to ensure a profit. The fate of these enterprises may very well rest in their success rate within empowered school districts.

Conclusion

All of these stakeholders, or interest groups, will play a role in the success or failure of a state takeover. Each stakeholder has the ability to obfuscate this high-stakes reform process. Regardless of the school takeover structure chosen by the state, all stakeholders must enter into a cooperative process for success to occur. Disagreements will occur, but issue mediation will be essential in melding the views of all of these different interested parties.

RECOMMENDATIONS

When the state has made the determination that a school district needs to be taken over, it must involve the mayor. The level of mayoral involvement needed for change is unknown at this time. Mayoral control can take many forms. Kirst (2002) outlined four forms: low, low-moderate, moderate, and high. The level of mayoral intervention ranges from careful prodding of elected boards to complete decision-making ability over the entire system. The higher the level of mayoral control the more effective a negotiator the mayor can be with the state legislature (Villegas, 2003). However, the highest level of mayoral control leads to dissatisfaction that can run through the urban school system (Batholomew, 2006). A balance between local and state control must be struck to satisfy all stakeholders.

Legitimate boards of control must be involved to enable local input to occur. Returning to Philadelphia, the current Philadelphia School Reform Commission has five members: two of these members are appointed by the mayor and three are appointed by the governor. For all of the important decisions, the Commission must approve the matter with a vote of at least 4–1. This essentially gives the Mayor of Philadelphia a veto over all important decisions (Kirst, 2002). This is not enough local control. How can students, parents, teachers, and administrators influence the mayor enough on issues that concern them? They can vote the individual out of office, but that can only occur every four years. Local stakeholders need to have direct access to the school board; they need their own elected representation.

A combination board of control should be developed. The exact composition of the board would need to be negotiated by the state and the mayor's office. The result of this negotiation must yield local representation that cannot be shut out of major policy decisions. This would provide a mechanism for local stakeholders to connect with the political mechanism that is now directing the school system. A teacher, administrator, parent, or student cannot be expected to gain access to the mayor, governor, or their representatives, but it is possible to gain access to someone living in their locality.

For this board to function, clear objectives must be defined in the state takeover. Districts that endure state takeovers face more challenges than governance. The community cannot be blocked out of this process. Alienation will not breed success. Stone (2001) is right: community capacity must be built to fix urban schools. The first step in doing this is to incorporate the community into the school restructuring process. Perhaps this will allow the development of community leaders who are not only part of the community but also the school community. The alternative is the continuation of state or city hall centered reconstitution efforts that yield few results (Cuban & Usden, 2003).

A board of control that incorporates local input has the opportunity for capacity building to occur. Urban environments face many more challenges than just failing schools. Anyon (2005) suggests that the core problem of urban schools is one of economics, not the fact that the schools do not receive enough funding, which they do not. Urban areas need reform on many levels. Anyon suggests a new social revolution, akin to the American Civil Rights movement, will be needed to change urban schools. Though compelling, Anyon's proposal is far beyond the scope of choosing the state takeover structure for a school district.

In reality, the research does not yield a best state takeover leadership structure. What few documented successes exist occur under direct mayoral control. These successes are very limited and only focus on limited increases in test scores. No method is effective at improving graduation rates or employment opportunities (Cuban & Usden, 2003). The current way of thinking when it comes to boards of control or mayoral control does not yield better schools.

Creating boards of control that have state, mayoral, and local input will make them more meaningful. However, the problems with such a board could be plentiful. Disputes among members may cause a powerful entity, either the state or the city, to pull support from the board. This would undermine the authority of the board and discredit the entire process. The strength of this board composition is also a potential weakness. By having multiple voices in the decision process there is more of an opportunity for the corruption that has plagued cities like Detroit (Hula, 1997) to enter the environment of a reconstituted school district.

When state governments decide to reconstitute a school district, they must be open to new ideas. They must embrace a school community perceived to be damaged. These communities cannot be discounted from the school district reconstitution process. If communities are discounted, the continued poor performance of school takeovers will continue. Incorporation of community members and interests, in some meaningful way, may lead to the possibility of honest reform taking hold and making actual differences.

REFERENCES

Anyon, J. (2004). *Radical possibilities: Public policy, urban education, and a new social movement.* New York: Routledge.

Bartholomew, B. (2006). Transforming New York City's public schools. *Educational Leadership, 63*(8), 61–65.

Cuban, L., & Udsen, M. (Eds.). (2003). *Powerful reforms with shallow roots: improving America's urban schools.* New York: Teachers College Press.

Fuhrman, S. H. (2004). Less than meets the eye: Standards, testing, and fear of federal control. In N. Epstein (Ed.), *Who's in charge here? The tangled web of school governance and policy* (pp. 42–74). Washington, DC: Brookings Press.

Gross, S. J. (1998). *Staying centered: Curriculum leadership in a turbulent era.* Alexandria, VA: Association for Supervision and Curriculum Development.

Gultz, M. (1999). *Here we are together . . . together at school* (Report No. PS025560). (ERIC Document Reproduction Service No. ED409985).

Hammer, P. C. (2005). *Corrective action: A look at state takeovers of urban and rural districts.* AEL policy brief. (ERIC Document Reproduction Service No. ED486081).

Hula, R. C., Jelier, R. W., & Schauer, M. (1997). Making educational reform: Hard time in Detroit 1988–1995. *Urban Education, 32*(2), 202–232.

Kleiner, R. E. (1990). *Assessing the holding power and attractiveness of a school system for at-risk students.* [Abstract] (ERIC Document Reproduction Service No. ED319753).

Kirst, M. W. (2002). *Mayoral influence, new regimes, and public school governance.* CPRE Report. (ERIC Document Reproduction Service No. ED468346).

Kohn, G. (2006, July). Urban reform, governance, and success: The Harrisburg School District story. In C. K. McGuire & V. W. Ikpa (Chairs), *Meeting the challenges of urban schools: Policy, research and practice.* Symposium conducted at the Education Policy Leadership Summer Institute, Harrisburg, PA.

Portz, J. (2000). Supporting education reform: Mayoral and corporate paths. *Urban Education, 35*(4), 396–417.

Research for Action, Inc., Philadelphia, PA. (2005). *The "original 86"* (ERIC Reproduction Service No. ED489428).

Ricci, D. (1993). *The transformation of American politics*. New Haven, CT: Yale University Press.

Ryan, J. E. (2004). The tenth amendment and other paper tigers: The legal boundaries of educational governance. In N. Epstein (Ed.), *Who's in charge here? The tangled web of school governance and policy* (pp. 42–74). Washington, DC: Brookings Press.

Sewall, A. M. (1996). *New school governance: The school board and its future*. Arkansas. (ERIC Reproduction Service No. ED403465).

Sloane, W. (2006). The legal and political environments influencing the distribution of power in education: Who decides? Legal issues in school governance. In C. K. McGuire & V. W. Ikpa (Chairs), *Meeting the challenges of urban schools: Policy, research and practice*. Symposium conducted at the Education Policy Leadership Summer Institute, Harrisburg, PA.

Steiner, L. M. (2005). *State takeovers of individual schools: School-restructuring options under No Child Left Behind*. Naperville, IL. Learning Point Associates. (ERIC Reproduction Service No. ED489527).

Stone, C. N., Henig, J. R., Jones, B. D., & Pierannunz, T. (2001). *Building civic capacity: The politics of reforming urban schools*. Lawrence: University Press of Kansas.

Villegas, M. (2003). *Leading in difficult times: Are urban school boards up to the task? Policy trends*. WestEd, San Francisco. (ERIC Reproduction Service No. 478513).

Whittle, C. (2005). The promise of public/private partnerships. *Educational Leadership, 62*(5), 34–36.

Ziebarth, T. (2002). *State takeovers and reconstitutions. Policy brief*. Colorado: Education Commission of the States. (ERIC Reproduction Service No. ED473720).

Ziebarth, T. (2004). *State polices for school restructuring. Policy brief*. Colorado: Education Commission of the States. (ECS Clearinghouse #5702).

CHAPTER 3

A RESEARCH-BASED PROFESSION IS NEEDED TO MEET THE CHALLENGE OF URBAN SCHOOLS

David M. Gates

A rising tide lifts all boats.
—John F. Kennedy

In an era of accountability and high-stakes testing, the words of President Kennedy would seem to have particular appeal. Originally used to address economic matters, the aphorism in an educational context suggests that universal educational reform will benefit all students. This would seem to be the logic upon which No Child Left Behind is predicated. While such a conclusion is appealing, it should be noted that the axiom is based upon the assumption that all boats are seaworthy. Considering the disparity of student achievement acknowledged along ethnic lines, it would appear that in reality, all students may not benefit equally. It is doubtful that there is a simple panacea to ameliorate this significant and complex problem; however, an educational profession that is driven by research may offer effective solutions.

Policy, Leadership, and Student Achievement, pages 29–35
29

As with so many other terms in the language, "research" is frequently used equivocally. The "research" typical of most students is the production of a paper citing "authorities." Such citations may be referencing fact, opinion, or theory. While acceptable for the substantiation of theoretical observations, such "research" does not necessarily present valid data from which informed decisions can be made. Consequently, the assumption that such papers constitute valid research would appear to be an overstatement.

Another misleading aspect of research in education is that while certain research data may document and identify a problem, these data do not support specific interventions for solving the problem. Knowing that there is an "achievement gap" is one thing; identifying a solution is a completely different matter. The validity of using problem identification data to justify interventions aimed at solving the problem is, at best, questionable.

In order to define "research" for the purposes of this discussion, two categories of research are identified, descriptive and experimental. The former is characterized by the use of descriptive statistics, determining correlations, and performing research studies such case studies and action research. In contrast, experimental research is characterized by hypothesis testing, determining intervention efficacy, and utilization of control and test groups. These two categories should not be confused with qualitative and quantitative research methodology. Descriptive research in general and case studies in particular can utilize quantitative methodology for data collection and analysis (Yin, 1994). While there are many advocates of each form, an unbiased observation would be that each is best suited for a different purpose and both have unique validity threats that need to be addressed.

Using the case study as an example, descriptive research is a good choice to examine what exists in a specific location over a given period of time. The use of descriptive statistics facilitates identifying what exists and is useful in determining problems and identifying what is happening in a bounded event. A significant tool in describing what exists is the correlation. Correlations assist in making predictions and summarizing data (Fraenkel & Wallen, 2003). However, it is significant to note that a demonstrated correlation between two variables does not suggest a direction of causality. This is an error typically made by the uninitiated in an attempt to "prove" the efficacy of a particular intervention if there is a correlation between the intervention and improved performance. Are there any other variables that could have caused the improvement? Is it possible that the improvement is an unintended consequence of another activity? Ultimately, correlations cannot "prove" a hypothesis; however, if there is no correlation between two variables, a hypothesis can be rejected.

In order to determine the efficacy of a particular intervention, experimental research is a favored model. Does the intervention provide better results than the one it is intended to replace? In order to test the hypothesis, or more accurately to reject the null hypothesis, the researcher attempts to control all variables with the exception of the intervention. Using control and test groups, the experiment is conducted and data are collected. Using statistical analysis, the significance of the results is determined in order to report the probability of rejecting the null hypothesis.

There is one other significant difference between descriptive and experimental research, the ability to generalize results. Descriptive research results are typically difficult to generalize to a larger population. Because this type of research is concerned with describing a bounded event, it would be possible to generalize the results to populations with similar characteristics, e.g., student intelligence, economic levels, teacher qualifications, etc. Creswell (2003) suggests that this inability to generalize is one of the reasons for the increased use of the mixed methodology research approach. Experimental research permits testing samples of a large and diverse population. Although accounting for independent variables would be complex, it is possible to collect data based on state, national, or international assessment results. Consequently, it is easier to justify the generalization of experimental results than those of descriptive research.

The significance of the previous discussion is that both descriptive and experimental research methodologies are well suited for different purposes. It would be prudent for educators to be able to recognize the differences both for the application of research methods and the analysis of research reports. The profession would be well served if teachers and administrators were prepared by pre-service programs to make informed judgments concerning the validity and accuracy of research results. This would tend to diminish the number of instructional methods included in the professional knowledge base that were validated by descriptive research.

Experienced educational professionals are very familiar with instructional methodologies that have become the "flavor of the month." Possibly more than any other profession, education has been plagued with fads, i.e., methods that are extremely popular and implemented nationwide during their "fifteen minutes of fame" and then recede into oblivion. Many of these "new" methods are seen as a repackaging of previously established pedagogy complete with new buzzwords to provide novelty and facilitate proliferation. Such perceptions may contribute to a cynical view of educational reform, thus increasing the inherent turbulence of change. Whatever happened to "The New Math," "The New Science," "Competency-Based Education," "Behavioral Objectives," "Outcome-Based Education," or "The Hunter Model?" What is happening with "Block (Intensive) Scheduling," "Reading Recovery," "Cooperative Learning," "Direct Instruction," and "Learning Focused Schools?" The merit of the preceding methodologies is not being questioned; however, there is one important question that should be addressed. What experimental testing has provided the data necessary to make informed decisions concerning the efficacy of these methods? While all are significant, three of the methodologies mentioned above seem particularly salient for improving student achievement in urban schools: Reading Recovery, Cooperative Learning, and Direct Instruction.

Reading Recovery is an early intervention program designed to assist children who have difficulty learning to read. Identified by their teachers, these children receive short-term, individual instruction intended to move the children from the bottom of their class to the class average where they will be able succeed in regular classroom reading instruction. The success rate of Reading Recovery is claimed to be 75–85% (Swartz & Klein, 1994). At face value, such an assertion is impressive; however, the program's definition of success is relative to the class average reading ability. What if the class is reading at the 25th percentile? It would be difficult to describe reading at this level a "success." In urban schools where this scenario is likely to be encountered, measuring the success of economically disadvantaged children with low criteria raises significant equity concerns. Additionally, some experimental research findings concerning the efficacy of Reading Recovery suggest the claimed success rate is significantly overstated (Center, Freeman, & Robertson, 2001) and the program's efficacy is doubtful (Chapman & Tunmer, 2003; Chapman, Tunmer, & Prochnow, 2001). Even though Reading Recovery has been widely acclaimed and adopted, it would appear that the efficacy of the program is less than compelling.

Cooperative Learning comprises teaching strategies in which students work together on common projects. With a significant amount of favorable literature and research, it would seem appropriate that Cooperative Learning be a recommended pedagogy. Indeed, some advocates of this strategy marginalized teacher-centered activities, e.g., lectures, to such an extent as to replace them completely with cooperative activities. Although Cooperative Learning can be successful, "one does not have to look hard for negative findings" (Genovese, 2005, p. 573). In his article, Genovese cites experimental research studies that found no differences in student achievement between lecture, programmed instruction, and cooperative learning (Kromrey & Purdon, 1995) and found that while students prefer cooperative learning, they had higher achievement in individual learning (Snyder & Sullivan, 1995). While such studies do not negate the value of cooperative learning, they do suggest it may not be prudent to use it as a replacement for other methods. Additionally, cooperative learning comprises a set of teaching strategies; consequently, teacher training is imperative for its success. It is not simply another name for "group work."

Direct Instruction is an instructional model that focuses on the interaction between teachers and students. Its design principles "include the framing of learner performance into goals and tasks, breaking these tasks into smaller component tasks, designing training activities for mastery, and arranging the learning events into sequences that promote transfer and achievement..." (Magliaro, Locklee, & Burton, 2005, p. 41). Frequently discounted in student-centered educational reform, Direct Instruction has a favorable history in experimental research, most notably in Project Follow Through.

Cited as the largest controlled comparative study of teaching methods, Project Follow Through involved 700,000 students in 170 communities across the United States (Kim & Axelrod, 2005). Started in 1967, this national study was part of the Johnson administration's War on Poverty and was funded until 1995. It was an experimental study that utilized a "test" school and a "control" school within the same community in order to identify best practices for educational reform. Including both teacher-centered and student-centered models, 12 models of instruction were compared. In measuring student achievement, the study results found Direct Instruction to be effective and superior to the other compared models (Magliaro et al., 2005). "In other words, Direct Instruction, a model classified as teacher-centered and basic skills-oriented, outperformed other models—models deemed to be cognitive or affective in nature—not only in basic skills achievement, but in cognitive and affective achievement as well" (Kim & Axelrod, 2005, p. 112). With such impressive results, it would seem that Direct Instruction should be among the most recognized teaching methodologies in the professional knowledge base. This does not appear to be the case.

The findings of Project Follow Through were largely dismissed by the educational community. While it is beyond the purview of this discussion to examine the reasons for this action, it is noteworthy that Kim and Axelrod (2005) state, "Advocates of Direct Instruction have maintained that the educational establishment had—and has—a strong philosophical bias favoring child-centered pedagogy that is almost dogmatically held regardless of research results" (p. 112). In support of this observation, they cite a study commissioned by the Manhattan Institute for Policy Research in which 56% of surveyed teachers reported having a "student-directed" teaching philosophy and only 15% of surveyed teachers believed it important to teach "specific information and skills."

The point of the preceding discussion is neither to advocate for a specific teaching strategy nor to marginalize any form of research. The teaching methodologies mentioned are presented as examples to demonstrate how educational research can be used, misused, and/or ignored. If educators are seeking to identify best practice and make data-driven decisions, it is paramount that they recognize research that is valid and accurate. In order to do this, knowledgeable educators need to understand the strengths and weaknesses of different research models and the appropriateness of their application with regard to the purpose of the research. Educators should also be able to identify the threats to validity inherent to each research model. In order to be a research-based profession, educators must be able to take a hard and critical look at the research, determine its quality, and develop strategies appropriate to its findings.

It is highly doubtful that a single panacea exists to improve the performance of all students. What is not doubtful is that the preponderance of evidence identifies an achievement gap in this country with a disproportionate percentage of underperforming students with Black and Latino ethnicities. This gap represents a true crisis in American education. A profession based on research to facilitate student learning rather than focused on raising test scores may stem a tide that only seemingly raises all boats.

REFERENCES

Chapman, J. W., & Tunmer, W. E. (2003). The Reading Recovery approach to preventive early intervention: As good as it gets? *Reading Psychology, 24*(3/4), 337–361.

Chapman, J. W., Tunmer, W. E., & Prochnow, J. E. (2001). Does success in the Reading Recovery program depend on developing proficiency in phonological-processing skills? A longitudinal study in a whole language instructional context. *Scientific Studies of Reading, 5*(2), 141–176.

Center, Y., Freeman, L., & Robertson, G. (2001). The relative effect of a code-oriented and a meaning-oriented early literacy program on regular and low progress Australian students in year one classrooms which implement Reading Recovery. *International Journal of Disability, Development & Education, 48*(2), 207–232.

Cresswell, J. W. (2003). *Research design: Qualitative, quantitative, and mixed methods approaches* (2nd ed.). Thousand Oaks, CA: Sage.

Fraenkel, J. R., & Wallen, N. E. (2003). *How to design and evaluate research in education* (5th ed.). Boston: McGraw-Hill.

Genovese, J. E. C. (2005). Why educational innovations fail: An individual difference perspective. *Social Behavior and Personality, 33*(6), 569–578.

House, E., Glass, G., McLean, L., & Walker, D. (1978). No simple answer: Critique of the "Follow Through" evaluation. *Educational Leadership, 35*(6), 462–464.

Kim, T. & Axelrod, S. (2005). Direct instruction: An educators' guide and a plea for action. *The Behavior Analyst Today, 6*(2), 111–120.

Kromrey, J. D., & Purdom, D. M. (1995). A comparison of lecture, cooperative learning, and programmed instruction at the college level. *Studies in Higher Education, 20*(3), 341–350.

Magliaro, S., Locklee, B., & Burton, J. (2005). Direct instruction revisited: A key model for instructional technology. *Educational Technology Research & Development, 53*(4), 41–55.

Snyder, T., & Sullivan, H. (1995). Cooperative and individual learning and student misconceptions in science. *Contemporary Educational Psychology, 20*(2), 230–235.

Swartz, S., & Klein, A. (1994). Reading Recovery: An overview. *Literacy, Teaching, and Learning, 1*(1), 3–7.

Yin, R. (1994). *Case study research: design and methods* (2nd ed.). Thousand Oaks, CA: Sage.

PART 2

THE HIGHER EDUCATION CONTEXT
AND STUDENT PERFORMANCE

CHAPTER 4

PROFESSIONAL IDENTITY FORMATION

Socialization and Mentoring of Pre-Service Teachers in Urban Communities

Roselynn U. Obi

Professional development and Identity formation are the correlates of socialization of pre-service teachers during the junior internship. This chapter examines how pre-service teachers involved in initial field experience acquire the knowledge, skills, and dispositions of the profession of teaching, and the impact of the process in teacher identity formation. The junior interns' perceptions of the relationships between them and their mentors/ cooperating teachers, as well as, the socialization process are very crucial to how the interns perceive themselves, What values are adopted, and what professional skills are developed (Obi, 2004a).

The urban field experience and mentoring activities assist the pre-service teachers' development as teachers, as well as, understanding of the teaching and learning process in general, and urban public schools in par-

Policy, Leadership, and Student Achievement, pages 39–54
Copyright © 2008 by Information Age Publishing

ticular. Internships provide where, when, and how student teachers learn to relate to students (Putnam & Borko, 2000), as well as, understand how they behave and learn. What impressions, interests, and knowledge they develop in this preliminary experience are important determinants in entering the profession of teaching. Putnam and Borko, (1998) assert, among other things, that in the education of teachers, field experiences play an important role in helping to teach and influence pre-service teachers' beliefs and knowledge about teaching.

The impact of initial relationships between the junior intern and the cooperating teacher is often overlooked in the education and training of teachers. Most of the studies on the socialization of teachers, and the relationship between mentors and mentees are centered on senior student teachers, and beginning teachers (Ashton, 1996; Elliott, 2000; Feiman-Nemser & Beasley, 1977; Hawkey, 1997; Kagan, 1992; Koerner, 1992; Odell, 1986, 1989; Putnam & Borko, 2000; Stanilus & Russell, 2000; Waldschmidt & Coxen, 2000; Zeichner, 1985; Zeichner & Gore, 1990). Initial teacher preparation is one place to institute the type of mentoring practice that will lead to positive socialization of pre-service teachers into the profession of teaching (Obi, 2003, 2004b). The process of socializing the junior interns into the profession of teaching helps in acquiring a professional identity. Similarly, (McGowen & Hart, 1990), point out that professional identity is achieved from professional socialization and development. The field experience affords the pre-service teacher the rare opportunity of understanding and acknowledging the relevance of the gradual developmental process inherent in this context.

The features and background, the ecological aspect of professional development are exposed. The pre-service teacher is now captivated by various dimensions of professional development; namely, personal dimension which includes such things as stimulating the intellect, developing and experiencing a sense of self worth and accomplishment, as were identified in the themes that emerged. For the urban teacher, the ecological dimension, as espoused by Vonk and Schras (1987), accounts for the nature of demands, constraints, conflicts and motivation, that characterize the teacher's work environment, particularly that of the urban setting. The entire socialization experience provides the intern insights and awareness to the complex nature of the teaching learning process, and to the multiple forms of knowledge, as well as the various dimensions of professional knowledge to be acquired.

PURPOSE OF THE STUDY

The purpose of this study is to ascertain how the socialization of the pre-service teachers (junior interns), a process, which enables the interns' acquisition of the knowledge, skills, and dispositions that will enable them participate as more or less effective members of the teaching profession, influence their professional identity formation as teachers. This begs the question of how the junior interns perceive themselves as teachers, as well as, how they construct their identities as teachers. In their first field experience as student teachers, the interests and knowledge they develop in this preliminary experience are important determinants in entering the profession of teaching. For the junior interns and the diversity encountered in urban public schools, there has to be a necessary positive experience in their initial encounter. The junior field experience is a critical period in the education of urban teachers, because it determines whether or not the junior intern will opt to undertake the senior internship in an urban school, and subsequently teach in an urban school. For these pre-service teachers, this initial field experience in their junior year serves as a bridge between theory and practice, and the idealistic notions and resolutions in the college classroom versus the naked truth in the public school classroom. The cooperating teacher whether he or she realizes it or not, plays a defining role in the nature, quality, and direction of this neophyte. The interpersonal relationship between the junior intern and the cooperating teacher is one aspect of the field experience that leaves on the student intern, a memory that is indelible. This initial experience frames the beginning of the intern's identity formation as a teacher. This study is of crucial importance to the nature of the learning environments and socialization of pre-service teachers and their impact on developing identity as teachers in the inner cities/urban areas.

These junior interns are in transition, and are still considering whether or not to choose teaching as a profession. Furthermore, they are also considering whether or not to choose the urban environment as the place to start their career. Majority of the interns in this study received their K–12 education in the parochial or suburban public schools. This stage in the profession is a reflective stage for the junior intern, who can still opt out of education as a career, or change their certification level. They rely on the mentor teacher to guide them, and point them to the correct ways of being a teacher, as opposed to studying in the college classrooms about being a teacher. In other words, they are being introduced to the procedural knowledge of teaching, instead of the semantic knowledge of teaching, and moving them from theory to the practice of teaching. This is a critical period in the interns' professional development, career choice and adopting the values of the profession. Interns may or may not identify with the teaching profession. This self development process of socialization, involves examining oneself as a teacher and questioning one's choice and adoption of values, as well as, developing the knowledge skills and dispositions inherent in the profession of teaching. The learning environments have changed for the junior teacher interns. They have now moved from the secure, familiar campus environments with their peers and professors, to an unfamiliar neighborhood, unfamiliar urban schools with unfamiliar teachers and students. The factors mentioned affect the social and emotional well being at this entry point into the profession of teaching. Whatever happens at this stage, serves as building blocks for the acceptance of the values of the profession, as well as, acquisition of the profession's knowledge, skills and dispositions. This stage is the beginning of the development of professional identity.

THEORETICAL FRAMEWORK

The theoretical framework guiding this research is Erikson's psychosocial theory of Identification and Identity formation. Papalia and Olds (1992), describe identification as a process by which a person acquires characteristics, beliefs, attitudes, values, and behavior of another person or of a group. To Erikson (1968), Identification with the mentor/cooperating teaching who is the model, depends on the intern's satisfactory interaction, as well as the trustworthiness of the mentor/cooperating teacher. According to Erikson (1968), Identity formation begins where the usefulness of identification ends, and that the community, in this case, (schools, mentor/cooperating teachers) often not without some initial mistrust, gives recognition with a display of surprise and pleasure in making the acquaintance of newly emerging individual (the intern). Maier (1978) describes a sense of identity to mean a sense of being at one with oneself as one grows and develops; and it means a sense of affinity with a community's sense of being at one with its future, as well as it history or mythology. A sense of identity for the junior intern carries with it, a sense of mastery of the knowledge, skills, and disposition of the profession; it implies a genuine readiness to face the challenges of the teaching profession. This study looks at the identity elements, and uses the identity theory to analyze the interns' socialization experiences in their quest for professional identity.

METHODOLOGY

The basic premise for collecting data in natural settings according to Hittleman and Simon (1992) is that people do not act in isolation. Their behaviors and actions occur in specific social context or situation, and therefore these behaviors and actions must be studied in their natural settings, as it applies to the junior interns as participant observers in the urban setting to gain deeper understanding of the process socialization, the context in which it occurred, and the junior interns' experiences, data for this study were gathered in three ways. The interns documented weekly, the interpersonal relationships, and interactions between them and their cooperating teachers. Exit interviews were conducted, and they consisted of structured interviews and the administration of questionnaires. Additionally, classroom observations were conducted during the semester. The data were coded, triangulated and emergent themes were identified.

PARTICIPANTS

This study was delimited to 30 pre-service teachers attending an urban university in the North East, and enrolled in different sections of educational psychology course taught by the same instructor, and concurrently engaged in an urban setting field experience, as participant observers for the whole semester. The students in this study are of two categories: (a) junior interns pursuing baccalaureate degrees in either the arts or sciences, and (b) the certification only students, who already have their baccalaureate. The certification specialties are: Elementary and High school. The junior field experience lasted the whole semester that is (15) fifteen weeks. The student interns visited the urban schools every Wednesday for a whole day throughout the semester.

FINDINGS

The pre-service teachers' reflections of their experience and progress yielded important information. The following 10 themes and patterns emerged from the data:

Theme 1: Feeling Welcome

"She made me feel as if I belong because she approached me in smiling manner."
"She designed an area in the back of the room for me to sit at."
"Mrs. C told me that she wanted me to feel at home."

Theme 2: Acceptance

One student had written the following with mixed emotions. "Mrs. G did not have much to say to me and I wasn't sure if she wanted me there or not.

She has never been a mentor teacher before and I think that she just didn't know what to do with me.". . . by the 3rd visit, "so far, I feel as though Mrs. G and I have a good relationship and I believe that as time passes we will become more comfortable with each other. She is easy to get along with and is open to suggestions that I make. She has already allowed me to direct the students in their lessons and is willing to let me do more. . . ."

". . . she was very excited to see me and she greeted me with open arms."

". . . sometimes I did not feel as though I was accepted as a teacher or as a student who was trying to become a teacher."

Theme 3: Inclusion

". . . she gave me a book so I could follow along with the review . . ."

". . . when and if I am ready I can help teach lessons along with her or on my own."

". . . she gave me the opportunity to help the students in so many ways."

Theme 4: Support

". . . my mentor teacher was supportive, patient, and understanding . . . There was always a positive attitude towards everything I would do, whether correctly or incorrectly . . . one thing I do remember clearly is how she always said, 'Let them know whose boss.'" Keeping that in the back of my mind, it was the determining factor within my reach to control the classroom. . . . In the time that she would leave to attend other classes or situations, I felt my "security blanket" had left. . . . After the conclusion of the day, I sighed heavily and she tapped me on the back and said, "You were born to do this" needless to say I left the building with a desire to return the next day.

". . . she seemed as though she wanted me to follow my dream as a teacher"

". . . Mrs. X went over a few notes with me that she jotted down while I was teaching the lesson. She said that my lesson was good, but wanted to give me a few suggestions on how I might improve it. She was concerned that I might feel a little insulted While the students were doing some desk work, she proceeded to show me some of the lesson plans and explain the thematic units, so I could understand how the lessons were planned."

Theme 5: Feeling of importance

"She asked my opinion on what I would like to gain from these experiences and also made suggestions."

"...my mentor teacher referred to me with certain student situations."

"...she asked my opinion on what I would like to gain from these experiences and also made suggestions."

"My mentor teacher always praised me and told me that I am of those people born to teach."

Theme 6: Dependence

"...I have been able to explain directions to students who need additional explanation."

"...She told the students that I could answer questions they had and help them with their work."

Theme 7: Appreciation

"...she has never said thank you for anything I have done for her."

"...I have decided that since they were gracious towards me last week, that I would make brownies for them and pass it to them at snack time."

"...my mentor teacher always praised me and told me that I am one of those people who was born to teach."

Theme 8: Attention

"My mentor teacher helps me and gives me attention because she constantly advises me in what she is doing."

Theme 9: Respect

"...she introduced me to the students and told them that they should give me the same respect that they give her."

"...that she did not interfere or interrupt me when I was in front of the class teaching."

She was concerned that I might feel a little insulted by the feedback. (I assured her that any constructive criticism she could give me would be greatly appreciated).

Theme 10: Responsibility

"...she said if I felt comfortable may be I would like to tutor some of the children have some trouble."

"...Mrs. X asked me if I was comfortable with math yet. She encouraged me to ask any question or to work around the room and check on the children while they are doing their work."

The 10 themes are then placed under four categories, namely, acceptance, responsibility competence and Confidence. The four categories are used to explain this Competency identity construction model. This competence model shown on Tables 4.1 and 4.2, is not strictly hierarchical in

TABLE 4.1   A Competency Model of Identity Formation in Pre-Service Teachers

Level	Response category	Themes description
1	Acceptance	Comments from themes 1, 2, 3, 9
		Theme 1. Welcome: "She made me feel as if I belong because she approached me in smiling manner."
		Theme 2. Acceptance: "She was very excited to see me and she greeted me with open arms." or "...sometimes I did not feel as though I was accepted as a teacher or as a student who was trying to become a teacher."
		Theme 3. Inclusion: "...she gave me the opportunity to help the students in so many ways."
		Theme 9. Respect: "...she introduced me to the students and told them that they should give me the same respect that they give her." "...that she did not interfere or interrupt me when I was in front of the class teaching."
2	Responsibility	Comments from themes 3, 4, 5, 10
		Theme 5. Support: "...my mentor teacher was supportive, patient, and understanding.... There was always a positive attitude towards everything I would do, whether correctly or incorrectly. After the conclusion of the day, I sighed heavily and she tapped me on the back and said," You were born to do this" needless to say I left the building with a desire to return the next day." "...she seemed as though she wanted me to follow my dream as a teacher"
		Theme 10. Responsibility: "...she said if I felt comfortable may be I would like to tutor some of the children have some trouble."

TABLE 4.2   A Competency Model of Identity Formation in Pre-Service Teachers

Level	Responsibility	Themes description
3	Competence	Comments from themes 4, 5, 6, 7, 8, 9, 10 Sense of mastery **Theme 6. Dependence:** "…I have been able to explain directions to students who need additional explanation." "…She told the students that I could answer questions they had and help them with their work." **Theme 7. Appreciation:** "…I have decided that since they were gracious towards me last week,…that I would make brownies for them and pass it to them at snack time." "…my mentor teacher always praised me and told me that I am one of those people who were born to teach." **Theme 8. Attention:** "My mentor teacher helps me and gives me attention because she constantly advises me in what she is doing." **Theme 9. Respect:** "She was concerned that I might feel a little insulted by the feedback.(I assured her that any constructive criticism she could give me would be greatly appreciated)." **Theme 10. Responsibility:** "Mrs. X asked me if I was comfortable with math yet. She encouraged me to ask any question or to work around the room and check on the children while they are doing their work."
4	Confidence	Comments from **themes, 1 through 10.** Engendering feelings of confidence is recursive and runs through themes 1 to 10.

structure, but recursive. The competency identity formation model helps to illustrate sequence of events and types of experiences encountered by the interns. Additionally, the competency model allows for the understanding of the interns' interpretations of their experiences affect the construction of their identities as teachers. Throughout this professional identity development, the results of the study suggest that the affect, emotional aspects of the self tended to be at the fore of the interns initial professional development. The first category dealt with being accepted into the fold of teaching. The second category related to being respected, valued, trusted, and assigned responsibility, this in turn gave rise to the last category that emphasizes competence. Competence in carrying out the responsibilities using the knowledge, skills, and dispositions acquired up to this point, especially during the internship and the socialization in the new complex learning environment. Throughout this competency model, Confidence serves as a Velcro that ties all the levels together, as it weaves in and out of the levels.

The competency model is a confidence-building model. This confidence is derived from the very beginning when the intern encounters the urban learning community.

It appears from the findings that the interns go through varying levels of identity formation. The acceptance level is crucial to the beginning of self-awareness as a teacher. Acceptance as a teacher is a big deal for the interns, bearing in mind that they are just beginning to move from student to student teacher and then finally to full-fledged teacher. Acceptance by both the cooperating/mentor teacher and the students serve as information function. The quotations in themes 1 and 2 of the findings are supportive of this notion.

Further analysis of the themes deals with the next level of the interns' identity formation, the concept of competence to successfully carry out their responsibilities. The welcoming and acceptance feelings are important, but not enough in their process of constructing a competent and confident professional identity. They are concerned with the provocative question of having what it takes to become a teacher. This is evidenced in their responses depicted in the themes. Additionally, findings in this study suggest confidence building as an outcome of this experience. The junior interns are more concerned about the relationship they have with their cooperating teacher. The fact that the interns derived much confidence in this initial experience is apparent in the following statements:

> I have learned what it takes to be a teacher in an urban environment. My level of confidence has increased, and any doubts before the internship of becoming a teacher, have been erased. I also see myself teaching for the rest of my life. I learned that I really do want to become a teacher, that I would enjoy teaching in a public school in an urban area; I learned that I have gained confidence to teach especially in urban school without doubt. I have learned many ways to manage my future class.

The Shift

An emergent thought in this study, is the shift in the interns. A shift has occurred in how the interns perceive themselves. Some have aligned themselves with the students. They empathize and express sympathy for the students: "I saw many things I wanted to change. Inner city schools are failing to educate their students because the teachers are lazy . . . I don't want to be like the teacher in my internship." This particular intern is now aware of what it takes to be effective in an urban school. The intern becomes aware and internalizes that to be effective and successful in an urban school, the teacher has to be motivated to work in the urban community.

The process of socializing the junior interns into the profession of teaching helps in acquiring a professional identity. Similarly, (McGowen & Hart, 1990), point out that professional identity is achieved from professional socialization and development, as evidenced by the many interns who reported the following transformative experiences:

> I learned that I have what it takes to become a teacher. I realized how important the job is and feel so inspired to make my best effort in becoming an effective teacher. I learned how to properly act and present myself in order to be respected as a professional.

> . . . I learned that I have had an impact on children's lives and as a teacher I will continue to do so. More important, I learned that I can be a good teacher. My confidence level has risen.

> The most important thing I learned from my experience was that after this experience I am surer than ever that I want to become a teacher.

> I realized that I loved to be around young kids and deal with any problems they are going through . . . I discover how enjoying it is to work with kids and teach them, making a difference in their lives. . . . I observed in this class how students look up to their teacher as their role model. I have confirmed my goal to be an Art Educator and to never stop learning ways to be a competent, caring teacher.

> I am a hard worker when I care about something. I really love children, and I picked the right field to go into. I love everything about teaching. The smile of a child is worth a million dollars, when they are smiling because you taught them something. I love the way the students think you are up there with their heroes. I cannot wait to graduate, have my classroom decorated to my liking, and receive my master in Education. The best thing about it all is that I can see myself doing this for the next 50 years of my life.

The findings in this study help in the understanding of how the interns' experiences help them construct their identities as teachers.

DISCUSSION AND CONCLUSION

It is by studying how cooperating teachers mentor and socialize pre-service teachers that we can be informed. How and why the cooperating teachers do what they do are essential to the professional development of would-be teachers. The classroom is a living entity, and the events in the classroom are fluid. Cooperating teachers are vital to the process of socialization and enculturation of pre-service teachers into the teaching profession. The findings discussed in this paper will be beneficial in the education of our teachers, particularly those whom we are educating to work in urban schools. A positive socialization is able to adequately deal with the anxieties, attitudes and emotions of the intern. A sizeable number of the teacher candidates who are junior interns have never been in an urban classroom. The mentors will play a large role in influencing the quality of the interns' experience. This winning experience affords the intern insights into, and awareness of the complex nature of the teaching learning process, to the multiple forms of knowledge, as well as the various dimensions of professional knowledge that are to be acquired to be successful in the profession of teaching.

Themes, such as feelings of acceptance, welcome, inclusion, support, importance, dependence, appreciation, attention, respect, and responsibility that emerged in the study are similar to those found by Maynard (2000) to be significant features of 'good' mentoring practice. These good mentoring practices will assist the interns through a positive and successful process of their professional identity formation. The difference in this study is that such themes as Responsibility and Respect are absent from Maynard's findings. The patterns of the themes are also open to various interpretations. The themes relating to responsibility and respect could have been a function of the group in this particular study, the junior interns. Unlike the first year teachers, and senior student teachers studied by Maynard and others, for the interns in the present study, this is their first experience as "student teachers." They have at this point in their professional education, very little rudimentary skills, knowledge, and disposition, unlike the much-studied group of senior student teachers and first year teachers. As some interns commented, "I wish my mentor teacher remembers what it was like for her." For some interns, they felt left out of the experience. One student put it this way; "I was left to observe most of the time." The experience of not being included in the daily routine of the class may have caused the interns the desire to be assigned more responsibilities and be respected.

The author particularly found an intern's observation very interesting, in the sense that the intern reported that he did not feel accepted by the students because they did not even look at him. This observation coming out of the high school is quite fascinating to note. It brings to the fore the point that it is not necessarily the relationship with their mentors that the interns are concerned about, rather, it's the relationship with students that is crucial to their motivation to become teachers. In accordance with Phinney's (1996) contention, that an individual's experience in society as a member of a given culture significantly affects the strength of his or her identity. Accordingly, relationships with the inner city students are very important to the interns. Acceptance by the inner city students is crucial to the interns' motivation to teach in the urban setting.

The interns' perceptions and expectations changed with time. For example, the intern who reported that she felt tolerated at the beginning, reported much acceptance by mentor teacher later in the experience. Forging an optimal mentor/mentees relationship could be a function of time for some. For the intern who said that he felt quite unwelcome because the school did not know that he was coming on that day, it took him a longer time to feel wanted, included, and accepted. One intern who was placed in a high school was not satisfied with his experience because he reported not being allowed to get involved with the lessons. He felt alienated in the classroom and had to endure weeks of observation. He perceived the teachers as unaware of their responsibilities because they did not read the packets given by the college. In all his comments, the intern who had to work with three teachers had the following observations: "I saw many things I wanted to change. Inner city schools are failing to educate their students because the teachers are lazy. I do not want to be like the teacher in my internship. (The) high school cared very little about my progress during the internship. Only schools who really want to help interns should take on the responsibility." It can be inferred from the above statement from the intern that he is now identifying with the inner city student. Both the students and the intern are being neglected by the teachers who are according to the intern, are neglecting their responsibilities of educating their students. This experience is the nexus of the intern's affinity to the inner city students. He can empathize with them, and "saw many things he wanted to change." The interns cited respect, responsibility, encouragement, and importance as extremely essential to their becoming teachers. The positive experiences of the interns were derived from the interpersonal relationships between the interns and their cooperating teachers. Results suggest that a successful and positive junior field experience produces another level of attitudinal change. It confirms their career choice. They are convinced that they have chosen the correct profession, and they are willing and prepared to do whatever it takes to succeed at this calling. The interns become self-regulated and determined to acquire whatever knowledge, skills and dispositions that will enable them become effective in the classroom in general, and the urban classrooms in particular.

In some instances, interns come with preconceived notions about the urban schools. Acquisition of a mindset to work in this environment requires the mentor to demonstrate positive dispositions and values about urban workplaces. It calls on mentors to make the implicit explicit. Once the intern identifies with the context; the environment and the students, the intern begins a personal journey and professional development that will help her succeed. They view their profession with passion, a passion to help the students succeed, and a passion that fuels and sustains their professional development. It is this professional commitment at this beginning stage that could reduce the attrition of teachers in urban schools. Central to findings in this study, is the information function of the junior field experience. The interns are introduced to the urban classroom. They are let into the professional details, the professional secrets, "You Are In" By the end of this experience, the junior interns believe that "they are in" indeed. They feel accepted into the profession as they all reported. This feeling of acceptance into the profession came in large part from being accepted by their cooperating teachers. The interns interpreted the mentoring behaviors as indications of their being accepted into the profession of teaching. Perhaps this explains the high reporting of improved confidence in their choice and ability to teach, but also to become teachers in urban settings.

EDUCATIONAL IMPORTANCE OF THE STUDY

The findings of this study yielded information that will be beneficial in the education of our teachers, particularly those whom we are educating to work in urban schools. A sizeable number of the teacher candidates who are junior interns have never been in an urban classroom. The mentors will play a large role in influencing the quality of the interns' experience. Risk-taking is a factor in achievement motivation. If pre-service teachers, junior interns are to function with minimal anxiety and stress, they should be eased into some of the unknown terrains in the urban schools. This approach is recommended because for a high proportion of the interns, this experience will be their first encounter of the urban schools and the students who are educated here. It is a new community for the interns, and the experience should be a positive one. Mentoring teachers should make sure that these junior interns are exposed to the best practices of the profession. Additionally, they should be aware of the role they play in the nurturing of both the professional and personal development of these most sensitive and impressionable pre-service teachers.

Since the ecological dimension deals largely with concerns relating to process and features that have to do with socialization, enculturation, and negotiation of the features, place, and practice into the norms of the local school districts and community. The junior interns should be assigned only to schools where they are wanted, as well as, only to teachers who want them. There should be clear articulation by the colleges and the public schools as to the requirements for the experience. All constituents should view internships in general and junior internship in particular, as serious ventures. They should foster school partnerships, and view the role of the cooperating teachers as that of a mentor. Exposing pre-service teachers to ethnic minorities, cultural diversity, diverse learners, and settings is essential to forming a realistic and healthy professional identity.

To promote the education and training of teachers in today's global community, it is imperative that teacher educators acknowledge that race, ethnicity, culture and diversity are societal issues that are pivotal to the sense of whom we are as individuals, as well as, who we are as educators in today's global community.

REFERENCES

Anderson, J. R., Greeno J. G., Reeder, L. M., & Simon, H. A., (2000). Perspectives on learning, thinking, and activity. *Educational Research, 29*(4), 11–13.

Ashton, P. (1996). Improving the preparation of teachers. *Educational Researcher, 25*(9), 21–22, 35.

Carter, K. (1990). Teachers' knowledge and learning to teach. In W. R. Houston, M. Haberman, & J. Sikula (Eds.), *Handbook of research on teacher education* (pp. 291–310). New York: Macmillan.

Collins, A., Brown, J. S., & Newman, S. E. (1989) Cognitive apprenticeship: Teaching the craft of Reading, writing, and mathematics. In L. B. Resnick (Ed.), *Knowing, learning, and instruction: Essays in honor of Robert Glaser*. Hillsdale, NJ: Erlbaum.

Daloz, L. A. (1999). *MENTOR: Guiding the journey of adult learners*. San Francisco: Jossey-Bass.

Elliott, R. L. (2000). *Mentoring preservice mathematics teachers: A sociocultural perspective*. Paper Presented at AERA, New Orleans.

Farnham-Diggory, S. (1992). *Cognitive processes in education* (2nd ed.). New York: Harper Collins.

Feiman-Nemser, S., & Beasley, K. (1997). Mentoring as assisted performance. A case of co-planning. In V. Richardson (Ed.), *Constructivist teacher education: Theory and practice*. New York: Palmer Press.

Hawkey, K. (1997). Roles, responsibilities, and relationships in mentoring: A Literature review and Agenda for research. *Journal of Teacher Education. 48*(5), 325–335.

Kagan, D. M. (1992). Professional growth among preservice and beginning teacher. *Review of Educational Research, 62*(2), 129–169.

Koerner, M. E. (1999). The cooperating teacher: An ambivalent participant in student teaching. *Journal of Teacher Education, 43*(1), 46–56.

Maier, H. W. (1978). *Three theories of child development* (3rd ed.). New York: Harper & Row.

Maynard, T. (2000). Learning to teach or learning to manage mentors? Experiences of school-based teacher training. *Mentoring & Tutoring, 8*(1).

McGowen, K. R., & Hart, L. E. (1990). Still different after all these years: Gender differences in professional identity formation. *Professional Psychology and Practice, 21*,118–123.

Obi, R. U. (2004a, April). *An examination of mentoring behavior of cooperating teachers in urban schools*. Paper presented at the American Educational Research Association in San Diego.

Obi, R. U. (2004b, April). *The apprenticeship model in the mentoring and socialization of pre-service teachers in urban schools.* Paper presented at the Annual Meeting of American Educational Research Association (AERA) in San Diego.

Obi, R. U. (2003, April). *Pre-service teachers' perceptions of mentoring behaviors and the interpersonal relationships between the interns and their cooperating teachers in urban public schools.* Paper presented American Educational Research Association in Chicago.

Odell, S. J. (1986). Induction support for new teachers; a functional approach. *Journal of Teacher Education, 37*(1), 26–29.

Odell, S. A. (1989). *Developing support programs for beginning teachers. Assisting the beginning teacher.* Reston, VA: Association of Teacher Education.

Papalia, D. E., & Olds, S. W. (1992). *Human development* (5th ed.). New York: McGraw-Hill.

Phinney, J. S. (1996). When we talk about American ethnic groups, what do we mean? *American Psychologist, 51,* 918–927.

Putnam, R. & Borko, H. (1998). Teacher learning: Implications of new views of cognition. In J. Biddle, T. I. Good, & I. F. Goodson (Eds.), *The international handbook of teachers and teaching.* Dordrecht, the Netherlands: Kluwer.

Putnam, R. T., & Borko, H. (2000). What do new views of knowledge and thinking have to say about research and teacher learning? *Educational Researcher, 29*(1), 4–15.

Stanislus, R. N., & Russell, D. (2000). *A mentor's story: A full time mentor works with three intern teachers in a career ladder program.* Paper presented at AERA, New Orleans.

Vonk, J. H. C. & Schras, G. A. (1987). From beginning to experienced teacher: A study of the professional development of teachers during their fist four years of service. *European Journal of Teacher Education, 10,* 95–110.

Waldschmidt, E. D., & Coxen, P. (2000). *A mentor's story: A full-time mentor works with three intern teachers in a career ladder program.* Paper presented at AERA, New Orleans, LA.

Zeichner, K. M. (1985). The ecology of field experience: Toward an understanding of the role of field experience in teacher development. *Journal of Research and Development in Education, 18*(3), 44–51.

Zeichner, K. (1996). Designing educative practicum experience for prospective teachers. In K. Zeichner, S. Melnick, & M. Gomez (Eds.), *Currents of reform in preservice teacher education* (pp. 215–234). New York: Teachers College Press.

Zeichner, K. M., & Gore, J. (1990). Teacher socialization. In W. R. Houston (Ed.), *Handbook of research on teacher education* (pp. 329–348). New York: Macmillan.

CHAPTER 5

CARIBBEAN STUDENTS' ADJUSTMENT TO COLLEGE

Implications for Higher Education Policy

D. Bruce Campbell, Jr.

The migration of foreign students to the United States to pursue degrees in higher education represents a consistent trend. Caribbean students and other foreign students are slowly becoming a significant part of college populations. In 1999, more than 481,000 foreign students enrolled in U.S. colleges, a significant increase from the 286,000 that enrolled in 1980 (U.S. Department of Census, 1999). This study investigates the college adjustment of Caribbean students[1] who attend a small, liberal arts college in the United States and focuses on their experiences of adjusting to their college environment.

The United States is one of the leading nations in the world in granting academic degrees to foreign students. Both the institutions of higher learning and the foreign students benefit from this process. Colleges and universities gain enrollments and maintain higher competitive standards by drawing on a larger student pool. Foreign students obtain an opportunity for higher education they might not have at home.

Policy, Leadership, and Student Achievement, pages 55–76
Copyright © 2008 by Information Age Publishing
55

The research question guiding this study was:

What are the Caribbean student's experiences as they adjust
to a liberal arts college?

A qualitative design is used to provide an in-depth account of Caribbean students' experiences, as well as to obtain a student perspective to college adjustment. Participants of the study will be interviewed on the college campus.

THE RESEARCH

The study of Caribbean students' adjustment to college in the US is the focus of this study. In the United States, the experience of going to college is often associated with leaving home, joining other individuals of the same age on a residential college campus, and living and learning in a campus setting. Postsecondary education is, for many, an education not only in the humanities, the social sciences, and the sciences, but also an education in living with peers in a temporary and transient environment that constitutes a formative influence on individual development. Residential learning recognizes that postsecondary studies are not only intellectual, but also bear potential for emotional, psychological, and interpersonal growth, in addition to providing an opportunity to learn how to live with those who are like us and with those who are different, distant, and unfamiliar.

This new setting may be overwhelming and intimidating for some students or refreshing and rejuvenating for others. Whatever emotions these students may be experiencing one might imagine the additional reactions an international student may be encountering. Coming to a new country for an education carries the thoughts of so much promise and hope for one's successful future. However, besides looking ahead to the future, these students have to deal with relevant issues of adjustment that they encounter.

First, the institution's approach to diversity draws from different studies as to what different institutions describe as the problems of having a diverse student population and what needs to be done to better serve the diverse population. The institutions recognize the adjustment these students need to make and are working to address this issue.

Second, assimilation, accommodation, and acculturation are all relevant topics to the study of student adjustment, especially in the work of Milton Gordon (1964). His work could be the necessary research link to help international students and American institutions. Third, in the discussion of student adjustment, the researcher has included several studies that are relevant to the topic of the adjustment of Caribbean students. A better understanding of what students have experienced can help predict what future students will encounter as well as assist colleges and universities and make the necessary improvement to institutions' environments.

Assimilation and Accommodation

There has been little research on the culture of Caribbean students and how it has been affected when they come to the United States to attend college. Nevertheless, there are a number of theories that can be used to describe the culturally pluralistic nature of the Caribbean student's role on college campuses in the United States. One of these theories is assimilation, related to Caribbean students accommodating into the culture of colleges in the United States. Milton Gordon (1964) is one of the founders of the assimilation and accommodation theory and his ideas have been cited numerous times in sociology and psychology research. According to Gordon (1964), the accommodation process develops through stages in which the new cultural group: (1) changes its cultural pattern to those of the dominant group; (2) develops large-scale primary-group relationships with the dominant group; (3) collaborates fully with the dominant group; (4) loses its sense of individuals being separate from the dominant group; (5) encounters no discrimination; (6) encounters no prejudiced attitudes; and (7) does not raise any issues that would involve value and power conflict with the dominant group. Each of these stages also represents a degree of accommodation.

Acculturation

If acculturation is distinguished from assimilation, even second-generation principles may have become almost entirely acculturated. They still retain a significant number of ethnic social ties, particularly familial ones, and cannot be said to have assimilated. "Acculturation refers mainly to the newcomer's adoption of the culture (i.e., behavior patterns, values, rules, symbols etc.) of the host society [or rather an overly homogenized and reified conception of it]" (Gans, 1997, p. 877).

Acculturation and assimilation are slightly different if acculturation is viewed as an international student's complete embrace of the new culture he or she lives in. Using an international student as an example, accommodation would be the student changing to a specific aspect of the culture. This specific aspect is what Gollnick and Chinn (1994) refer to as the "dominant" culture, the lifestyle of the majority group in a particular culture.

Two reasons explain why acculturation is always a faster process than assimilation. American culture is a powerfully attractive force for immigrants (Gans, 1997). Therefore, it easily appeals to children and young adults, particularly those coming from societies that lack their own commercial popular cultures. Second, ethnic groups can acculturate on their own, but they cannot accommodate unless they are given permission to enter the "American" group or institution. Since discrimination and other reasons often lead to denial of that permission to the immigrant and even the second generation, assimilation will always be slower than acculturation (Gans, 1997).

The speed and succession of the acculturation process depend on several factors, including location and discrimination. If a minority group, like Caribbeans, are spatially isolated and segregated on a college campus (whether voluntarily or not), the acculturation process is very slow. Oppressed groups are usually marked with discrimination; it deprives group members of educational and occupational opportunities and primary relationships with members of the dominant group (Gordon, 1964).

When two groups share primary group relationships, including membership in the same cliques and social clubs, it is referred to as structural assimilation (Gordon, 1964). For most groups, success in becoming acculturated has not led to structural assimilation. It has neither eliminated prejudice and discrimination nor led to large-scale collaboration with the dominant cultural group (Gans, 1997).

A characteristic, such as race, prevents assimilation for people of African descent. Unfortunately, many people view members of different races with prejudice and make assimilation difficult for members of oppressed groups. However, when assimilation process is effective, it leads to the disappearance of a cultural group that is distinct from the dominant group.

It is important to note that acculturation is determined in part by the individual (Gans, 1997). International college students can decide how much they want to dress, speak, and behave like members of the dominant group since the dominant group determines the extent of structural assimilation. The ideology of assimilation comes from a larger issue of adjustment, specifically, a Caribbean student's adjustment to the college culture in the United States. Caribbean students' adjustment can be measured (via surveys, interviews, and observations) by an evaluation of the experiences these students encounter with individuals in their college community. The new surroundings these students are in is a major factor in their level of adjustment.

Cultural Identity

Culture provides the foundation for an individual's identity that mediates the way an individual thinks, feels, and behaves in society. At the same time, "culture develops within 'unequal and dialectical relations that different groups establish in a given society at a particular historical point'" (Giroux, 1988, p.116). Giroux's statement provides insight into interactions between students on college campuses.

Unequal relations among individual groups powerfully impact their ability to state and accomplish their goals (Giroux, 1988). The dynamics of these power relationships and the effect they have on the development of groups must also be an integral part of the study of culture. "Culture gives us our identity through acceptable words; through our actions, postures, gestures, and tones of voice; through our facial expressions; through our handling of time, space, and materials; and through the way we work, play, express our emotions, and defend ourselves" (Hall, 1977, p. 215). Traits and values learned as part of each individual's ethnic background form the basis of cultural identity. The phrase cultural identity refers to individual characteristics, traits, and values that an individual embodies pertaining to his/her personality and culture. Traits and values learned as part of one's ethnic origin, religion, gender, age, socioeconomic status, primary language, geographical region, and place of residence all aspects of one's cultural identity (Gollnick & Chinn, 1994).

A person learns how to become a functioning adult within a specific society through culture (Gollnick & Chinn, 1994). The processes of enculturation and socialization begin at birth. The term socialization is the general process of learning the social norms of the culture (Abercrombie, Hill, & Turner, 1984). Enculturation is the process of acquiring the characteristics of a given culture and generally becoming competent in its language. This initiation process of enculturation and socialization occurs from interactions with parents, siblings, doctors, teachers, and neighbors.

A second characteristic of culture is that culture is shared (Gollnick & Chinn, 1994). Shared cultural patterns and customs bind people together as an identifiable group and make it possible for them to live together and function with ease.

An individual is placed in a new setting where their cultural identity becomes strengthened and weakened to some degree. This is part of the adjustment process. For instance, freshman college students coming to the United States from the Caribbean are involved in these cultural adjustments.

THE PROBLEM

Based on the literature presented in this study there are several disparities around the issue of college adjustment that international students encounter in their college communities. In the midst of the college adjustment, a student's development takes place.

College is the time when most students are beginning to understand whom they are and what type of values they have. Although this can occur any time, various aspects of college adjustment, culture, acceptance, withdrawal, and cooperation of college students and the institutions they attend affect the experiences and perceptions students have of college and themselves.

The institution's approach to diversity may impact how a Caribbean student adapts to the campus. Several studies (Allen, 1992; Clark & Crawford, 1992; D'Augelli & Hersberger, 1993; Davis, 1991; Fleming, 1995; Haniff, 1991; Mio, 2000; Nieto, 1994) suggest that schools need to look at policies and practices, as well as the curriculum, counseling, and cultural resources and events available for Caribbean students to make their occurrences at the college comfortable enough to fulfill a rewarding academic and social college experience.

Some aspects of their adjustment depend on the institution the student is attending. Research from Ana Maria Villegas (1998, 1991) challenges schools to be culturally responsive, that students' backgrounds are important and need to be taken into consideration in the decision-making process with the interest of the student in mind. Villeagas and others (A.P.A., 1992; Dwyer & Villegas, 1993; Floden, 1991; Glaser, 1984; Resnick, 1989; Tharp & Gallimore, 1988) have made linkages to students' background knowledge, ethnicity, and culture and how it is relevant for these students to keep and bring this body of knowledge and values with them to college. The university's level of cultural responsiveness to all cultures makes the process of a student's assimilation and acculturation as well as the institution's commitment to accommodation much easier. These issues of re-definition and change are particularly interesting when one ascribes social identity to categories such as ethnicity or gender, which might be thought to be particularly resistant to change. The importance of ethnic identity is well documented. Ethnic identity is embedded in a multidimensional context, related to factors such as language, cultural background, geographic region, social class, and political conflict (Gollnick & Chinn, 1994; Saylor & Aries, 1999; Wilson & Constantine, 1999). If a person's group identification is supported by a particular context, what happens when the person leaves that context and moves into another? This is what Caribbean students face when they come to the United States to attend college. The study will take a closer look at all of these pertinent issues on Caribbean students' experiences and share their stories.

METHODOLOGY

The methodology of the study follows a qualitative research design. A single site, descriptive methodology was utilized. The research questions focused on the voice of the students and school community that are not expressed in the literature to date. Participants had the opportunity to speak on their experiences on this subject as well as how these experiences were related to the research topic. In addition, the research questions locate Caribbean students at the center of the research and speak to the possibility of effecting change in the lives of these students as well as future students based on the telling of their stories.

Site Selection

Thompson College is a pseudonym to protect the participants and institution used in this study. Thompson College is a secluded campus tucked away in a residential community where it is easy to get caught up in the natural quietness of the surroundings. Thompson College is a private, predominantly White, coed, liberal arts college. Thompson College has more than 1,000 full-time students. There is an average of 70 international students a year and a little less than 25% of the entire student population are students of color, 14% of these students are of Asian ancestry, around 14%. African American and Latino/a students each make up about 6%, and other groups, such as Native Americans, etc., make up less than 0.5%. These percentages seem to be high for a college community in terms of a diverse student body. In fact, Thompson College has one of the highest percentages of student diversity in the country for a liberal arts college.

This small, liberal arts college was selected as the research site for two reasons. First, the institution for the research site is located in a secluded suburban area. That means students' main form of social activity occurs on the college campus. Secondly, the experiences of Caribbean students at small colleges are underrepresented in the literature. This study puts the Caribbean students as the focus of the study through the investigation of their experiences of adjustment. This research site provides an accessible environment and a naturally bounded system of a college.

Description of Participants

The study focused on the student population on the college's campus that identifies as having Caribbean roots. The first interview session that each Caribbean student participated in was called the Focused Life History (Campbell, 2001). The definition of a Caribbean (for this study) is a citizen of a Caribbean country or is a first or second-generation child of Caribbean origin (Table 5.1).

TABLE 5.1   What the Methods Measure

Methods	Measures
Interview Protocol (Campbell, 2001)	The in-depth interviews explore the participant's backgrounds, views, and experiences relevant to their adjustment to college.
Survey Sheet (Campbell, 2001)	The survey sheets the students filled out shed light into the daily interactions these students have with the college community, answering questions as to where they socialize, with whom, and how often.
Focus Group	The focus group sessions encouraged discussion among the participants so they generate a better understanding of their different and similar experiences on campus and how they cope.

TABLE 5.2   Categories that Impact Student Adjustment

Aspects of Caribbean Student Adjustment	Subgroups
College Environment	Other students, geographic location of the college, faculty/administrators, curriculum, social activities, etc.
Background	1st or 2nd generation Caribbean, family background, previous social environments
Identity	Ethnic, Cultural

TABLE 5.3   Biographical Data of Participants

Category/Question	Response	Number of Participants	Percentage of Participants
Gender	Male	3	50%
	Female	3	50%
Year in college	Sophomore	3	50%
	Senior	3	50%
Where were you born?	United States	3	50%
	Caribbean	3	50%
Where were your parents born?	United States	0	0%
	Caribbean	6	100%
Where did you grow up?	United States	3	50%
	Caribbean	3	50%
What was the ethnic makeup of the neighborhood you grew up in?	Predominantly White	0	0%
	Predominantly minority	6	100%
	Mixed	0	0%
What was the ethnic makeup of your elementary, middle, and high school?	Predominantly White	1	17%
	Predominantly minority	3	50%
	Mixed	2	33%
How would you describe your friends?	Predominantly White	0	0%
	Predominantly minority	5	83%
	Mixed	1	17%

Every college student goes through some form of adjustment period when they attend college. College is usually a new environment for them to learn and grow as individuals. Results of the adjustment of the Caribbean college students can be viewed in three categories: Initial, Student Commitment, and Social.

FINDINGS

Initial Adjustment

The initial adjustment phase is the time of early transition for students. These are the initial thoughts and allure of the college for students even before setting foot on campus. The initial adjustment phase also focuses on the time the students have actually moved on campus and begun their college careers. What has that time been like for these Caribbean students? This phase takes a closer look at the beginning level of adjustment for these students as they deal with issues of expectations and building a social network at college.

Daily Campus Life Makes a Difference

As the students began to settle into the surroundings of the college, several students had initial adjustments to make to Thompson College. Five of the students experienced a drastic change in environments. While four of the participants went to high schools that were predominantly minority if not mixed, only one went to a primarily White institution. Students shared their initial issues of feeling isolated and unwelcome at Thompson College from fellow students and some faculty. In the classroom, they expressed a pressure of representation.

> I'm sick of being in different courses and I am one of few Black students and I'm there in a class discussion on race, ethnicity, or culture. Why is it that all the White students and the professor look at me to represent the Black race....As if we (people of African heritage) all think the same. One time I was in a humanities course and the topic of slavery came up. I'm Caribbean born and raised there. Of course there was slavery in the Caribbean but did anyone ever consider that my perspective on slavery would be different from an African American? No! (Caribbean Student)

At different times, all six participants commented on having similar experiences that this student described. They also expressed their belief that these occurrences would continue until changes take place on campus. As one

Caribbean student described, the minority student population is so small on this campus that minorities stick out like a sore thumb when they are in a setting where they are the only minority in the room or one of few.

> I see it in classes all the time. It is like some of the White students on campuses only perceptions of Black people are what they have seen on television. In sociology and history classes, whenever issues of race and class come up the White students look to the Black students for guidance and knowledge.... Like these students are the spokesperson for their ethnic groups [said sarcastically] (White Student).

Other non-Caribbean students, as well as faculty, have commented to suggest that occurrences similar to the one this student has just described have happened a few times in different courses over the years and were brought to the attention of the provost's office.

In the past, there was a minority student run event on campus set up like an open mic where students (mostly students of African heritage) would speak out concerning different issues that affected the college community in a positive or negative way. This event was held in the spring semester and heavily attended by the entire college community: students, faculty, administrators, and college employees of all races. The power of such an event may have brought about positive change on campus. For example, some of the Caribbean students and college community believe that the "open mic" (microphone) event played a role in the opening of a multicultural office on campus as well multicultural events and faculty searches. Some of the Caribbean students shared their experiences in the focus group.

> **Caribbean Student 1**—"I can remember my freshman year when Black students had 'Speak Out.' There was actually a voice on campus and the college community was concerned because they would show up to the event in big numbers.
> **Caribbean Student 2**—"Now it's practically extinct. Low attendance and little interest, especially by minorities."
> **Caribbean Student 3**—"Times are different now. Students are lazier and always thinking 'oh someone else will speak up.' Also I'm sure the administration feels they have enough things in place for minorities that they should be comfortable here."

However, the luster of such an event has tarnished as students' interest in speaking out has changed and their commitment to change has been redefined. Students felt they would be targeted by faculty and administrators on campus as a "troublemaker" if they spoke out. Moreover, students have redirected their commitment to their academics and small social networks instead of invoking change on campus.

Focus Group

Many of the Caribbean students commented that they were pleased to have the opportunity to participate in the focus group. They all felt that the issues were important and rarely do they get the chance to discuss them on campus.

Student Commitment

The second phase of the Caribbean students' adjustment was their commitment to the institution. A different level of involvement on campus also appears to affect social adjustment. Austin (1975) demonstrates that the level of involvement in college activities is positively associated with college persistence, student satisfaction, and connectedness to college. Most of the Caribbean students who participated in the study are fairly active. However, the stories they share reveal that their adjustment has not always been positive. The only noticeable exception is the Minority Scholars Program (MSP) that Thompson College students can enjoy.

All minority students are contacted and introduced to MSP prior to their first semester at the college. This is a program that began in the 1980s for minority students majoring in the Humanities and the Social Sciences.

> The Minority Scholars Program in the Sciences, Humanities, and Social Sciences offers students of color four years of guidance, support, and opportunity, ensuring academic success at Thompson College and fulfillment of academic potential at the best graduate and professional schools afterward. (MSP Web site)

MSP is successful because since it was established, it has created numerous workshops, tutoring programs, internships, counseling, and advising opportunities. Furthermore, faculty members are very involved in the program. In fact, during the 2001–2002 school year 37 faculty members were a part of MSP, which is a large number for such a small campus. One important aspect of MSP is that it is funded by an outside foundation. This is an important part of MSP's success as all the participants (6 Caribbean students and 10 members of the college community) have stated that several resources, activities, events, etc. are not a reality or possibility on campus for minorities because of a lack of funding. "The funding that MSP gets has helped MSP build the resources and staff necessary to service students" (Administrator).

With such a successful program for more than 20 years, it appears that Thompson College is addressing the academic needs of minority students from the moment they step on campus. With numerous programs, counseling, and support, minority students have available resources to make them a successful "academic" student. However, there are many ways students that do not take advantage of this program and the services it provides. Most of the students that fell into this category blamed campus politics once again for not attending MSP events. As one Caribbean student stated:

> Some of the workshops that MSP has are very beneficial so I use the program for those reasons. MSP wants to build a community where all minorities get along and help one another. That does not happen in the real world so why would you expect it to work here. The politics of how the program is run seems shady so it seems better to stay out of all that mess and use the program for what it's worth.

Student Organizations Impact

Even though MSP is a successful "academic" program for minority students, there are other opportunities for students to work on their social success. Students may find social support through the MSP program, but that is not the focus of the program. There are several other opportunities the school offers for these students to have a positive social experience. There are more than 100 student activities and organizations on campus. Of this number, 11 are official minority student organizations.

The Caribbean organization on campus has a short history since it was created in the fall of 1997. However, the Caribbean organization's leadership, described by members as on the "border of dictatorship" caused low membership and poor organization.

> The organization is still fairly new. These students have no example to follow. Some of their leaders have gone away for semesters abroad. I would imagine it will take the commitment of a faculty member or administrator to serve as a mentor to the organization for the Caribbean organization to really make an impact on this campus. (Administrator)

Interestingly enough two other members of the organization made the same statement in their own way. The fascinating aspect was that one was non-Caribbean and the other was a freshman.

Now, the Caribbean organization is in the process of rebuilding the organization and its reputation. Just this semester the organization missed the deadline for student organization budgeting. The organization still received money but not the full amount they could have obtained if it had filed when it was supposed to. This recent mishap sparked an array of conflict and hostility among members of the organization. The most revealing result was that the annual Caribbean Week (the organization's biggest event of the academic year) was canceled. Continuous mistakes and then name-calling like this only hurts the organization more and more.

> It's frustrating when members of the organization can't pull their weight. Then the whole organization suffers. This was a case where someone wanted sole control of a project because they didn't like the person who was previously handling it but they dropped the ball. (Caribbean student)

Several of the minority student-run organizations have little impact because of the low turnout at meetings. The only time there is a substantial turnout is when there is a party. Students have stated there are two major reasons for the low attendance rates. First, students do not particularly care for the egos and politics of the leaders and members of the different minority organizations. "Too much time of the meeting is devoted to nonsense and I'd rather spend time doing my schoolwork or hanging out with friends." (Caribbean Student). Students get so wrapped up with the "soap opera" of the small campus with "he said" and "she said" incidents that they lose the focus of what the organizations and events are supposed to be about.

The second reason students attribute low attendance at minority events and organizations is all six Caribbean students felt the college is not truly interested in diversity. After being invited to a few Caribbean organization meetings and events, students' comments about the lack of involvement became apparent. There were only a handful of individuals at these meeting and events. More noticeably, it was the same few students in attendance. It is hard for students to build an organization and conjure up support for the organization when the college community (including Caribbean students) does not attend the organizations' functions.

> The only time the student population "seeks" diversity is when one of the Black or Latino organizations throws a party. This is when all students come out to the event because this campus loves to party and the students know they will hear good music. (Caribbean Student)

This student's statement came to life as one of the only Caribbean student parties, which was held during MSW, was overflowing with minority and non-minority students. With free food and good diverse music, "the party was a big hit" on campus as several students reported. Despite the cries of lack of support from the campus community, some of the participants of the study do not participate in their own functions and those of other minority organizations. The results from the survey questions reflected a lack of organization and lack of support. One survey question was, "How many Caribbean organization meetings did you attend this month?" (Campbell,

2001) More than half of the respondents admitted to not knowing there was an organization meeting until the next day. As one student explains,

> We were supposed to have a meeting last Tuesday. I only knew about the meeting because other members were asking where I was that night and updated me on what was discussed at the meeting. The sad part is I asked the co-president the week before if there was going to be a meeting and that person said no.

This student was not the only person to comment about such an experience. These incidents also did not happen in the same month. Another important question in the survey was "What campus events did you attend this month?" (Campbell, 2001). Usually students would have the one and only minority campus party that occurred that month. Alternatively, they would not have anything at all. Nevertheless, the Multicultural Office, MSP, the actual college, and different academic departments would have different events on campus such as guest speakers, special dinners, and workshops. For some reason the Caribbean, students did not have the interest to attend these numerous events.

> Some of the events are honestly just a conflict with my schedule. I have classes all day and sometimes at night. Then there are meeting for organizations and then these social events? Sometimes it is just too much and I cannot go to everything! I need time for myself, time to study, time to relax. (Caribbean Student)

Caribbean students' social events seemed to take place during their everyday occurrences. Students filled the pages answering questions asking about social events off campus, social activities, and where they ate their meals. These students were very active in going to parties at different institutions in the area other than their own institutions.

Most of them commented that eating lunch and dinner on a daily basis with their closest friends was very important to them. One student summed it up this way:

> We are so busy with classes, studying, jobs, and commitment to campus organizations sometimes at the dining center is the only time we get to catch up with others and hang out. If not, we might not be able to see our friends until people are done with their obligations and ready to relax for the night before the next day starts. (Caribbean Student)

The Caribbean students place a significant amount of emphasis on their close friends as their social outlet and support. These groups of individuals that surround and support these students are known as their social network. The impact of a college student's social network seemed crucial to the success of their social adjustment.

Social Life

The final phase of adjustment for the participants of this study was their social life. Social adjustment assesses how one is dealing with the success of interpersonal relationships and social support, the extent and success of social involvement, and satisfaction with the social environment (Baker & Sirky, 1989). The major source for these students' adjusting to Thompson College is their social network. The social network is the group of individuals the student feels are friends, mentors, and individuals they can confide in and engage in social activities with together. The participants mentioned that members of their social networks included Caribbean students, other minority students, and a few White students. For some participants their social network was not limited to just students. A few of the students had deans, faculty, and other college employees as part of their social network. Some of the students' social networks were initiated during the Summer Institute. Others were formed during classes or through social organizations and events.

Research has consistently found that social supports have a positive effect on adjustment (Solberg, Valdez, & Villarreal, 1994). Interviews from this study revealed a difference in satisfaction and tolerance of the college based on the student's social supports. Those that had an extensive support network appeared to have an easier time adjusting and spoke more about the joys they experience on campus. However, a number of participants with a smaller and possibly weaker social network spoke freely about the frustrations they had as a student and laying a great deal of the cause of their problems on the institution.

One of the students that have had a positive adjustment experience summed up his experience by stating, "The whole experience (college) is what you make of it" (Caribbean student). This student is very active at the college but has a balance of students, faculty, and administrators of different ethnic backgrounds that make up his social network.

This study found the same results regarding cultural pride. All the participants talked about their cultural pride and how they were pleased to express it. This expression usually came to light at Caribbean parties (or other parties where Caribbean music was played), Caribbean organization meetings, and decorating their dorm rooms.

POLICY IMPLICATIONS FOR COLLEGE AND UNIVERSITIES

Colleges and universities need to develop and implement policies that are being culturally responsive when it comes to serving the entire student body academically and socially. Thompson College is separating the student body through individual programs and possibly hindering cultural awareness on campus, which affects every student's adjustment. Ana Maria Villegas (1991, 1998) refers to an ideology of an institution being "culturally responsive." Culturally responsive is when colleges and universities find ways to adjust, accept, and appreciate different cultures. For an institution to be culturally responsive, they have to provide support of all of the ethnic groups they serve. A college that is receptive to all forms of diversity enables students to be themselves and enjoy their college experience.

Thompson College and several other institutions across the country have programs where they have a separate orientation for minority students and then another orientation for the entire student body. Besides separate orientations, there are different programs throughout the school year tailored toward different ethnic groups, which sometimes make other students feel unwanted. This separation of services can be beneficial, however, there needs to be some inclusion. For instance, some of the minority orientation topics may discuss cultural differences of the population on campus. Minority students usually know about other minority cultures. However, White students might get more understanding of cultures if they were included in the discussion during orientation and throughout the school year. These types of policies reflect what Ana Maria Villegas refers to when she talks about institutions being culturally responsive.

The institution's approach to diversity may affect how a Caribbean student adapts to a college campus. Several studies (Allen, 1992; Clark & Crawford, 1992; D'Augelli & Hersberger, 1993; Davis, 1991; Fleming, 1995; Haniff, 1991; Mio, 2000; Nieto, 1994) suggest that schools need to look at policies and practices, as well as the curriculum, counseling, and cultural resources and events available for Caribbean students to make their occurrences at the college comfortable enough to fulfill a rewarding academic and social college experience. This study is no different as Caribbean students, non-Caribbean students, and the majority of the faculty and administrators that participated have all commented that there needs to be more action taken toward diversifying all aspects of college life on Thompson College's campus.

The third conclusion is that the students' commitment to and level of involvement with the institution and the social network they create for themselves plays a significant role as to whether their adjustment is pleasant or frustrating. Participating students' different levels of adjustment can be attributed to what activities and individuals surrounding them. Students who were active members of the college community and surrounded themselves with a diverse social network that includes other students (of different ethnic backgrounds), faculty, and administrators stated their college adjustment has been enjoyable. However, students who were less active in the college community and social networks limited their social network to other students (usually minority students) and reported their college adjustment as quite frustrating.

The goal for most colleges and universities is to provide a rich nurturing environment for a student to grow academically and socially. Most of the Caribbean students at Thompson College have assimilated, but it has been a daily challenge. The results from this study emphasize the need for the college's commitment to being culturally responsive in all aspects of college life to assist these students with the assimilation process. Furthermore, all students need to take responsibility for their own adjustment and create change if that is what they need.

NOTE

1. For the purpose of this study, students are from the Caribbean and/or are American students of first or second generation Caribbean origin.

REFERENCES

Abercrombie, N., Hill, S., & Turner, B. S. (1984). *Dictionary of sociology.* New York: Penguin Books.

Abi-Nader, J. (1993). Meeting the needs of multicultural classrooms: Family values and the motivation of minority students. In M.J. O'Hair & S. Odell (Eds.), *Diversity and teaching: Teacher education yearbook* (Vol. 1, pp. 212–236). Fort Worth, TX: Harcourt Brace Jovanovich.

Allen, W. (1992). The color of success: African American college student outcomes at predominantly white and historically black public colleges and universities. *Harvard Educational Review, 62,* 1, 26–44.

American Heritage college dictionary (3rd ed.). (1997). New York: Houghton Mifflin.

American Psychological Association. (1992). *Learner-centered psychological principles: Guidelines for school redesign and reform.* Washington, DC: Author.

Austin, A. (1984) Student involvement: A developmental theory for higher education. *Journal of College Student Personnel. 26,* 197–308.

Baker, R. W. & Siryk, B. (1989) Measuring adjustment to college. *Journal of Counseling Psychology, 31*(2), 179–189.

Beckham, B. (1988). Strangers in a strange land: The experience of blacks on white campuses. *Educational Record,* 74–78.

Berreman, G. D. (1985). Race, caste, and other invidious distinctions in social strati-fication. In N. R. Yetman (Ed.), *Majority and minority: The dynamics of race and ethnicity in American life* (4th ed., pp.21–39) Boston: Allyn & Bacon.

Bogdan, R., & Biklen, S. (1992). *Qualitative research for education: An introduction for theory and methods* (2nd ed.). Boston: Allyn and Bacon.

Campbell, D. B. (2001). *Taking a close look at Caribbean students social adjustment to a small college campus.* Unpublished dissertation, Drexel University.

Chickering, A. W. & Assoc. (1981). *The modern American college.* San Francisco: Jossey & Bass.

Clark, S. & Crawford, S. (1992). An analysis of African American first-year college student attitudes and attrition rates. *Urban Education, 27,* 1, 59–79.

Cookson Jr., P. W. (1994). *School choice: The struggle for the soul of American education.* New Haven, CT: Yale University Press.

Cox, O. C. (1948). *Caste, class, and race.* Garden City, NY: Doubleday.

Creswell, J. (1994). *Research design: Qualitative and quantitative approaches.* Thousand Oaks, CA: Sage.

Creswell, J. (1998). *Qualitative inquiry and research design; choosing among five tradi-tions.* Thousand Oaks, CA: Sage.

Cross, W. E., Jr. (1971). The negro-to-black conversion experience: Toward a psy-chology of black liberation. *Black World, 20,* 13–27.

D'Augelli, A. R., & Hershberger, S. L. (1993). African American undergraduates on a predominantly white campus: Academic factors, social networks, and cam-pus climate. *Journal of Negro Education, 62*(1), 67–81.

Davis, R. (1991). Social support networks and undergraduate students' academic-related-success outcomes: A comparison of black students on black and white campuses. In W. Allen, E. Epps, & N. Haniff (Eds.), *College in black and white: African American students in predominantly white and historically black public uni-versities.* Albany: State University of New York Press.

Dwyer, C. A., & Villegas, A. M. (1993). *Guiding conceptions and assessment principles for the Praxis series: Professional assessments for beginning teachers.* Princeton, NJ: Educational Testing Service.

Flavell, J. H. (1963). *The developmental psychology of Jean Piaget.* New York: D. Van Nostrand Co.

Fleming, J. (1995). *Blacks in college: A comparative study of students' success in black and in white institutions.* San Francisco: Jossey-Bass Publishers.

Floden, R. E. (1991). What teachers need to know about learning. In M. Kennedy (Ed.), *Teaching academic subjects to diverse learners* (pp. 181–202). New York: Teachers College Press.

Gans, H. (1997). Toward a reconciliation of "assimilation and pluralism": The in-terplay of acculturation and ethnic retention. *International Migration Review, 31*(4), 875–892.

Giroux, H. A. (1988). *Teachers as intellectuals: Toward a critical pedagogy of learning.* Granby, MA: Bergin & Garvey.

Glasser, R. (1984). Education and thinking: The role of knowledge. *American Psy-chologist, 39,* 93–104.

Glesne, C. & Peshkim, A. (1992). *Becoming qualitative researchers: An introduction.* New York: Longman.

Gollnick, D. M. & Chinn, P. C. (1994). *Multicultural education in a pluralistic society.* (4th ed.) New York: Macmillan College Publishing Co.

Gordon, M. (1964). *Assimilation in American life: The role of race, religion, and national origins.* New York: Oxford University Press.

Gossett, B., Cuyjet, M. & Cockriel, I. (1996). African Americans' and non-Americans' sense of mattering and marginality at public, predominantly white institutions. *Equity and Excellence in Education, 29*(3), 37–42.

Grant, G. & Breese, J. (1997). Marginality theory and the African American student. *Sociology of Education, 70,* 192–205.

Hall, C. C. I. (1980). *The ethnic identity of racially mixed people: A study of Black-Japanese.* Unpublished doctoral dissertation, University of California, Los Angeles.

Hall, E. T. (1977). *Beyond culture.* Garden City, NY: Anchor Press.

Haniff, N. (1991). Epilogue. In W. Allen, E. Epps, and N. Haniff (Eds.), *College in black and white: African American students in predominantly white and historically black public universities.* Albany: State University of New York Press.

Hedegard, J. (1972). Experiences of black college students at predominantly white institutions. In E. Epps (Ed.), *Black students in white schools.* Worthington, OH: Charles A. Jones Publishing Company.

Hoaglin, D. C., and others. (1982). *Data for decisions.* Cambridge, MA: Abt Books.

Holcomb-McCoy, C. C. (1997, June 29-July 1). *Who am I? The ethnic identity of adolescents.* Paper presented at the Annual Meeting of the American School Counselor Association Nashville, TN.

Hollins, E. R., King, J. E. & Hayman, W. C. (1994). *Teaching diverse populations: Formulating a knowledge base.* Albany: State University of New York Press.

Krueger, R. A. (1994). (2nd ed.). *Focus groups: A practical guide for applied research.* Thousand Oaks, CA: Sage.

Lee, Winfield, & Wilson A. (1991). Academic behaviors among high-achieving African American students. *Education and Urban Society, 24*(1), 65–86.

Lincoln, Y. & Guba, E. (1993). Postpositivism and the naturalist paradigm. In C. Conrad, J. Haworth, & A. Newman (Eds.), *Qualitative research in higher education: Experiencing alternative perspectives and approaches.* Needham Heights, MA: Ginn Press.

Lofland, J., & Lofland, L. (1995). *Analyzing social settings: A guide to qualitative observation and analysis* (3rd ed.). New York: Wadsworth Publishing Co.

Lucas, T., Henze, R., & Donato, R., (1990). Promoting the success of Latino language minority students: An exploratory study of six high schools. *Harvard Educational Review, 68,* 315–340.

McClelland, K., & Auster, C. (1990). Public platitudes and hidden tensions: Racial climates at predominantly white liberal arts colleges. *Journal of Higher Education, 61*(6), 607–642.

Merriam, S. (1998). *Qualitative research and case study applications in education: A qualitative approach.* San Francisco: Jossey-Bass Publishers.

Merriam, S. (1988). *Case study research in education: A qualitative approach.* San Francisco: Jossey-Bass Publishers.

Mio, J. S. (2000). *Resistance to multiculturalism: Issues and interventions.* Philadelphia, PA: Taylor & Francis.

Moffatt, M. (1996). *Coming of age in New Jersey: College and American culture*. New Brunswick, NJ: Rutgers University Press.

Moll, L. (1992). Bilingual classroom studies and community analysis: Some recent trends. *Educational Researcher, 21*(2), 20–24.

Moll, L., & Diaz, S. (1993). Change as the goal of educational research. In E. Jacob & C. Mjordon (Eds.), *Minority education: Anthropological perspectives* (pp. 67–79). Norwood, NJ: Ablex.

National Coalition of Advocates for Students. (1988). *New voices: Immigrant students in U.S. public schools*. Boston: Author.

Newmann, F. M. (1993). Beyond common sense in educational restructuring: The issues of content and linkage. *Educational Researcher, 22*(2), 4–13, 22.

Nieto, S. (1994). Lessons from students on creating a chance to dream. *Harvard Educational Review, 64*(4), 3–36.

Ogbu, J. (1988). Class stratification, racial stratification, and schooling. In L. Weis (Ed.), *Class, race, and gender in American education*. Albany: State University of New York Press.

Oliver, M., Rodriguez, C., & Mickelson, R. (1985). Brown and black in white: The social adjustment and academic performance of Chicano and black students in a predominantly white university. *The Urban Review, 17*(1), 3–23.

Olsen L. (1998). *Crossing the schoolhouse border: Immigrant students and the California public schools*. San Francisco: California Tomorrow.

Omi, M., & Winant, H. (1986). *Racial formation in the United States: From the 1960s to the 1980s*. New York: Routledge & Kegan Paul.

Parham, T.A. (1989). Cycles of psychological nigrescence. *The Counseling Psychologist, 17*, 187–226.

Pascarella, E. & Terenzini, P. (1991). *How college affects students*. San Francisco, CA: Jossey & Bass.

Peshkin, A. (1988). In search of subjectivity—one's own. *Educational Researcher, 17*,17–21.

Phinney, J. S. (1996). Understanding ethnic diversity: The role of ethnic identity. *American Behavioral Scientist, 40* (2), 143–52.

Piaget, J. (1950). *The psychologist of intelligence*. London: Routledge & Paul.

Piaget, J. (1970). *Science of education and the psychology of the child*. Coltman, D. (Trans.) New York, Orion Press. (Original work published 1970).

Piaget, J. (1977). *The essential Piaget*. In. N.R. Guber, H. E. & Vonèche J. J (Eds.) New York: Basic Books.

Pratte, R. (1979). *Pluralism in education: Conflict, clarity, and commitment*. Springfield, IL: Thomas.

Resnick, L. B. (1989). Introduction. In L. Resnick (Ed.), *Knowing, learning, and instruction: Essays in honor of Robert Glaser* (pp. 1–42). Hillsdale, NJ: Erlbaum.

Rossman, G. B., & Rallis, S. F. (1998). *Learning in the field: An introduction to qualitative research*. Thousand Oaks, CA: Sage.

Rubin, H. J., & Rubin, I. S. (1995). *Qualitative interviewing: The art of hearing data*. Thousand Oaks, CA: Sage.

Rudestam, K., & Ima, K. (1987). *The adaptation of southeast Asian refugee youth: A comparative study*. San Diego, CA: Office of Refugee Resettlement.

Rudestam, K., & Newton, R. (1992). *Surviving your dissertation: A comprehensive guide to content and process*. Newbury Park, CA:. Sage.

Saylor, E. S., & Aries, E. (1999). Ethnic identity and change in social context. *The Journal of Social Psychology, 139*(5), 549–566.

Seidman, I. E. (1998, 1991). *Interviewing as qualitative research*. New York: Teachers College Press.

Smedley, B. D., Meyers, H. F., & Harrell, S.P. (1993). Minority-status stresses and the college adjustment of ethnic minority freshmen. *Journal of Higher Education, 64*(4), 434–452.

Solberg, V., Valdez, J., & Villarreal, P. (1994). Social support, stress, and hispanic college adjustment: Test of a diathese-stress model. *Hispanic Journal of Behavioral Sciences, 16*(3), 230–239.

Solorzano, D., & Villalpando, O. (1998). Critical race theory: Marginality and the experience of students of color in higher education. In C. Torres & T. Mitchell (Eds.), *Sociology of education: Emerging perspectives* (pp. 211–225). Albany: State University of New York Press.

Spradley, J. (1979). *The ethnographic interview*. New York: Holt, Rinehart & Winston.

Stake, R. E. (1995). *The art of case study research*. Thousand Oaks, CA: Sage.

Stein, A. (1971). Strategies for failure. *Harvard Educational Review, 41*, 133–179.

Sutherland, P. (1999). The application of Piagetian and neo-Piagetian ideas to further and higher education. *International Journal of Lifelong Education, 18*(4), 286–294.

Taylor, S. J. & Bogdan, R. (1984). *Introduction to qualitative research methods* (2nd ed.). New York: Wiley.

Terenzini, P. T. (1992). *Out-of-class experiences research program. The transition to college*. (ERIC Document Reproduction Service. ED357710).

Tharp, R., & Gallimore, R. (1988). *Rousing minds to life: Teaching, learning, and a schooling in social context*. Cambridge: Cambridge University Press.

Tinto, V. (1975. Dropout from higher education: A theoretical synthesis of recent research. *Review of Educational Research. 45*(1), 89–125.

Trueba, H. T. (1989). *Raising silent voices: Educating the linguistic minorities for the twenty-first century*. Cambridge, MA: Newbury House.

Upcraft, M. L., & Schuh, J. H. (1996). *Assessment in student affairs*. San Francisco: Jossey-Bass.

U.S. Department of Census. (1999). *Statistical abstract of the United States 1998* (118th ed.). Washington, DC.

Villegas, A.V. (1998). *In pursuit of equity and excellence in education*. Washington, D.C.: American Association of Colleges of Teacher Education. Princeton, NJ: Educational Testing Service.

Villegas, A. V. (1991). *Culturally responsive teaching for the 1990s and beyond*. Thousand Oaks, CA: Sage.

Waters, M. C. (1999). *Black identities: West Indian immigrant dreams and American realities*. New York: Russell Sage.

Weigel, V. B. (2002). *Beyond the virtual classroom*. San Francisco: Jossey-Bass.

Willie, C., & Cunnigen, D. (1981). Black students in higher education: A review of studies, 1965–1980. *American Review of Sociology, 7*, 177–198.

Willie, C. (1978). *The sociology of urban education: Desegregation and integration.* Lexington, KY: Lexington Books.

Willie, C., & Cunnigen, D. (1981). Black students in higher education: A review of studies, 1965–1980. *American Review of Sociology, 7,* 177–198.

Wilson, J. W., & Constantine, M.G. (1999). Racial identity attitudes, self-concept, and perceived family cohesion in black college students. *Journal of Black Studies, 29*(3), 354–36.

Wolcott, H. (1988). Ethnographic research in education. In R. Jaeger (Ed.), *Complementary methods for research in education* (pp. 185–212). Washington, DC: American Educational Research Association.

Wu, X. (1993). *Patterns of adjustment concerns and needs perceived by international students in a community college environment in Iowa* (University of Iowa). Dissertation Abstract International, 54 (07), AT 9334678.

Yin, R. K. (1994). *Case study research: Design and methods* (2nd ed.) Thousand Oaks, CA: Sage.

CHAPTER 6

ADDRESSING THE NEEDS OF HISPANIC STUDENTS IN K–16 SETTINGS

Demographic changes and the increased number of Hispanic people in the United States and institutions of higher education have created interest in public debates and institutions of higher learning. Policy leaders, administrators, and researchers are facing a serious challenge of educating and training this rapidly increasing subgroup whose dropout rate seems to be less than satisfactory (Leon, 2002). Hispanics are one of the nation's fastest-growing populations in the United States (Hernandez, 2002).

Despite these increases, Fry (2002) noticed that there is a large discrepancy when graduation rates were considered between Hispanic students and their counterparts. Cabrera and La Nasa (2000) noted that young Hispanic high school graduates are just as likely as their White counterparts to enter college, yet half are not as likely to finish a bachelor's degree. If this trend continues, Vernez and Mizell (2001) predicted that a large number of Hispanics without higher degrees would influence the economy negatively because they are not earning the higher wages that postsecondary degrees often command in the marketplace. The focus of this paper is on

Policy, Leadership, and Student Achievement, pages 77–89

factors that promote retention and success of Hispanic students K–16. Understanding the issues that determine why some Hispanic students decide to stay enrolled in school until the completion of a bachelor's degree may be the link to narrow the disparities in educational levels and income of Hispanic people.

The first section of this chapter examines the increasing Hispanic population in American society and the achievement gap between Hispanics and their White counterparts. Also in this section, it is stated how these trends affect us as Americans on a social and economic level. The second part reviews factors that influence educational success such as culture, finance, academic preparedness and language. The third section examines educational approaches that support student learning, retention, and success. The final section provides implications for higher education policy.

The nation's demographic landscape and the composition of students in higher education have changed dramatically in recent years, and will continue to grow, according to a report by the New Jersey Commission on Higher Education (2000). The report also noted that the U.S. Department of Labor predicts that the country's population will increase by 50% in the first half of the 21st century with ethnic minority groups, particularly Hispanic people, making up nearly half of the total population. Clearly, this shift has major implications for the nation's leaders and institutions of higher education. Findings from a report submitted to the President, *From Risk to Opportunity* (White House Initiative on Educational Excellence for Hispanic Americans, 2003), a plan to close the achievement gap for minority students, showed that Hispanic Americans are now the largest minority group in the nation. According to Ramos (2004), the Hispanic population is washing over everything including institutions of higher education, "Nothing, absolutely nothing, will remain untouched by this Hispanic wave" (p. 15). However, the White House Initiative on Educational Excellence for Hispanic Americans (2003) found that the nation is losing Hispanic Americans throughout all lines of the educational continuum, especially in higher education. Only 10% of Hispanic Americans graduate from four-year colleges and universities. The report noted that the federal government does not adequately monitor, measure, and coordinate programs and research that benefit Hispanic students in higher education despite their rapid growth in the United States population. The report also mentioned that the nation's Hispanic American population totals more than thirty-seven million and increased 4.7% from April 2000 to July 2001. These figures did not include foreign-born Hispanic people who entered the United States in large numbers.

Research conducted by Hernandez (2000) showed that the Hispanic population increased 53% from 1980 to 1990, and 27% from 1990 to 1996. In 2002, the Hispanic people accounted for 13.5% of the United States population. As this trend continues, by 2010, Hispanic people will make up one out of every five young people of high school age, compared with one in 10 in 1999 (Ramos, 2004).

Scholars (Cabrera and La Nasa, 2000; Fry, 2002; Hernandez, 2002) noted that the number of minority students entering the United States and going for institutions of postsecondary education is on the rise and political attention has been given to the success of these students. A college degree allows for higher salaries than for people with only a high school diploma, increases their chances of employment, improved working conditions, easier adjustment to technological advances, improved health, and longer life (The Institute for Higher Education Policy, 1998).

Why the interest in education success of Hispanic students in the United States, particularly in the area of higher education? Higher education institutions play a vital role in the intellectual and economic growth of the American people, which in current times are viewed as declining with more and more talented Hispanic students lagging behind other subgroups in obtaining a bachelor's degree. Approximately 40% of Hispanic college students' ages 18 to 24 years of age enroll in two-year colleges compared to about 25% of White and African American students. Of them, Fry (2002) found that only 20.8% of Hispanic full-time students had attained an associate's degree within three years of study, while 32.7% were no longer enrolled. The percent for Hispanic students enrolled in four year institutions of higher education were vastly lower, and these students make up the majority of the fastest growing populations in the United States (Barnard, 2007).

While retention and graduation concerns of Hispanic students in schools of higher education are on the rise due to the number of Hispanic students entering American schools and institutions of higher learning, Fry (2002) reported that native-born Hispanic high school graduates are enrolling in college at a higher rate than their foreign-born counterparts. This is especially true of the second generation Hispanics, the U.S. born children of immigrants. About 10% of all Hispanic high school graduates were reported to be enrolled in some form of college compared to 7% of the total population of high school graduates. In the 2000 U.S. Census, the Hispanic population made up 12.5%, an increase of 57.9% from the 1990 Census (Longerbeam, Sedlacek, & Alatorre, 2004). In a recent report from the Pew Hispanic Center found that while large numbers of Hispanic students are enrolling in postsecondary educational institutes, retention and graduation are still a concern (Fry, 2002).

Furthermore, the overall presence of Hispanic students, K–16, have politicians concerned about the disparity in the educational levels and income of Americans as they continue to increase along a continuum of ethnicity and race, with Hispanic people and African Americans on the lower end and non-Hispanic Whites and Asians on the upper end (Vernez & Mizell, 2001). This concern suggests that major minority students are not obtaining the intellectual knowledge, expertise, and language proficiency that are needed to secure the social and economic benefits that are associated with a college degree.

Based on the literature, research revealed that efforts to understand Hispanic students' cultural values could be used to develop programs that promote retention and success of minority students in schools and higher education. Whereas there are policies established and programs developed for the success of all students K–16, research revealed that more could be done to facilitate the learning experiences of minority students to help them succeed.

Traditionally, the Hispanic family is a close-knit group and the most important social unit. In the Hispanic family, individuals feel a sense of moral responsible for aiding other members of the family experiencing difficulty with life issues. While there seems to be a popular but erroneous belief that Hispanic parents do not care about the education of their children, a number of studies reveal that Hispanic parents do indeed appreciate and understand the importance of their children's education and, in most cases, encourage academic attainment (Clutter, 2006). Family support is the leading factor that helps Hispanic students overcome the negative consequences of educational risks (Hernandez, 2002). This same study revealed that even those parents, who could not help their children financially or academically while they were in college, provided moral, spiritual, and emotional support. Pidcock, Fischer, and Munsch (2001) explained that Hispanic students might undermine their academic careers when family issues at home produce demands to return home to help manage the affairs of the household. When these findings were compared with White students' reasons for leaving school and not returning, the findings did not appear to be influenced for the same reasons. The study indicates that colleges do not provide the necessary support for Hispanic students to be retained, which limits Hispanic students' options to seek alternative solutions to resolving their personal and family matters. The study also suggests that family ties and the need of mentors at the college impacts retention of Hispanic first-year college students. Hernandez (2000) noted that the strength of the family was the main reason Hispanic students stayed at the college. "Oh my God, what an incredible disappointment I'd be for my parents" (p. 3).

Hispanics value family and education. Ninety-eight percent viewed education as important despite the rumors that Hispanic parents do not care about the education of their children (Fry 2002). In fact, almost all of the literature pertaining to Hispanic student retention in one way or another discussed the importance of family members' contribution to emotional support and commitment to education as the most influential bridge between Hispanic college students' persistence and college achievement. In a study conducted by Ramos (2004), Hispanic students who received continuous encouragement toward their education by their family members were more likely to persist in their educational endeavor. Ortiz (2004) noted that Hispanic parents express becoming a role model for their children. Consequently, many Hispanic parents return to college to show their children that no matter what obstacles may be present in higher education, a college degree was still possible. Richard Fry (2002), Senior Research Associate at Pew Hispanic Center, reported clear evidence that Hispanic parents and Hispanic youth know the importance of a college degree and are willing to make the necessary sacrifices to help their children achieve that goal. The findings were the results of a national survey by the U.S. Department of Education's National Educational Longitudinal Survey consisting of 25,000 Hispanic college students. Consistent with Fry's study, Hernandez's (2002) qualitative study of 10 first-year Hispanic college students showed that family concerns and support for a college degree encouraged their persistence until completion. To sum up what most of the participants articulated in this study, mothers played the most influential role in student achievement. Latino mothers who value schooling believed in their child's ability to succeed and constantly encouraged them to participate actively in their schools to give them a better chance at academic success. As is true for many Hispanic family members regardless of their national origins (e.g., Mexican American, Central American, Cuban American, Puerto Rican, etc.), Hispanic students rely heavily on their family members as the only source of emotional support. According to Ramos (2004) the definition of family is not only limited to the nuclear family but also includes extended family members, university faculty, and administrators who show interest in Hispanic students' learning and success, and college peers to be successful in college. Padilla (1998) noted that Hispanic students learned how to overcome college barriers by creating a supportive family with members of the college.

In an effort to meet the educational needs of Hispanic students K–16, a closer look at issues that prevent educational success for Hispanic students was examined. These issues were outlined as educational funding, finances, academic difficulty, and language.

The major opposition to retention of Hispanic students in K–16 settings comes from distributions by the federal government and its limited funding, to have the new teaching methods material to give to teachers, and professors, and the lack of support to fully provide the teaching community research and the theory behind these supposing successful practices to increase students' critical thinking and performance. For example, The National Science Foundation has been the leading sponsor in financing projects to broaden the knowledge of new teaching methods through programs in education directed toward courses, curriculum, and laboratory improvement in schools. The program's budget of $34 million this year is down from a high of $56.4 million in 2002, a consequence of a declining budget for the NSF's education division overall (Brainard, 2007).

In 2001, Vernez and Mizell noted that while Hispanic youths are entering college at a comparable rate to Non-Hispanic Whites, many Hispanic youths lack the funds to pursue a college degree. In the same study, it was stated that financial difficulties was the most cited explanation for Hispanic students leaving college. Cabrera and La Nasa (2000) noted that Hispanics are more likely than students of other ethnicities to be part-time students, work after high school, or are far more likely to be enrolled in two-year colleges than any other group for want of finances. Fry's (2002) report showed that a greater number of Hispanics are attending two-year colleges, delaying or prolonging their college education into their mid-20s and beyond due to lack of money. Another in-depth examination of Hispanic youth ages 18–24 revealed that many Hispanics perceived the cost of attending a four-year public or private college as beyond their financial means. Ninety-eight percent of respondents felt it was important to have a college education, but the cost of tuition was too high. Thirty-eight percent of the respondents did not feel the benefits of a college degree outweighed the college costs. Furthermore, many did argue that a number of Hispanics do not readily find a job to pay the incurred debts (Padilla, 1998). The research also revealed that many Hispanic students, especially those who were not United States citizens, had misperceptions about financial aid eligibility requirements, i.e., the application and financial aid process and deadlines. These studies suggested that the low trend of college achievement among Hispanic students would remain unchanged if actions were not taken to address the issues of misinformation and misperceptions about financial aid procedures and college costs.

In addition to financial issues, a strong high school curriculum was related to retention and success in college. In a study conducted by Warburton, Bugarin, Rosio, and Nunez (2001) showed that there is also a strong correlation between high school curriculum and GPA in postsecondary education, and the amount of remedial courses students need to take and their retention rate. Research by Seidman (2005), shows that approximately 30 to 40% of all entering freshmen are academically underprepared for college level reading and writing courses and approximately 44% take at least one remedial course in math, writing or reading. In addition, there seems to be a strong indication that a rigorous high school curriculum, defined as advance sciences (chemistry, biology, and physics), four years of math (algebra 1, algebra 2, geometry, and pre-calculus), three years of foreign language and one honors (advance placement) course, help achieve greater success for students in postsecondary education retention and completion

(Warburton et al., 2001). Furthermore, Nora and Cabrera (1996) conducted a quantitative study that showed that a strong academic preparation is a much more potent predictor about college success than external factors.

Consequently, many Hispanic college students in the United States, particularly first-generation Hispanic students, have difficulties in higher education due to factors such as academic preparation, separation from family and community, adjustment to college environment, and lack of minority role models contribute to retention and success in high education (Nora & Cabrera, 1996). Even though results from a quantitative study on the relationship between academic comfort and persistence among Hispanics, African American and White college students showed that difficulty in academic work was not a deterrent to retention for Hispanic students. In this study, the academic comfort scale was used to measure interests that predict persistence in educational settings. Students with high scores are usually well educated or intend to become well educated. Low scores indicate that the students are less comfortable in an educational setting and find intellectual exercises boring. These students are generally dissatisfied with their entire educational experience and may be thinking about leaving school (Tomlinson-Clark, 1996).

In addition, another factor that hinders the success of Hispanic students comes from a variety of issues such as people's attitudes toward changing standard practices to a rewards system based on good research above good teaching of students. In other words, research universities care more about research than success of students in higher education. Due to this understanding, it is not surprising that the strongest resistance to updated teaching methods in higher education would come from the nation's research focused universities, which gives out most of the degrees in science, math and engineering (Brainard, 2007). This approach is largely in part associated with the attitudes of instructors who pride themselves on using introduction courses to weed out students they view as lazy or lack the ability to succeed (Brainard, 2007). Seidman (2005), *Talking About Leaving: Why Undergraduates Leave College,* noted that in reality many students who leave college are highly motivated and prepared and those that do remain do so despite obstacles presented in teaching from these professors.

The literature also revealed that universities need to build a more inviting and comfortable environment for Hispanic freshman. Universities also need to incorporate the Hispanic family into the college admission process and retention efforts, which provides essential linkages for Hispanic students and their parents (Green, 2007). Not providing literature in Spanish requires Hispanic parents and family members to suppress their mother tongue, which is usually associated with giving up their heritage, culture and identity. Culture is the essence of many different groups. For most native-born and foreign-born Hispanics, the likelihood that adult family members will adopt a new culture may be delayed or never occur. The success of learning a new language is a long and hard journey, especially for Hispanics who recently moved to the United States and speak no English or know very little English, although many researchers argue that many immigrants lose their native language after the second generation (Suro & Passel, 2003). Suro and Passel (2003) showed that second-generation immigrant children from Latin America, without exception, display a continuous effort to preserve their parental language. This characteristic is especially true in second-generation Hispanics. The Pew Hispanic Center (2000) showed that most first generation and approximately 50% of second-generation Hispanics are bilinguals. Similarly, Hispanic's multidimensional access to speak Spanish and English at home and in their ethnic communities constantly limits the adoption process of assimilation. Hispanic families in the United States know the advantages of being bilingual for academic and career purposes and advocate that their cultural heritage and mother tongue remain strong (Arriagada, 2005). For example, Cook's (2005) research on language shows that there is a difference between monolingual and bilingual speakers, which plays a significant role in whether or not students are successful in higher education. Cook (2005) explains that monolingual or bilingual cognitive processes affect the students' higher learning experience and perception. Cook (2005) points out those bilingual speakers have knowledge of two or more languages in ones mind. A monolingual speaker is understood to be someone who is raised with one language and does not learn a second language. This concept of knowing more than on language is called "multi-competence" which emphasizes that bilingual students may have misconceptions of their environment such as college procedures or institutional practices, which may account for the times bilingual students use institutional services (p. 3). For example, a bilingual student may need assistance with tuition payment and two services are present: financial aid office and student services office. The student may view the financial aid office as a bank service offering checks and savings accounts, whereas, the student services department may be viewed as services given to students for an array of situations including help with tuition payment. On the other hand, the financial aid office could be viewed as supplemental office or handout only given to the poor. Due to the student's misconception about the services of the department, the student goes to the wrong department to meet his or her needs. When the student is referred to the right department, the student may view the situation as being ignored and may find the experience offensive. This negative misconception about the university services may cause the student to become frustrated and increase his or her tendency to leave the college.

In the United States, two major aspects of the dominant culture are prevalent for success, education and the English language. The multifaceted factors that relate to students' persistence and performance are usually associated with the level of education, social status, income and health, which are heavily tied to education. This entails the myth that the more education one has the better opportunity for a career one will get at a higher income level. A postsecondary education further promotes higher recognition in the community as a whole and leads to better health and longevity. The other aspect of success in America is the English language. It is believed that English is the only language that entails unity among the population, solidarity in the eyes of foreign nations, and elimination of barriers that are so restricted within cultures, such as color of skin and lifestyle. In contrast to the United States, in all Spanish-speaking countries, the two major aspects of success in these countries are family and the Spanish language. In the family, the notion of reciprocity, respect, family responsibilities and in some countries religion, have been an intricate part of the Hispanic lifestyle, which constitutes that sacrifice to meet those needs supersede any other goal. The other aspect of success in these countries is the Spanish language for many of the same reasons that English is preferred in the United States.

Green (2007) describes two major principles to retain Hispanic students in higher education. First, incorporating the family in all aspects of the college admission and retention activities, and secondly, Green further noted that colleges could greatly assist Hispanic parents and students by creating a more welcoming and comprehensive front door and comfortable environment by providing literature and messages in a "language-accessible" format. Language-accessible information is a method of constructing a positive schema about the university and makes the college dream more of a reality for Hispanic families. Many organizations such as the Pathway to College Network, Sallie Mae Fund and the National Association for College Admission Counseling are producing educational materials in Spanish to attract Hispanic students. Research from the University of Washington indicated that universities have a central role of informing students and parents about campus programs and services at a level that is comprehensive to people from ethnic/minority groups, which represent a significant and visible portion of those seeking information about colleges. Despite these odds, many Hispanic families continue to seek information about higher education for their children (Longerbeam et al., 2004).

In an effort to establish effective retention strategies in higher education, each higher education institution must engage in continuous planning of activities with leaders at all levels of the educational spectrum to establish programs that increase students' awareness of their academic potential and increase faculty and family involvement. New methods of teaching in these programs primarily focus on what has been called "student centered" or "inquiry-based learning." Instead of one-way lecturing methods, Vincow (1995) emphasized constant interaction between both teachers and students to help answer and understand the ideas and material for classes. As of now, besides outside programs such as Sister of Science, this method has only been adopted at liberal colleges which accounts only for about 10% of degrees in this field and the lower education of K–12 learning across the country (Brainard, 2007).

Another focus on these methods relies on a concept known as double-looped learning which states that you evaluate success based on what students retain from learning and not the resultant score of learning. This double loop allows for change to have direct impact on learning by evaluating the process that leads to the desired or failed result and make changes. This process does not evaluate the material used or test the students to evaluate changes to teaching, but evaluates the routine process in learning and understanding that students use in learning the material. As a result, the materials they learn are better focused on students' retention of knowledge and not the result of short-term success. This is often limited to time issues but the results in retention of learning results in a higher GPA per student, and more students are likely to succeed in real life applications (Tagg, 2007).

A growing factor in these community programs is the concept known as Critical Mass, which has been adopted by the educational community, especially for retention purposes. In science, critical mass is explained as adding a substance to an existing compound until a result occurs. In higher education, this term refers to how many people of an ethnic social background are needed before that group becomes successful in college (Hagedorn et al., 2007). In an effort to test these new methods several programs have been established at the elementary, high school and college level such as The Sisters in Science Equity Reform Project (SIS). SIS is a multifaceted educational school intervention, which includes programs designed to increase female interests, achievement, self-esteem and positive attitudes toward science and mathematics; enhance female awareness of academic and career opportunities in sciences and mathematics; and educate in-service and pre-service teachers about the relationship between gender and the design and implementation of science and mathematics and increase parental involvement and awareness in science and mathematics.

IMPLICATIONS FOR HIGHER EDUCATION

Research on the factors that influence student retention in higher education found that integration in higher education starts at the high school level and continues throughout their educational undergraduate career:

(1) Institutions of higher learning need to bridge the relationships between prospective college students and college faculty and administrators through innovative retention programs. (2) More should to be done to incorporate prospective college students' families in the learning and retention process. In order words, recruiting and retaining college students in higher education is not an isolated recruitment event. It is a slow and involved process through a continuum of learning and college experiences. (3) Recruitment and retention programs should be tailored to include family members throughout the students' educational career. (4) Create a more welcoming environment by providing literature in Spanish for parents who know little or no English. (5) The learning process should incorporate the learning experience to real life situations. In other words, teachers and professors should develop lesson plans where students could be more interactive in the learning process as they apply real life situations to the concept or at the least call for an internship to their requirements. These findings revealed that these items should be reconsidered as factors that encourage student retention and graduation.

REFERENCES

Arellano, A. R., Padilla, A. M., (1996). Academic invulnerability between a select group of Latino university students. *Hispanic Journal of Behavioral Sciences, 18,* 1–13.

Arriagada, P. (2005). Family context and Spanish-language use: A study of Latino children in the United States. *Social Science Quarterly, 86*(3), 599–619.

Astin, A. W. (1999). Involvement in learning revisited: Lessons we have learned. *Journal of College Student Development, 40,* 587–598.

Astin, A. W. (1984). Student involvement: A developmental theory for higher education. *Journal of College Student Personnel, 25,* 297–308.

Brainard, J. (2007). The tough road to better science teaching—Chronicle.com. *Chronicle of Higher Education, 53,* 48.

Braxton, J. M., Milen, J. F., & Sullivan, A. S. (2000). The influence of active learning on the college student departure process: Toward a revision of Tinto's theory. *Journal of Higher Education, 71,* 569–590.

Cabrera, A., & La Nasa, S. M., (2000). Understanding college choice among disadvantaged Americans. *New Directions for Institutional Research, 107.* San Francisco: Jossey-Bass.

Cabrera, A. F. (1996). The role of perceptions of prejudice and discrimination on the adjustment of minority students in college. *The Journal of Higher Education, 67,* 119–148.

Clutter, A. W., & Nieto, R. D. (2006). *Understanding Hispanic culture.* Retrieved October 9, 2006, from http://ohioline.osu.edu/hyg-fact/5000/5237.html.

Cook, V. (2005). *Universal grammar and multi-competence.* Retrieved October 9, 2006, from http://homepage.ntlworld.com/vivian.c/Writings/Papers/multi-competence &UG.htm.

Fry, R. (2002). *Latinos in higher education: Many enroll, too few graduate.* U.S. Department of Labor, Pew Hispanic Center. Washington, DC.

Green, V. (2007). *Nature and the marketplace: Capturing the value of ecosystem services.* Retrieved August 18, 2007, from http://www.vivagreen.com/taxonomy/term/512/all.

Hagedorn, L. S., (2005). *How to define retention: A new look at an old problem.* Paper presented at the meeting of Council for the Study of Community Colleges (CSCC), Mineapolis, MN.

Hagedorn, L. S., Chi, W. C., Rita, M., & McLain, M. (2007). An investigation of critical mass: The role of Latino representation in the success of urban community college students. *Research in Higher Education, 48,* 73–91.

Hernandez, M. (2003). *A profile of Hispanic Americans: Executive summary.* Princeton, NJ: Population Resource Center.

Hernandez, J. C., (2002). A qualitative exploration of the first-year experience of Latino college students. *NASPA Journal, 40,* 69–84.

Hernandez, J. C. (2000). Understanding the retention of Latino college students. *Journal of College Student Development, 41,* 575–588.

Hurtado, S., & Ponjuan, L. (2005). Latino educational outcomes and the campus climate. *Journal of Hispanic Higher Education, 4,* 235–251.

Hurtado, S., & Carter, D. F. (1997). Effects of college transition and perceptions of the campus racial climate on Latino college students' sense of belonging. *Sociology of Education, 70,* 324–345.

Kraemer, B. A. (1997). The academic and social integration of Hispanic students into college. *The Review of Higher Education, 20,* 163–179.

Leon, D. (2002). *Latinos in higher education.* Sacramento, CA: Elsevier Science & Technology.

Longerbeam, S., Sedlacek, W. E., & Alatorre, H. M. (2004). In their own voices: Latino student retention. *NASPA Journal, 41,* 538–550.

New Jersey Commission on Higher Education. (2000). *Status of minorities in New Jersey higher education.* Retrieved October 9, 2006, from http://www.state.nj.us//highereducation/minoritystat.htm.

Nora, A., & Cabrera, A. F. (1996). The role of perceptions on prejudice and discrimination on the adjustment of minority students to college. *Journal of Higher Education, 67,* 119–148.

Noel, R., & Smith, S. (1996). Self-disclosure of college students to faculty: The influence of ethnicity. *Journal of College Student Personnel,* 512–524.

Ortiz, A. M. (2004). Addressing the unique needs of Latino students. *New Directions for Student Services, 105.* San Francisco: Jossey-Bass.

Padilla, R. V., (1998). *Chicana/o college students: Focus on success.* Report prepared for the Hispanic Association of Colleges and Universities. San Antonio, TX.

Pidcock, B. W., Fischer, J. L., & Munsch, J. (2001). Family, personality, and social risk factors impacting the retention rates of first-year Hispanic and Anglo college students. *Adolescence, 36*(144), 803–818.

Ramos, J. (2004). *The Latino wave. How Hispanics will elect the next American president* (p. 257). New York: Harper Collins Publishers Inc.

Seidman, A. (2005). *College student retention: Formula for student success.* Westport, CT: Praeger.

Seidman, A. (1997). *Why students leave college.* Westport, CT: Praeger.

Smedley, B. (1993). Minority-status stresses and the college adjustment of ethnic minority freshmen. *The Journal of Higher Education, 64,* 434–452.

Spady, W. G. (1971). Dropouts from higher education: An interdisciplinary review and synthesis. *Interchange, 1,* 64–85.

Suro, R., & Passel, J. S. (2003). *The rise of the second generation: Changing patterns in Hispanic population growth.* Washington, DC: Pew Hispanic Center.

Swail, W. S., Kenneth E. R., & Perna, L. W. (2003). *Retaining minority students in higher education: ASHE Higher Education Report, 30.* San Francisco: Jossey-Bass.

Tagg, J. (2007). Double-loop learning in higher education. *Change, 39,* 36–41.

The New Millennium Project on Higher Education Costs, Pricing, and Productivity. (1998). Reaping the benefits defining the public and private value of going to college. *The Institute for Higher Education Policy, 3,* 58–63.

Thomas, L. (2002). Student retention in higher education: The role of institutional habitus. *Journal of Education Policy, 17,* 423–442.

Tinto, V. (1993). *Leaving college: Rethinking the causes and cures of student attrition* (2nd ed.). Chicago: University of Chicago Press.

Tinto, V. (1975). Dropout from higher education: A theoretical synthesis of recent research. *Review of Educational Research, 45,* 89–125.

Tomlinson-Clark, S. (1996). A longitudinal study of the relationship between academic comfort, occupational orientation and persistence among African American, Hispanic and White college students. *Journal of College Student Development, 35,* 25–28.

Vernez, G., & Mizell, L. (2001). *Goal: To double the rate of Hispanics earning a bachelor's degree.* Washington, DC.:RAND Publisher.

Vincow, G. (1995). *The student-centered research university. Annual report to the faculty.* Syracuse, NY: Syracuse University.

Wasley, P. (2007). A secret support network. *Chronicle of Higher Education, 53,* A7–A29.

Warburton, E. C., Bugarin, R., & Nuñez, A. M. (2001). *Bridging the gap: Academic preparation and postsecondary success of first-generation students* (NCES 2001–153). AAAS-benchmarks for Science Literacy-Project 2061 and the NCTM-Standards for School Mathematics.

White House Initiative on Educational Excellence for Hispanic Americans. *From risk to opportunity. Fulfilling the educational needs of Hispanic Americans in the 21st century. Final report submitted to President Bush, March 31, 2003.* Retrieved October 9, 2006, from http://www.yic.gov.paceea/final.html.

PART 3

SPECIAL POPULATIONS AND STUDENT ACHIEVEMENT

CHAPTER 7

MEETING THE ACADEMIC NEEDS OF URBAN POPULATIONS

Homeless Families and Students

Kimberly D. Matthews

INTRODUCTION

Homeless student populations throughout the nation, particularly in urban areas, are suffering academically at the local and district level. When you are worrying about daily crises, it is very difficult to focus on how to obtain a quality education and to make sure it is meeting the academic needs of students. The federal policy, McKinney-Vento Homeless Education Assistance Act, which is supposed to guarantee students access to public schools paired with No Child Left Behind, is lacking in structure and implementation. In addition, government funding allocated for this national problem is at a minimum, causing state compliance to be uneven and educational program reform to go unevaluated or to be nonexistent in many states across the country. As the numbers of homeless children continue to rise, and the allocated funds supplied to each state in the country continue become

Policy, Leadership, and Student Achievement, pages 93–99
Copyright © 2008 by Information Age Publishing
All rights of reproduction in any form reserved.

less, barriers and obstacles are becoming a major issue. If funds are not allocated to certain Local Education Agencies for local liaisons to disburse for services, then those entities must then find funding through private institutions to support their homeless education program.

This urban issue facing many schools across the country at times goes unnoticed: with barriers in place, students are not gaining access to the quality education that they deserve to succeed academically.

POLICY CONTEXT

As homelessness became an epidemic in the early 1980s, the federal government felt this was a local problem that did not require federal intervention; their response was to form a task force to provide local agencies with information on how to obtain federal funds to decrease the number of homeless people in given areas. After many frustrating years of advocacy and policy action, homelessness was recognized as a national problem requiring immediate action.

In 1986, the Homeless Persons' Survival Act was introduced in both houses of Congress, which focused on relief measures, preventive measures, and long-term solutions to homelessness. However, only small portions of this Act were enacted into law. After intense advocacy on behalf of the homeless, large bipartisan majorities in both houses of Congress passed, legislation in 1987 that was renamed the Stewart B. McKinney Homeless Assistance Act after its chief Republican sponsor. It was then reluctantly signed into law on July 22, 1987 by President Ronald Reagan.

According to the National Coalition for the Homeless, in 1999 it was estimated that 57% of homeless school aged children did not attend school regularly, and many homeless children were experiencing difficulty obtaining and maintaining access to a free public education. The McKinney Act contains nine titles within its context that focus on various issues pertaining to homeless individuals and families. Title VII of the McKinney Act was implemented and authorizes four programs for the education of homeless persons: Adult Education for the Homeless, Education of Homeless Children, and Youth, Job Training for the Homeless, and Emergency Community Services Homeless Grant Programs. In 1994, Congress amended the Education of the Homeless Children and Youth program to give flexibility in the use of funds to local educational entities. In 2001, Title VII-B of the McKinney Act was amended by the No Child Left Behind Act, then reauthorized on January 8, 2002 and renamed the McKinney-Vento Homeless Education Assistance Improvements Act, which was signed by President George W. Bush.

As stated by the United States Department of Education, the purpose of this program is to:

> Address the problems that homeless children and youth have faced in enrolling, attending, and succeeding in school. Under this program, State educational agencies (SEAs) must ensure that each homeless child and youth has equal access to the same free, appropriate public education, including a public preschool education, as other children and youth. Homeless children and youth should have access to the educational and other services that they need to enable them to meet the same challenging State student academic achievement standards to which all students are held. In addition, homeless students may not be separated from the mainstream school environment. States and districts are required to review and undertake steps to revise laws, regulations, practices, or policies that may act as a barrier to the enrollment, attendance, or success in school of homeless children and youth. (Subtitle B of Title 7, of the McKinney-Vento Homeless Assistance Act-42-U.S.C 11431, etseq. pp. 21–17)

By complying with these guidelines students should be making academic strides and to be able to keep up and compete with their educational peers.

The term "homeless children and youth" has a certain definition outlined by the McKinney-Vento Act. It is defined as individuals who lack a fixed, regular, and adequate nighttime residence. This definition and term include various situations that children and youth face, such as those who are sharing housing with other persons, living in motels, hotels, and etc., living in emergency or transitional shelters, abandoned in hospitals, awaiting foster care placement, and those in inadequate living accommodations such as cars, buses, parks, and train stations. As agencies identify individuals who fit this definition, they can begin the process of utilizing the program to service students.

As these steps have been taken to create, develop, and set policy into motion, the funding of this movement for the education of homeless children is lacking. While it is part of the No Child Left Behind initiative, it does not rank very high on the importance scale of education. While there are funds allocated for each state, additional funding must be obtained in other ways for local programs to operate fully and effectively.

BALANCING PUBLIC VALUES

Equity versus equality is a key issue when looking at this educational policy from a financial perspective. The Department of Education awards funds to states by a formula. "The amount that a state receives in a given year is based on the proportion of funds allocated nationally that it receives under Title I, Part A of the Elementary and Secondary Education Act of 1965 for that year" (United States Department of Education, 2004). Each state, which includes the District of Columbia and Puerto Rico, will receive the minimum allocation of $150,000, according to the budget allocation for the 2004 fiscal year; the maximum was not stated. However, after each state has been granted funds, the state then disburses sub grants to local education agencies to uphold the law's reauthorized stipulations. A state may use the allocated funds for the purposes of state activities. States that receive more than the minimum allocated funds may reserve 25% of allocated funds for state activities. States that receive the minimum allocated funds may reserve up to 50% for their state activities.

School districts can then offer many services based on the allocated funds they have received. The points that give rise to the equity versus equality issue are that depending on the needs of each school district, the size of each school district and the services already in place in those schools have a major effect on the equality issue. Not every school district or local education agency that has applied for funding should receive the same dollar amount, especially for those areas that have higher populations of homeless children to educate and service.

As the state follows through with the Tenth Amendment in assuming responsibility for education for the "general welfare," it seems that Pennsylvania has a heavy load to carry. After the state receives its nominal amount, it is then disbursed to eight Regional Sites around the state, and then disbursed again to a maximum of 501 school districts. Philadelphia County, incorporating the School District of Philadelphia itself, is its own region due to high numbers of homeless children. The other urban school districts in the state fall under the other seven Regional Sites. The school districts not requiring immediate district-level attention receive services through their local Intermediate Units. Having the School District of Philadelphia be its own region is a testament to the financial resources needed. However, if a region services 17 counties with a high financial request, their need seems to be just as great as the one-county region. Increasing the budget allowance for this program can begin to solve some of the problems. Also, providing ways for state agencies and local agencies to obtain outside funds for their budget would be helpful as well.

One of the positive areas of this educational program is the prescribed parent, student, and teacher involvement. The fact that this program takes the entire family issue into account says a lot about helping the "whole" child, and not parts of the child. When the family unit begins to come together and repair, the child can better focus attention on academics in a successful manner.

INTEREST GROUPS

In this educational program, other than the federal government being a relevant player and acting as a director, the state and the local education agencies are the producer and assistant producers of funding and developers of programs; the local liaisons are the actors who perform the act waiting for audience feedback. The State Coordinator has many responsibilities to fulfill making sure that the program is running the way the federal government has designed. The primary responsibilities of the State Coordinator for Education of Homeless Children and Youth are to:

> Develop and carry out the State's McKinney-Vento Plan; Gather valid, reliable, and comprehensive information on the problems faced by homeless children and youth, the progress of the SEA and LEAs in addressing those problems, and the success of McKinney-Vento programs in allowing homeless children and youth to enroll, attend, and succeed in school; Coordinate services on behalf the McKinney-Vento program; Provide technical assistance to LEAs in coordination with the local liaisons to ensure that LEAs comply with the McKinney-Vento Act; and collect and transmit to the U.S. Department of Education, upon request, a report containing the information that the Department determines is necessary to assess the educational needs of homeless children and youth. (Subtitle B of Title 7, of the McKinney-Vento Homeless Assistance Act-42-U.S.C 11431, etseq. pp. 21–17)

In short, the State Coordinator's job is to also work very closely with the LEAs in their state making sure that any assistance they need is given to help their local programs run effectively. On the local level, every Local Education Agency, whether they receive McKinney-Vento funds or not, must designate a local liaison for homeless children and youth. The LEA's job is to work in the best interest of the homeless student. This means that they try to maintain a stable education environment and do their best to keep students in their school of origin. In working toward this effort, the LEA must be in constant contact with the local liaison to overcome obstacles, utilize limited resources, and reach desired goals. The local liaison serves as the contact between families, school staff, district personnel, shelter staff, and other service providers. The liaison coordinates services to ensure that homeless children enroll in school to have successful academic opportunities.

Along with these responsibilities, local liaisons assist homeless children with various activities ranging from enrolling students in school to collaborating and coordinating with the State Coordinators for the Education of Homeless Children, community, and school personnel responsible for providing education and related services to children. The actual relationship between the State Education Agency, the Local Education Agencies, and the local Liaisons are that they provide information to one another on a continuous basis. The state is there to ensure that children and youth are receiving services that they need in order to enroll, attend, and succeed in school. The state also assists the LEAs in designating local liaisons. They provide guidelines and describe factors for a LEA to consider when choosing a local liaison.

Partnering and collaborating can help a program have a greater impact on those they are trying to serve than one that does not collaborate. Barriers and obstacles are easier to overcome and solutions quickly generated to ensure success for all.

RECOMMENDATIONS

In looking at the issue of homeless students receiving a quality education and succeeding in school, the policy itself is not the problem. The main problem is the issue of funding. As the numbers of individuals without a place to live or the ability to sustain their families increases, funding becomes the bottom line for the continuance of this educational program. As states are exceeding their allocated funding limits, some portion of services needed are now becoming barriers. At the federal and state level, transportation is the number one barrier for homeless students and youths. One must wonder how much of the budget is spent on this issue at both levels of the program. Since the cost of transportation is unstable and ever-changing, has the transportation budget been changed for the agencies to comply with services needed? This is just one example of many more to come as funds dwindle. A social movement on behalf of students and families is once again necessary to continue their rights to access a free public education. Not all parents will go to the mat for their children and some just do not know how to, or where to begin. Those in power or in charge should begin to take control of what are truly important, put children first, and stand up for their rights, rich or poor. This social movement can be started by building civic capacity and looking directly at the problems facing local communities. There is strength in numbers, and if people begin to band together to try to change some of the political systems, perhaps different and beneficial outcomes can happen.

ANTICIPATED OUTCOMES

In researching this topic and reviewing concepts and theories that have been introduced, I feel that the main question that needs to be answered is "Who is in charge?" When I ask this question, I ask in terms of financial allocation, plan development, budget implementation, and program evaluation. These areas of educational policy need to be examined in depth as well as clarified.

I believe with every Presidential change, and then subsequent cabinet changes, the unspoken rules for funding, plan development, and evaluation will be redesigned and unknown to those who require the most assistance. Furthermore, with the No Child Left Behind law approaching its deadline and unrealistic mandates set for schools and students, I wonder if the Homeless Education Program component will be changed as well. If it is changed, the funding portion will be changed to shift its funds to another needy area. If this situation occurs, then programs for educating homeless students will be dismantled and schools and intermediate units will be forced to add them into their regular budgets, which in the areas that need this law the most are already strained.

I agree with the Department of Education (2002) when they stated in an executive summary, "Homeless students are best served when promising practices are implemented as part of a comprehensive and coordinated homeless education program. Ultimately, the success of any homeless education program requires coordinated action by many individuals, and is measured by whether all homeless students are identified, enrolled, and educated appropriately."

REFERENCES

Epstein, N. (2004). *Who's in charge here: The tangled web of school governance & policy.* Washington, DC: Brookings Institution Press.

Pennsylvania Department of Education. (2005). *Pre K–12: Student services and programs: Program statistics.* Retrieved on July 24, 2006 from the Pennsylvania Department of Education at www.pde.state.pa.us.

Stone, C., Henig, R., Jones, B., & Pierannunzi C. (2001). *Building civic capacity: The politics of reforming urban schools studies in government and public policy.* Wichita: University of Kansas Press.

United States Department of Education. (2002). *Education for homeless children and youth program: Learning to succeed. Executive summary.* Available at http://www.ed.gov/offices/OUS/PES/eed/learnsucceed/exec sum.html

United States Department of Education. (July 2004). *Education for homeless children and youth program: Title VII-B of the McKinney-Vento Assistance Act; a non-regulatory guidance.* Subtitle B of Title 7, of the McKinney-Vento Homeless Assistance Act-42-U.S.C 11431, etseq. pp. 21–17.

CHAPTER 8

WORDSWORTH ACADEMY

Adapting Educational Reform to the Private Alternative School Setting

Roger Cadenhead

The year 1957 marked an important event in American education. Only three years after the famed *Brown v. Board of Education*, a court case that was to embark American educational institutions on an effort to correct racial inequalities in schooling, which is still a work in process, the Russians proved they were somewhat ahead of the United States. The launch of the Sputnik satellite had an immediate impact in American society. As a result, American schools became the topic of concern. The launch of Sputnik appeared to prove that American schools had fallen behind the schools in Russia. American schools must begin teaching more math and science to students, or the United States would fall further and further behind other nations in the rush to new technologies, and especially the rush to explore space. There needed to be a push in mathematics and science that would enable American students to catch up to the Russian students in the field of technology.

As a high school student in the early 1960s, I was caught up in this rush to have schools provide higher levels of math and science instruction to

Policy, Leadership, and Student Achievement, pages 101–122
101

students in the high schools of America. Teachers talked about Sputnik and what it would mean for America if we could not compete with the Russians technologically. Students were told that to compete with the Russians, American students must prepare themselves with more math and science knowledge. As such, my high school transcripts will show higher math courses such as calculus and analytical geometry, along with physics and various courses in science. I was encouraged by my teachers and guidance advisors to pursue a career in engineering, so that some day I might be a part of some technological enterprise that would put America back on top. The launch of Sputnik had inspired Americans to think about their schools, and to support efforts that seemed to be aimed at making them better.

After graduation from high school, I was accepted at an engineering college and went off to help make America more competitive with other nations. I shared this experience with a number of friends, since there were six of us who attended the same college in our freshman year. Some of my friends saw it through, and today are trained as engineers, but I doubt any of them think they have played a key role in returning America to international dominance in technology. But we were influenced by the message of that time . . . learn science and math in order to keep your country competitive. In some sense, national interest became a major influence in the lives of high school students of that time. Students were not encouraged to think solely in terms of what was best for them, but rather what might be best for the nation. This philosophy was summarized by President-elect John F. Kennedy in his inaugural speech on January 20, 1960, when he said: "And so my fellow Americans: Ask not what your country can do for you—ask what you can do for your country" (Clarke, 2004, p. 78).

Today, in 2006, those sentiments expressed by John Kennedy in 1960 are just memories, but there is still no shortage of concern in American society for our schools. The emphasis on science and math as a way to catch the Russians may have become a distant memory, but there are plenty of new voices and new ideas for making the schools in our society successful. There is no end of criticisms made about schools, and there is no end of ideas to make schools better. There is an ongoing discussion about schools that involves politics, business, and other forces of change. Some of those voices advocate systemic changes for the schools, and some have even advocated a total systemic change as the only hope for American education (Anyon, 2005). Today, there are advocates for more federal control of American schools, advocates for decentralizing control of schools, ideas about curriculum revision to make it more appropriate to the times, and the list goes on. Reforming American education has not only become a major issue in our culture, but school reform has also become big business in America. Nonprofit corporations have made fortunes promoting individual systems for school improvement and the state and federal governments have become more and more involved in making the schools of America better.

Often competing advocates for school reform lose sight of what may be in the best interest of the individual student. The current debate and discussion about school reform seems to prove that schooling in America are still in need of radical change, and the ideas for how to make those changes are numerous. The problem faced by school administrators today is how to decide which plans or models to follow, and which actions taken will result in the best outcomes for the students being served. The problem faced by students today is no different from the problem that I faced in high school. Like me, students today have little voice in what initiatives their schools are pursuing, what model or plan has been adopted for them. Time has passed since the 1960s and Sputnik, but students today often find themselves as pawns in someone else's system of reform. It is important to not lose sight of the students in every rush to reform American schooling. True reform should always be about providing what is best for the students in schools. No matter what systems or models or programs are used, the end result should be to meet the needs of the students, to assure both preparation for the future and success in the present.

MODERN REFORM IN AMERICAN EDUCATION

The Sputnik event of 1957 sparked a rash of examinations of American schools and its education system. In 1959, Admiral Hyman Rickover published Education and Freedom. In his book, he made an attempt to link the security of the American nation and the quality of its education. His contention was that if the educational system were allowed to weaken the educational capacity of our young students, then the result would be the eventual weakening of the security of the nation in the world. This was the beginning of a series of books and studies concluding that American education was failing to achieve what our society expected. Something had to be done. The schools had to be improved, or the nation would suffer the result. Rickover's book was a criticism of the inefficiency of American schools and their failure to properly prepare students by weakening down what they were learning. The weakening of the schools would inevitably lead to the weakening of the nation.

In 1966, with the publication of what became known as the "Coleman Report," America was told that schools had little influence on their students and did little to really improve student achievement. To believe the "Coleman Report" was to believe that the child's environment and genes, and parents and culture, determined the value and meaning of schooling. The report concluded that schools could do little to help students overcome limitations of experience and knowledge resulting from their backgrounds. The Coleman Report challenged the new goal of using American schools, a common experience for the races, as the mechanism to help America achieve some sense of racial equality. *Brown vs. Board of Education* sought to open up the promise of quality education to all, and the schools, it was hoped, could help those who society had left behind catch up. Schools were to be the means whereby the racially mistreated could achieve parity with the majority. But the Coleman Report cast a long shadow on that perspective. For if, the schools could really make little difference in a child's life and achievement, then nothing could be done in schools. Schools were doomed to remain ineffective agents of improving the lives of students. The resulting question was "Why should money and effort be invested in an agency that could not help students overcome inequalities current in our culture?" The Coleman Report led many to think that reforming the schools in America would just be a waste of resources. But the most significant critique of American education came out in 1983 with the report issued by the National Commission on Excellence in Education. The report, *A Nation at Risk: The Imperative for Educational Reform*, brought American education under a new microscope of examination. The report claimed that the nation's future was being jeopardized by a "rising tide" of mediocrity. A quote from the report stated: "If an unfriendly foreign power had attempted to impose on America the mediocre educational performance that exists today, we might well have viewed it as an act of war" (A Nation at Risk, 1983). This statement alone alarmed the American public, and immediately there was a call for reforming American education. The recommendations of the Commission for solving the deterioration of the educational system included reforms in five areas.

First, that graduation requirements should be strengthened, and that all schools require students take four years of English, three years of mathematics, three years of science, three years of social studies and at least a half year of computer science. Second, that four-year colleges and universities raise their admission standards and that students should be encouraged to prepare themselves to meet those standards. Third, that more time should be invested in teaching and learning, through lengthening the instructional day or year. Fourth, a seven-part plan to improve the preparation of a new generation of teachers to meet the new demands of the intensified curriculum and school program. Fifth, that elected school leaders and teachers are held accountable for implementing the suggested reforms, and that the citizenry provide whatever fiscal resources may be needed by the educational leaders.

The *Nation at Risk* report set the stage for a 24-year effort to reform American education. While not all of the reforms suggested in *Nation at Risk* were ever implemented, the report did give birth to a whole new national pursuit...reforming the American school system. This national pursuit of reforming American education has taken many different turns in the 24 years since the *Nation at Risk* report of 1983. And like the recommendations of that report, not all the recommendations and suggestions of the numerous reform initiatives in the last 24 years have proven to be the silver bullet that transforms American education into what everyone wants it to be.

A Nation at Risk was really the first time in the history of schooling in America that the federal government seemed to be taking the lead in finding fault with schools and then making recommendations to solve the faults. The report was supported by President Ronald Reagan, and his support and the support of others in his government seemed to signify that the report was the official position of the United States government. The alarm was sounded again, there was a crisis in our schools, and once more, the attention of the nation was turned to an examination of schools, how they functioned, what was being taught, and what outcomes were being accomplished. For the first time, the political will of the American people was called forth to work toward improving American schools, because the report claimed that the schools were failing miserably and the extension of that was that the schools were also failing citizens. Because the report was backed by the leader of the American government, it was accepted as a fact that the schools were failing. The report was the proof. It must be the truth, based upon facts that had been uncovered by those who wrote the report.

In a 1995 book, *The Manufactured Crisis: Myths, Fraud and the Attack on America's Public Schools*, authors David Berliner and Bruce J. Biddle took the main claims of *A Nation at Risk* to task. This report, the basis for a major change in education policy in America, was full of claims that are without merit. Many claims were made to prove that the schools were failing miserably, but yet the sources of the proof for the claims were never made known. It was a report without merit, full of myths, and unfounded statements. Berliner and Biddle take great pains to show that evidence abounds to contradict the hostile finding of the *Nation at Risk* report. The report, in their opinion, was full of myths that could not be supported (Berliner & Biddle, 1995, p. 6). The report was, in their opinion, motivated by political purpose, and that purpose was not directed at making sure that American education served the interests of all its citizens equally.

This mixing of politics into the debate about school improvement was to set the scene for future efforts by the federal government to direct efforts to reform American schooling. The apparent finding of the *Nation at Risk* report, the pretext for federal involvement in the issue of school reform in America, has been exposed as lacking substance when the issues are closely examined. But future efforts of the federal government to intervene in the debate about American schools would be grounded in research and facts.

REFORM EFFORTS SINCE 1983

The Nation at Risk report in 1983 started a reform movement in American Education that persists until today. While many of the original contentions about the failures of American schools found in A Nation at Risk have since been challenged (Berliner & Biddle, 1995) the report began a continuous rush to fault American schools and a relentless pursuit of ways to solve the problems being perceived. Over the period of 24 years since 1983, there have been numerous movements and efforts to change American education into the elusive model that will satisfy reformers. These efforts to modify, change, and improve American schooling have taken many forms and shapes during this period. The process has never been one that every stakeholder in education can agree upon. The result has been that while models and suggestions for reform have been numerous, agreement on which models to pursue and implement has been a problem. This has brought the whole process of reform into question. It does not appear that much has been accomplished despite the abundance of possible choices for school improvement.

A recent article from the *Arizona Star*, "Student-achievement Strategies' Effect in Question," made the observation that outside improvement plans for schools have had "either modest effects or no effects" on student achievement in Florida and Texas. The Rand Corporation study of 250 elementary and secondary schools in Florida and Texas found that schools were not implementing all of the changes incorporated in the various improvement plans that they had adopted. The four comprehensive School Reform (CSR) models studied were among the most popular in recent years, and include the models of The National Institute for Direct Instruction, the Success for All Foundation, Accelerated Schools, and Core Knowledge. These models were selected for the Rand study because they have been widely implemented in schools throughout the nation and differ significantly from one another. The study concluded that the adoption of these models in schools really had little impact on student achievement and overall school improvement. It appears that nothing, including some expensive models, is really working to make the schools better or to raise student achievement. The faults are still being noted, and the problem still exists. (This report can be retrieved from the Rand Corporation Web site at www.rand.org/pubs.)

Over the last 23 years, there have been efforts to revise, revamp, extend, and modernize the education process for American schools, but no single idea or model or plan, has been accepted as the panacea, the cure for all that ails American education. But that has not stopped the process. Models and plans continue to be created and all of them make some claims to success. Yet, again in an article from the *Time Magazine* Web site, dated

December 9, 2006, another panel of experts has again set forth to identify what schools in America must do if students are to be properly prepared for the 21st century. Of note is the opening line: The world has changed, but the American classroom, for the most part, has not (http://www.time. com Fischler, December 28, 2006). This is yet another panel, with another set of priorities, another set of goals, another set of models that will assure success for the ailing American education enterprise. The report claims to take a look at what must be done to help assure our students can compete in the global economy. This tone of this very recent report sounds very much like the report in 1983, but its recommendations are much more generalized. For instance, the report suggests that students need to know about the world, become more sensitive to other cultures, and be able to speak other languages than English. Additional mandates require that students be made more aware of linkages between various types of technology and that they develop excellent people skills along the way. And like the mandates of *A Nation at Risk*, these too will fall on some willing ears as well as some deaf ears. And this recent report again reinforces the notion that despite all of the efforts to modernize and improve our schools, the fault lines remain exposed to anyone willing to take a close look.

But this article helps make my point: there is an ongoing examination of American education because there is always some group who thinks the current system is not getting the job done. This process of examining and making recommendations for improvement has been going on for the last 23 years; where are we today, and what have we achieved? Not much, because if the goal lines continue to be moved from time to time, no one can know when there is success. This whole approach is terribly frustrating and confusing. Most people in education, such as teachers and administrators, are interested in helping the next generation learn how to succeed in life. However, as the constant drone of faultfinding with education continues, educators themselves are often the ones blamed for the substance of the criticisms. The distressing realization that efforts and money expended will probably not make much difference leads to paralysis and fear of trying new things. Criticism of America has become a national pastime. Criticism of education has come in many forms and from many people. In 1987, E. D. Hirsch, Jr. published his book, *Cultural Literacy*, in which he had argued that children in American schools were being deprived of basic knowledge necessary to their ability to function in modern society. His claim was that the schools were failing to teach cultural literacy to their students, and by failing to do so, those students were doomed to failure in modern society. He went so far as to include in his book an appendix called "What Literate Americans Know," which was a list of some dates and many terms and geographical locations, that he claimed should be taught in schools because doing so will help students to be prepared for the world they would face.

In the Vintage Books paperback version, the list can be found on pages 152–215 (Hirsch, Jr., 1988). It is no wonder that his original book met with hostility in the education community.

In 1996, Hirsch returned to his criticism of American education in *The Schools We Need and Why We Do not Have Them.* In the introduction to this new book, he writes that "... our K–12 education is among the least effective in the developed world," a conclusion he reached after reading three reports of various "authoritative studies" he references in his notes (Hirsch, Jr., 1996, p. 273). He argues that "despite recent public pressure for school improvement, there has been little movement toward rigor in American educational theories"(Hirsch, Jr., 1996, p. 2). In his book, he acknowledges the efforts of the "national standards movement" as a good first step to identifying the knowledge and skills that children should possess at various levels of their educational experience. He also dismisses any objection that the use of standardized tests in American education poses any problems for students or schools (Hirsch, Jr., 1996, p. 229). He also claims that "improving the effectiveness and fairness of education through enhancing both its content and commonality...will...diminish the economic inequities within the nation" (Hirsch, Jr., 1996, p. 238). In 1987, he was interested in identifying a list of things an educated person should know, and by 1996, he has identified what must be done to solve the economic inequities that area part of our culture and society.

In 1999, another book appeared that pointed to the clear failure of the American school system and condemned educators as well. In *The Conspiracy of Ignorance: The Failure of American Public Schools*, by Martin L. Gross, the author appeals to test scores by American students as proof that schools were failing to educate students adequately. In his book, he claims that the educational establishment is the real wall between American schools and success. As the author writes, "Simply stated, American public schools, from kindergarten through the senior year of high school, are miserably failing their students and the society" (Gross, 1999, p. 5). His basic premise in this book is that the educational establishment has stood in the way of genuine reform of American education. He lists the actions of two education Presidents, namely President Carter and President Clinton, as examples of the conflict that even those supporting public education face. President Carter had his daughter attend a public school in Washington, D.C. for four years, while President Clinton sent his daughter to a private school for eight years. He credits the Clinton's with knowing that private schools do a better job of teaching children than do public schools. He goes on to fault the entire structure of administration in the American education system, and accuses the system of promoting an "unscholarly anti-intellectual, anti-academic cabal which can best be described as a conspiracy of ignorance...that fosters...false theories and low academic standards" (Gross, 1999, p. 11).

And what are the solutions to the problems that Gross identifies? On pages 246–254, he lists 19 steps that must be taken if the public school system is to be reformed, rebuilt, and regained. Most people stop reading when they see that he advocates the closing of all undergraduate schools of education, eliminating "the inferior Doctor of Education Degree," and offering $4,000 vouchers for students in failing schools, enabling those students to choose to attend private schools with the vouchers (Gross, 1999, pp. 249–250). He also recommends a return to "tradition and superior curriculums that worked quite well," stop "grade inflation," and discontinue "ed psych courses for teacher training" (Gross, 1999, p. 253). The solutions to the problem, were one to believe Gross, is to simply return to a previous point in time, abandon efforts to improve understanding of the learning process through psychology, and eliminate certain aspects of the educational establishment. Eliminate all those things and American education will be better off. But authors such as Hirsch and Gross were not alone in finding fault with the way the education efforts of the country were going. Surely, the government could get involved and find the solutions to the problems. In 1994, Congress passed The Goals 2000: Educate America Act. The foundation for this act was laid by Governor George Bush of Texas and members of a government panel that had set forth their findings and suggestions in 1990. Goals 2000, as this act came to be known, sought to improve student learning in American schools by implementing a long-term and broad-based effort to promote coherent and coordinated improvements in the American education system. Goals 2000 sought to identify a set of National Education Goals and establish a set of voluntary national standards that would serve as benchmarks for accomplishment in the major academic subject areas. These standards would be used by parents, educators, and citizens as guides for school improvement (an archived copy of this entire report is found at http://www.ed.gov/pubs/goals). President Clinton was known as an "Education President" and he pushed the Goals 2000 as his major initiative in reforming American education. Just as President Reagan had stood behind *A Nation at Risk* and advocated for its recommendations, President Clinton stood behind the recommendations of Goals 2000. Two of the more interesting goals set forth were: that "every school in the United States will be free of drugs, violence and unauthorized presence of firearms and alcohol, and will offer a disciplined environment conducive to learning" and "every school will promote partnerships that will increase parental involvement and participation in promoting the social, emotional and academic growth of children." It is interesting that school reform, by Goals 2000, included far more than manipulation of curriculum and overcoming the "education establishment." It stated its goals in terms of generalities.

President George Bush has made his mark on the debate about reforming American education through his support of the No Child Left Behind

Act, signed into law on January 8, 2002. It is interesting to visit the official government Web site for this law found at http://www.ed.gov.nclb. The site lists four goals of the NCLB Act: first, strong accountability for results; second, more freedom for states and communities; third, encouraging proven educational methods; fourth, more choice for parents. Of course, this law, like every other effort to identify the needs of our schools and recommend reforms, has fallen prey to critics on every hand. Few critics would agree that the four goals established on the Web site are meaningful for the reform of the American education system. This law, like *A Nation at Risk*, Goals 2000, and other initiatives supported by the government, will suffer the same failure as the other plans. Why? Because it too, as the others, falls on some deaf ears, and meets the same fate . . . that of an unrealized potential. Few believe that this law will revitalize, re-energize, and reform American schooling. Taking a look at some of the initiatives over the last 23 years, efforts to make our schools better only reinforce the impression that there is really no answer for all the problems. Initiatives have been undertaken by local, state, and federal governments. There have been efforts to modernize the curriculum to reflect a changing world, as well as efforts to return the curriculum to its basics. There have been experiments with math and reading curricula, and there is no end of programs developed by curriculum companies, all of which claim to lead to academic success for students using the programs . . . for a price. There have been experiments with school scheduling such as block scheduling, to give more time to teachers and students in order to add depth of learning for the subject taught. Numerous efforts have been undertaken to prove that smaller classrooms will result in greater success for students. Innovations such as magnet schools, charter schools, and more recently "Internet" schools, have been thrown into the reform mix in the name of school reform. There has been the growth of a significant home-schooling movement in America as well. There has been constant pressure to improve teacher preparation, requiring more course work and the passage of competency exams. And all of this has been taking place in a period of time when attaining the spirit of *Brown vs. Board of Education* has supposedly been an important goal for the nation and its schools.

It should come as no surprise that reform of American education have been an elusive goal, and every initiative, every program, every model, has its supporters as well as its detractors. In the final analysis, each school must make up its own mind, each school administrator must make choices that best serve purposes and goals that have been identified. There will never be just one single identified system of study for all of the schools in America.

At the very best, 24 years of reform since *A Nation at Risk* proves there can be no single answer, because every system, model, and approach has its detractors and critics and so every new idea is doomed to failure eventually, as the history of these last 23 years demonstrates. With this background in mind, it is time to admit that no one model will fit all student needs and determine what is the best, sensible plan to pursue if schools are to be made better in what they deliver to the most important stakeholders . . . the students.

As far as reform of American education is concerned, it is both the worst of times and the best of times. It is the worst of times, because nothing seems to be working to solve the perceived problems in our schools. Programs, models and initiatives, and plans abound, and yet there is no clear sense of real change in American schooling. A recent article from *Time* magazine, "How to Bring Our Schools Out of the 20th Century" by Claudia Wallis and Sonia Steptoe, opens with this observation: " The world has changed, but the American classroom, for the most part, hasn't." So what these authors seem to be saying is that the more things change, the more they stay the same. This seems to be the growing consensus on what the last 24 years of reform efforts in our schools has really accomplished . . . seemingly, very little. For those interested in reforming our schools, it is the worst of times, because the will to change and keep working for improvement is being weakened by the constant criticism of the schools and those who work in them. The will to take action is being diminished by the promise of failure, because nothing is really getting the job accomplished the way reformers wish to see it happen.

But it may actually be the best of times. Instead of placing the emphasis on the fact that no single plan is going to be acceptable for all schools and all teachers and therefore change for the better is hopeless, why not consider that there have never been so many good ideas about how to make schools better? The push to reform American schools and make them better at meeting the needs of their main stakeholders has led to the explosion of models and plans, many containing excellent ideas and approaches. There is a wealth of information available to support efforts to change the way we do schooling. Any school administrator, seeking to make his school the best it can be in serving the needs of the students in the school, has an unlimited amount of information available to help inform decisions.

It is my contention that every school administrator, such as building principals and administrators, must cut his/her own path to reform and make individual decisions about how to have the best school program possible. It is very unlikely that the suggestion for the complete systemic change of Jean Anyon will ever be effected in America. So the answer will not be a total overhaul, but a school-by-school reform effort. Every school leader must make decisions in the best interest of the population of students being served. Models and approaches chosen must meet the needs of the chief stakeholders in the school, namely the students. School leaders must learn to ignore the constant criticism that shadows every effort to educate children and youth. Once the primary commitment is made to serve the needs of the children, then decisions can be made about aspects of the curriculum, how to manage the teaching process, how to deliver instruction, how to discipline the students, and how to best meet the needs of the students in the school. Such a view allows school administrators to implement suitable models based on research and with a record of success. The program can and must be individually adapted to the school's purpose and goals and shaped to best meet the needs of the students. This requires that the school leaders, the main decision makers, decide upon a plan and structure that the teachers and students can accept and support. The last 23 years of research make it possible for school administrators to pick and choose approaches that allow them to best serve their students. Reform of education for schools should not be just compliance to policy, but a genuine exploration and "acquisition of new knowledge and skills" (McElmore, 2006, p. 227). It is the acquisition of new knowledge and skills that enables a school to be as effective as it can be in this present time. Certainly the last 24 years of research allow school administrators the opportunity to pick and choose from the very best that researchers have discovered. Successful reform of schools will probably not result from strict adherence to every aspect of a various reform model, but rather to the conscious act of choosing the best aspects of various models and the adapting those aspects to best serve the students in the school.

The purpose of this chapter is to highlight a specific program in a private academic school in Harrisburg, Pennsylvania. While there is no end of ideas for making educational programs successful, the welfare of students should still be the overriding goal of education. This is especially true for students who are considered "at-risk," who have a history of failure in the public school setting, and who have been placed outside the public school setting. Education for these students takes on an increased sense of urgency and importance. Any program serving students who have been forced to accept alternative placement outside the public schools should set a high priority on helping these students learn to be productive and healthy citizens. For many of these students, placement in an alternative school, such as Wordsworth Academy in Harrisburg, Pennsylvania, entails a real opportunity for them to begin to succeed.

The state of Pennsylvania has a well developed alternative education program. The State Department of Education maintains a department to supervise the various alternative education institutions serving this unique purpose. In 1997, there were approximately 7,791 students in alternative placement in the state of Pennsylvania. By the year 2006, that number had increased to an estimated 23,772 of the Pennsylvania Department of Alternative Education. This growth in using alternative placement options in Pennsylvania is typical of what is taking place in other states throughout the nation. Reform in education must find its place in these schools as well in the mainstream public schools. Generally speaking, it is the students in alternative placement who need the benefits that reform efforts can bring to their schools. Reform of the schooling process, finding ways to better equip students for modern life, and teaching students skills that will lead to continuing success in their lives, is needed as much in schools outside the mainstream as do the mainstream schools.

BACKGROUND HISTORY OF WORDSWORTH ACADEMY

Wordsworth Academy, a licensed private academic school in Harrisburg, Pennsylvania, has been in operation in Harrisburg since 1999. The school is an affiliate of Wordsworth Academy of Pennsylvania, with corporate offices in Philadelphia, Pennsylvania. Wordsworth Academy as an organization was founded in 1952 and has been engaged in serving children and youth through various programs in the areas of mental health and education. The Harrisburg site is currently serving 70 students from the Harrisburg region and about 14 school districts by accepting alternative placement for students at risk. Most of the students are identified as Special Education and are placed in Wordsworth because of behavioral problems. These students are all deemed to need an alternative placement to the public school if they are to succeed in schooling. Wordsworth Academy is one of 654 different approved providers of educational services to disruptive youth in the state of Pennsylvania. In 2006, approximately 24,000 students have been placed in alternative placement outside the public school setting. Alternative schools, such as Wordsworth Academy, are an important part of the public school system, and must be full participants in the school reform movement. The public schools benefit from being able to remove highly disruptive youth from their programs. In many cases, placement outside the public school setting is very appropriate for students at risk and is a viable choice for their education. A student needs to be in a school where their behavior can be managed and their needs can be met. To address the educational needs and emotional needs of students with behavioral disorders is what alternative schools must be prepared to accomplish.

Wordsworth Academy promotes the following mission statement: "The Mission of Wordsworth, a not-for-profit institution founded in 1952, is to provide quality Education, Treatment and Care to children and families with special needs" (available at www.wordsworth.org). This philosophy places the students at the center of the educational process, and they are the chief stakeholders in the school's efforts to educate them and meet their emotional and social needs. Since 1999, a conscious effort has been made to develop an educational program at Wordsworth Harrisburg that assures that the special needs of students in the school are met. As the Harrisburg program has developed and grown from one student to the current enrollment of 70, attention has been paid to the best elements of what educational reformers are advocating. As reform efforts are taking place at local, state, and federal levels, and as various models and programs are being implemented as part of the national effort to reform American education and schools, Wordsworth has studied many of the various models and has adopted what is believed to be the best parts of those models. The idea has been to develop a program that avails itself of the best practices available for working with children at risk. Almost all of the students at Wordsworth are considered "at risk" because of behavior problems. Many have been placed outside the public schools because of a history of misbehavior that is disruptive to the educational program of their public school. Most of the students placed at Wordsworth have not experienced success in public school. Under Pennsylvania law, placement in Wordsworth Academy must be approved by the parents, and even though alternative placement is difficult for families to accept, Wordsworth is one of the options that parents are given. The administrative team of Wordsworth is committed to making the school an example of the best program that it can be. The program that Wordsworth follows is one that is informed by research and utilizes an eclectic mix of various features from a number of reform models and programs.

Wordsworth Academy has pursued many research-based reforms in an effort to be a quality educational experience for its students. Research has informed many of the decisions made by Wordsworth administration as it has sought to develop a holistic approach to schooling for its students. The research behind the Small School model has led to many innovations in school administration. The educational program has attempted to deliver instruction to the students at their achievement levels, and has committed to the use of a Direct Instruction model for Reading in the form of Corrective Reading. Counseling services have been enhanced to help with the emotional needs of the students. The use of Effective Curriculum (as structured in Effective Curriculum for Students with Emotional and Behavioral Disorders, 2001) enables the school to address the growing emotion al and social needs of the student population. Every effort has been made to develop a program that is holistic in approach and attempts to meet the varying needs of the student population. Wordsworth Academy seeks to address the continuing educational needs of every student, while also addressing the emotional and social development of the students in its care.

Reforming the American school system by making schools better and suited to serve the needs of all students has been an elusive goal. Wordsworth Academy has not adopted any single Comprehensive School Reform Model for its program. The program has turned to various sources of research for information and taken aspects of program design from many of the Comprehensive School Reform models that are current in reform circles. The instructional program and ancillary programs that serve the students, such as counseling and discipline approaches, have been based upon the best of several different approaches and models. The balance of this paper will take a look at those approaches and explain how research has informed their development. The three specific areas of focus will be the approaches to school administration, student discipline, and use of a nontraditional curriculum.

WORDSWORTH ACADEMY: PROGRAM DISTINCTIONS IN MANAGEMENT

Site-based management has been one aspect of school reform that has influenced school districts to decentralize management of their schools. It has been adopted by many school systems to increase school autonomy and to share decision-making with teachers, parents, and community members. Site-based management typically involves the formation of a leadership team or committee empowered to make decisions affecting curriculum and other school management issues. Under site-based management, teachers are asked to assume leadership roles in staff development, mentoring, and curriculum development and to become partners in school and staff supervision and evaluation. Teacher involvement is a major theme in the implementation of site-based management philosophy. The model used to inform administrative practices at Wordsworth is the Comer School Development Program. The Northwest Regional Educational Laboratory (NWREL), maintains a Catalog of School Reform Models on its Web site at www.nwrel.org that sets forth various aspects of the entire school reform model of James Comer of Yale University. This program, called the School Development Program, lists a nine-element process of school reform. The Comer model was developed in 1968, and 30 years of research indicate that full implementation of the model leads to high levels of student achievement and development (Essential Understandings of the Yale School Development Program, 2004). Wordsworth Academy has not adopted all nine aspects of the model, but has selected the aspects that can best be adapted to the Harrisburg site. The strongest feature of the Comer model adopted by Wordsworth Academy in Harrisburg is the school planning and management team. This team develops the comprehensive school plan, which includes the following: setting academic and social goals for the school and coordinating all school activities, including staff development programs. The team is empowered to monitor the school program and modify it as necessary with oversight of curriculum, instruction, and assessment. The planning team meets weekly and cooperatively makes decisions concerning the daily administration of the school. Team members have assigned roles and work together to improve the school's management. The goal for the team is to constantly improve the effectiveness of the curriculum by constantly assessing student needs and teacher performance. The effect of the school planning and management team has been significant. The program has developed a capacity to respond to the dynamic aspects of working daily with students who have behavioral disorders. This capacity to respond to every behavioral event in a professional and appropriate manner creates confidence between the staff and the students. The management team works daily to create and maintain a safe and secure environment for staff and students. The success that the school staff has had in managing the school has been attributed, in great part, to the commitment to this aspect of the Comer model.

A second aspect of the Comer model adopted by Wordsworth Academy is the reliance on a student and staff support team. This team is made up of the school psychologist and the school nurse, along with other members of the counseling and administrative staff. The role of the student and staff support team is to provide cohesion between the school's student services, facilitate the sharing of advice across divisions of the school, address the individual needs of students, and help students access resources outside the school. The counseling team directs weekly team meetings with teachers to discuss student progress. These team meetings with teachers and teacher assistants is a key feature of how this aspect of the Comer model is being implemented by staff. Sharing information across divisions of the school is essential to helping students with their emotional needs. The Comer model has proven to be a key piece of the effort to make Wordsworth Academy responsive and effective in dealing with a difficult student population.

WORDSWORTH ACADEMY: PROGRAM DISTINCTIONS IN STUDENT DISCIPLINE

Wordsworth Academy of Harrisburg is an alternative placement option for students who have both special education needs and behavioral disorders. Most of the students at Wordsworth have experienced difficulty maintaining consistent participation in the public schools. Misbehavior is a disruptive influence in the public school setting. Most public school teachers and administrators try accommodating students with behavioral disorders to a certain point, but often reach a point where the student is marked for placement in a school environment that can help manage their inappropriate behavior. Almost 100% of the students placed at Wordsworth Academy have experienced behavior control problems in their public schools. Any child who can manage his/her own behavior in the school setting stands a chance of succeeding at school; but a child who cannot self-manage behavior at school will inevitably experience difficulty being successful. Inappropriate behavior, driven by emotional components and motivations, often leads a student to failure. An alternative school where a large percentage of students have behavioral disorders must maintain a student discipline program that meets the needs of the students while holding them accountable for their inappropriate behavior. The underlying philosophy is that situations requiring discipline can and should be opportunities for learning, growth, and community-building. Wordsworth Academy is committed to helping students understand their negative and inappropriate behaviors and to learn how those behaviors are harmful to the school community. Every student at Wordsworth is called upon to evaluate their personal behaviors in terms of what is best for the school community. Inappropriate behaviors at school are hindrances to the operation of a learning community. This concept of "shared community" is at the core of Wordsworth's student discipline system. The school management team at Wordsworth has adopted the best features of restorative discipline for schools (Stutzman & Mullet, 2005). Restorative discipline is defined as follows: "Restorative discipline, like punishment, concerns itself with appropriate consequences that encourage accountability—but accountability that emphasizes empathy and repair of harm" (Stutzman & Mullet, p. 13). The school management team has adopted principles of the restorative discipline approach to deal with the inappropriate behaviors of Wordsworth students. This approach fits the overall holistic approach that Wordsworth uses in helping its students develop appropriate responses to frustration and anger in community relationships. Restorative discipline comes out of the restorative justice culture that has been popular in recent years. Misbehavior in this model presents a learning opportunity, and a teachable moment that staff and students use to enhance the welfare of the community. Discipline, in the case of this model, is more than just stopping a student's bad behavior; it involves teaching the student to be responsible to other community members for bad behavior and making amends to the members of the community whom they have offended. This adds to students' socialization, holds them accountable to others outside of themselves, and teaches them to take responsibility for their own behavior. Restorative discipline helps offending students deal with the harm and inconvenience they have caused other members of their learning community. The cohesion of the entire learning community are valued and students are taught to be accountable to others in their learning community.

In an article by Paul McCold and Ted Wachtel, "In Pursuit of Paradigm: A Theory of Restorative Justice," the authors identify four possible responses to inappropriate behavior: neglect it, permit without comment, punish it, or use the offense as a teachable moment to restore what has been lost or damaged (McCold & Wachtel, 2003, p. 1). The key to restorative discipline is to find suitable and appropriate consequences for inappropriate behavior. The underlying principle of the student discipline of the Wordsworth system is to lead offending students toward an effort to repair harm done to other people and to the learning community. This view of restoring the damaged relationships within the community is the basic premise of to help them accept responsibility for their actions and be willing to take some action to repair the damage. An important aspect of the system is clear limit-setting followed by diligent and consistent enforcement of behavioral standards. Students are constantly reminded of their responsibilities to the school community. When a student's behavior offends the behavioral standards of the community—standards that are constantly rehearsed for them—then the student is given a plan to become reintegrated into the community without sustaining the label of the offender (Wachtel, 2000).

The structures for implementation of the restorative discipline model involve both a mental health staff and a counseling staff. These professional team members are committed to the same idea: that discipline is more than just punishing, that discipline involves responsibility of the offender to make amends to the members of the learning community whom they have offended. Student discipline, in the Wordsworth model, is more than isolation of the offender; it is an effort to reincorporate the offender back into the community as soon as possible. However, reincorporation into the community requires that the offending student be responsible for what they have done. In addition, the offending student must explore alternative courses of action that could have been used. The purpose of this approach is to help students understand that they have other choices available to them should they find themselves in a similar situation in the future, and where possible, immediate restoration is sought through verbal and written apologies. Additional efforts by staff have been made to use role playing and Web-based teaching through video streaming called United Streaming (Discovery Education). This Web site allows free downloads of video about topics such as conflict resolution, anger management, bus behavior, and other topics. These videos can be shown to offending students, and through processing by the mental health workers, the students are allowed the opportunity to explore alternative appropriate behaviors that could be chosen as opposed to the inappropriate behavior that was chosen. This approach has been very successful. The use of restorative discipline is further supported by implementation of the Positive Behavior Support Program developed by George Sugai, from the University of Oregon College of Education. Positive Behavior Support has six major components: a common approach to discipline, positively stated expectations of students, established procedures for teaching student expectations to the students, a continuum of procedures for encouraging and rewarding the demonstration of student expectations, a continuum of procedures for discouraging rule-violating behavior, and procedures for monitoring and evaluating the effectiveness of the discipline system (from Colorado Department of Education Web site, www.cde.state.co.us/pbs). An excellent overview of the program can be retrieved from www.pbis.org. The six elements of the PBS system work alongside the school's commitment to restorative discipline. The school management team is responsible for providing assistance with the implementation of the Positive Behavior Supports throughout the school. This requires staff training and constant monitoring of the program. The counseling team further emphasizes the positive aspect of student expectation by operating a school store. Students earn Wordsworth currency through demonstrating their personal commitment to the positive aspects of our discipline system.

WORDSWORTH ACADEMY: PROGRAM DISTINCTIONS IN USE OF EFFECTIVE CURRICULUM

Students who have failed to fit into their public schools, who have probably missed many days of school, and who experience behavioral disorders that have interfered with their education, are certainly in need of the traditional subjects of the school curriculum. Students need to know how to do math and read adequately. Commitment to these traditional aspects of the curriculum must not be abandoned just because the students have behavioral disorders. It cannot be denied that the presence of emotional factors and occurrences of inappropriate behavior tend to interfere with the teaching of traditional subjects; it is still important to teach them. This of course calls for teachers to be creative and flexible, and lessons in the traditional subjects of math and reading and science and social studies must be delivered in creative ways. But for children at risk, who have emotional issues and manifest behavioral disorders, there are nontraditional aspects of curriculum and learning that they must have opportunity to experience.

Wordsworth Academy has adopted a philosophy of creating instructional opportunities based on the individual needs of students with emotional and behavioral disorders. The guide for curriculum planning the school follows is adapted from *Effective Curriculum for Students with Emotional and Behavioral Disorders* by Beverly Johns, E. Paula Crowley, and Eleanor Guetzloe. This program views the teacher as the catalyst for change and establishes the importance of teaching social skills to students in their care. Children at risk, especially those with behavioral disorders, often are characterized by minimal social skills development. This places the teaching of the nontraditional curriculum, social skills, on a par with teaching elements that are more traditional. The teacher is to be the leading model for demonstrating social skills to students. Students are to be taught self-management strategies and are taught numerous acronyms for behaviors they are to actively choose as part of their self-management efforts (Johns, Crowley, & Guetzloe, 2002, pp. 87–91). Teachers must know as much as possible about their students if they are to help them develop the social skills that they lack. The ultimate goal of the Effective Curriculum is to build into students the social skills and sensibilities needed to succeed in the smaller communities of their family and neighborhood. This commitment to a nontraditional curriculum often appears to sacrifice the more traditional elements of the curriculum. But children who are at risk have greater needs in the area of self management and community living. Effective Curriculum allows the staff of Wordsworth Academy to help their students identify and develop the social skills that they lack. The school management team is responsible for working with teachers to help them implement the various school wide aspects of the Effective Curriculum.

CONCLUSION

Reform of American education and the improvement of American schools has been a serious national undertaking spread out over the last 23 years. Research into schooling has abounded during this 23-year period. Initiatives in almost every aspect of the schooling experience have been modified or adapted in the pursuit of some way to help our school meet the needs of all our students. Despite unprecedented research, despite the development of countless systems and models for reforming our schools, some reports indicate that little has been accomplished. Studies that are more recent seem to have the schools no better off now than when this reform effort began. Anyone in education who wants to have an excellent program of instruction and deal with the needs of students in a therapeutic manner has many places to look for guidance. The research culture is rich with suggestions and ideas about how to make schools more effective. Not every idea can be incorporated, and no single model is a fit for every school. It is therefore possible to be eclectic about what reform measures a school adopts, and which measures remain for someone else to adopt.

American schools can be divided into a large number of groups, and types of schools are very numerous. The focus of school reform has generally been the public schools. The public schools have invested large amounts of money in purchasing one system for reform or another system. Recent research shows that despite the adoption of models and programs to reform schools, little seems to be changing. This conclusion causes some educators to despair that reforming schools will ever be accomplished since no single model or program seems to be adaptable to every school setting. Instead of seeing the current reports as an indication that reform is a futile endeavor, school administrators should be prepared to adopt the best practices from the various models and programs for school reform. The last 23 years of research and experiment have produced a large source of findings about schools. It is important that school administrators of private schools search the literature in pursuit of answers making their schools the best they can be. School administrators should not be as concerned about following policy as they are about developing programs that are best for their students.

Reform of schools, whether those schools are public or private, should have the same goal . . . to serve the needs of the student population. With this goal in mind, school administrators can pick and choose reform elements that are best in helping them develop their program distinctions. This is the approach that Wordsworth Academy, a private licensed academic school in Harrisburg, Pennsylvania, has pursued. For reform efforts in school management, Wordsworth Academy has adopted many aspects of the Comer model. In the area of student discipline, Wordsworth Academy has adopted aspects of Restorative Discipline combined with aspects of the all-school Positive Behavior Supports system. As an alternative school, serving students at risk, Wordsworth Academy has attempted to keep the emotional and social needs of its students at the center of its curriculum reform efforts by adopting many aspects of the Effective Curriculum program.

Whether a school is a large public school, or a small private school, providing the best education for students and meeting their needs should still be the goals of the school. Reform of education must include every type of school, and schools must be free to adopt practices that research has shown to be effective. It is the practice of using research about models and programs to determine which ones are best for local student populations that will ensure that schools in America continue to change and improve. Reform that best serves the needs of student populations will not be served by administrative adherence to some unified policy. If meeting the needs of student populations is the real goal, then reform will best be accomplished by success at the level of the individual school. This has been the approach of the administration of Wordsworth Academy.

REFERENCES

Anyon, J. (2005). *Radical possibilities: Public policy, urban education and a new social movement.* New York: Taylor and Francis Group.

Berliner, D., & Bruce J. B. (1995). *The manufactured crisis: Myths, fraud, and the attack on America's public schools.* New York: Basic Books.

Clarke, T. (2004). *Ask not: The inauguration of John F. Kennedy and the speech that changed America.* New York: McMillan.

Essential understandings of the Yale School Development Program. (2004). Yale Child Study Center, reprinted from *Transforming Social Leadership and Management to Support Student Learning and Development.* Twin Oaks, CA: Corwin Press. Retrieved from www.nwrel.org.

Gross, M. (1999). *The conspiracy of ignorance.* New York: Harper Collins. (First Perennial Edition, 2000).

Hirsch, E. D., Jr. (1987). *Cultural literacy: What every American needs to know.* New York: Houghton-Mifflin. (First Vintage Books Edition, 1988).

Hirsch, E. D., Jr. (1996). The *schools we need and why we don't have them.* New York: Doubleday. (First Anchor Books Edition, 1999).

Johns, B. H., Crowley, E. P., & Guetzloe, E. (2002). *Effective curriculum for students with emotional and behavioral disorders.* Denver, CO: Love Publishing Company.

McCold, P., & Wachtel, T. (2003). *In pursuit of paradigm: A theory of restorative justice.* International Institute for Restorative Practices. Retrieved from www.restorativepractices.org

McElmore, R. (2004). *School reform from the inside out: Policy, practice and performance.* Boston: Harvard Education Publishing. (Third Printing, 2006).

Rickover, H. G. (1959). *Education and freedom.* New York: E. P. Dutton.

Statement of restorative justice principles as applied in a school setting. (2003). London: The Restorative Justice Consortium. Retrieved from www.restorative-justice.org/uk/

Stutzman, L., & Mullet, J. (2005). *The little book of restorative discipline in schools.* Intercourse, PA: Good Books.

Sugai, G., & Horner, R. (2003). *Overview of school-wide PBS: What is PBS and getting started.* Washington, DC: OSEP Center for Positive Behavioral Intervention and Supports. Retrieved from www.pbis.org.

Vernez, G., & Karam, R., Mariano, L. T., & DeMartini, C. (2006). *Evaluating comprehensive school models to scale.* Pittsburgh: Rand Corporation.

Wachtel, T. (2000). Restorative practices with high-risk youth. In G. Burford & J. Hudson (Eds.), *Family group conferencing: new directions in community centered child and family practice* (pp. 86–92). Hawthorne, NY: Aldine de Gruyter.

CHAPTER 9

STUDENT ACHIEVEMENT AND SCHOOL REFORM IN AN URBAN SCHOOL DISTRICT

Vivian Ikpa

INTRODUCTION

If an unfriendly foreign power had attempted to impose on America the mediocre educational performance that exists today, we might well have viewed it as an act of war. As it stands, we have allowed this to happen to ourselves. . . . We have, in effect, been committing an act of unthinking, unilateral educational disarmament.

—*A Nation at Risk* (1983)

Although this statement was written almost a quarter of a century ago in the introduction to the 1983 Reform Initiative, A Nation at Risk, one could argue that we are still at war. One may also contend that President Bush's focus on No Child Left Behind is an attempt to address the mediocre educational performance of all children, especially ethnic and racial minorities. The United States Senate approved the No Child Left Behind Act (NCLB) on December 2001 and the President signed this historic education reform

Policy, Leadership, and Student Achievement, pages 123–139
Copyright © 2008 by Information Age Publishing
All rights of reproduction in any form reserved.

initiative, into law on January 8, 2002. This Act was a reauthorization of the 1965 Elementary and Secondary Education Act and provided 26.5 billion dollars to education. NCLB elaborates and redefines the federal role in education policy. Specifically, this education policy mandate proposes a systemic testing program for students in grades three through eight. The primary goal of NCLB is to narrow the achievement gap between disadvantaged and advantaged children attending public schools. This federally sponsored policy attempts to eliminate gaps in achievement by balancing the public values of excellence, choice, adequacy, efficiency, and equity. This Act seeks to accomplish this objective by emphasizing four principles: accountability for results, increased local control, increased emphasis on successful teaching methods, and increased parental involvement. As educators and social scientists continue to debate the merits of NCLB, the achievement gap between minority and nonminority children continues to exist. Many continue to believe that this high stakes testing driven reform initiative does not adequately provide the resources that will allow educators to address the achievement gap. The proposed reauthorization of NCLB has generated extensive discussions between education policy makers and educators. On April 23, 2007, Secretary of education, Margaret Spellings presented a reauthorization proposal to the public. This document outlines five policy priorities:

1. Strengthen efforts to close the achievement gap through high standards, accountability, and more information for parents;
2. Give States flexibility to better measure individual student progress, target resources to students most in need, and improve assessments for students with disabilities and limited English proficiency;
3. Prepare high school students for success by promoting rigorous and advanced coursework and providing new resources for schools serving low-income students;
4. Provide greater resources for teachers to further close the achievement gap through improved math and science instruction, intensive aid for struggling students, continuation of Reading First, and rewards for teachers in high-need schools; and
5. Offer additional tools to help local educators turn around chronically underperforming schools and empower parents with information and options. (Spellings, April 23, 2007)

Under policy priority 1, states are required to narrow the achievement gap between minority and nonminority students. The reauthorization proposal details specifics for measuring the progress of all students and stipulates that all students and student subgroups should be performing at or above grade level by 2014. The blueprint also requires states to be accountable for performance in science, reading/language arts, and mathematics. Many are expecting the reauthorization of the No Child Left Behind Act to play a crucial role in reducing the achievement gap between minority and nonminority students.

THE RESEARCH

A review of student performance in mathematics, science, reading, and other content areas suggests that there is much work to be done in our nation's schools. Data from the United States Department of Education indicated that between 1970 and 1980, the African American–European American achievement gap declined by 50%; however, the gap began to increase in 1988 (Haycock, 2002). An analysis of data from the National Center for Educational Statistics (2001) reported that standardized achievement test scores of African American students increased significantly in the 1970s, and into the 1990s. The results suggested that the reading achievement test scores of 17-year-old African Americans increased throughout the 1980s and 1990; however, the achievement gap between African Americans and European Americans increased in the 1990s. Findings further indicated that the mathematics achievement test scores of 13-year-old African Americans and European Americans decreased significantly in the 1980s.

A review of findings from the National Center for Educational Statistics (2001) suggested that only 1 in 100 African American 17-year-olds can read and interpret technical data as compared with 1 in 12 of their European American counterparts. Analyses of these data also found that only 1 in 100 African Americans can solve multistep word problems and elementary algebra as compared to 1 in 10 European American students. It was sad to note that only 3 in 10 African Americans have mastered the computation of fractions, common percents, and averages, while 7 in 10 European Americans have mastered these skills. The gaps between these two groups continue to drive research agendas. Findings show that by the end of high school, African Americans have acquired skills in reading and mathematics that are the same as those of 8th grade European American students. Perhaps even more revealing, the statistics indicated hat African Americans are half as likely to complete a four-year college as European Americans. Further analyses of data from NAEP (2007) reported the following in mathematics, the average achievement gap between 9-year-old African American and European American students was 35 in 73 and declined to 23 points in 2004. Data also indicated that the average mathematics scores for 13-year-olds decreased from 46 points in 1973 to 27 points in 2004. Additionally, the gap between African America and European American 17-year-olds was 40 points in 1973 and declined to 28 points in 2004.

Analyses of mathematics and science achievement indicated that performance declined in the 1970s and increased during the 1980s and early 1990s. Findings suggested that most gains were evident in mathematics. The average science scores for 17-year-olds declined between 1969 and 1982; however, they began to increase slightly until 1992. The data also indicated that although the average science score was higher than the scores reported between 1977 and 1990, the score was lower than the average score in 1969. Data suggested that the science gap between African American and European American students has narrowed since 1970 for 9- and 13-year-old students. This was not true for 17-year-olds.

RESEARCH SETTING

The city of Norfolk is located in the southeastern region of the state of Virginia along the Elizabeth River and is home to the world's largest naval base. Its strategic location along the mouth of the Chesapeake Bay makes it both a cultural and financial regional power. The city has long been the center of trade, transportation, and military operations. Historically, the Norfolk Naval Base shipyards and seaport have been the city's major employers and have provided economic stability. According to the 2004 census, 241,727 individuals reside in the city and are linked by an elaborate network of highways, bridges and tunnels that connect the cities of Norfolk, Virginia Beach, Newport News, Hampton, Chesapeake, Portsmouth, and Suffolk. These seven independent municipalities have a population of just over 1.5 million and are located in a region known as the Hampton Roads metropolitan area. A review of Norfolk's demographic data revealed the following divisions: European Americans, 48.4%; African American, 44.1%; Latino American, 3.8%; American Indian, 0.5%; Asian American, 2.8%; Biracial or Multiracial, 2.5%; Native Hawaiian and Pacific Islanders, 0.1%; and Other Race, 1.7%.

The Norfolk Public Schools is the largest urban district in the state of Virginia and ranks 70th in size among urban districts nationally. An analysis of 2002 enrollment data indicated that approximately 37,565 students were enrolled in grades Pre-K through 12. Additionally, less than 10% of the school age children in the city attended private school. However, just before the desegregation of the Norfolk Public Schools in 1970, 57% of the district's 56,830 students were European American and 43% were African American. However, after more than 15 years of mandated desegregation, enrollment dropped to 34,803 students. Of this number, 42% were European Americans and 58% were African American. As a result of this shift and a loss of more than 18,000 students, the Norfolk School Board suggested a new approach to desegregation. The school board voted to abolish cross-town busing for elementary school children. The revised desegregation plan assigned students to neighborhood schools, creating 10 elementary schools that were more than 99% African American. By 2001, 67.1% of the 37,349 students were enrolled in the Norfolk Public Schools.

Currently, there are approximately 37,000 students enrolled in 62 educational facilities in the districts. These facilities include: 35 elementary schools; 9 middle schools; 5 high schools; auxiliary facilities, alternative magnet and specialty programs: These specialty programs include: world studies; technology; communications, arts, languages; military science; International Baccalaureate; Medical/Health professions, Engineering; Gifted and special education and numerous others (Norfolk Public Schools Division Performance, 2006).

HISTORY, POLITICS, AND THE ACHIEVEMENT GAP

Historically, resistance to integrated schooling is not new. It is believed that the doctrine of "separate but equal" originated in 1849 (Levy & Phillips, 1951). One of the earliest challenges to segregated schooling can be traced to an African American community in 18th century Boston, Massachusetts. After the American Revolution, the city of Boston developed the first urban school district in the nation (Schultz, 1973). This urban school district established three writing schools and three reading schools for all children between the ages of 17 and 14. During this time, African American children were allowed to attend school with their European American counterparts (Cubberly, 1947). Although the schools were integrated, the parents of African American children contended that European American teachers and students were treating their children unfairly (Shultz, 1973). Due to the perceptions of unfair treatment, parents of African American students requested that the city of Boston provide publicly funded, separate educational facilities for their children (Schultz, 1973). In 1787, Prince Hall delivered a petition on behalf of the African American parents to the Massachusetts Legislature. This petition requested that the Boston School Committee establish a separate school for African American children in the community (Aptheker, 1969). The Commonwealth rejected this petition; however, the African American parents continued their fight for separate and equal schools.

In 1798, Elisha Sylvester established a school for African American children in the home of Prince Hall (Woodson, 1919). Two years later, the African American community requested funding from the Boston School Committee in order to support the separate schools for their children. The committee refused to fund these racially segregated schools; however, the board members agreed to fund a private school established by African

American parents. By 1830, a segregated school system for African American children was in place in the city of Boston (Schultz, 1973). Although the request for separate schools was granted, the parents of African American children were not pleased. They complained that these schools were inferior in every way to those attended by European American children. In essence, the separate schools were unequal (Schultz, 1973).

During the 1840s, the city of Boston established one grammar school and two primary schools specifically for African American children. In 1883, the Boston Committee conducted a study to examine the effectiveness and quality of education in the city's schools. The results of the study indicated that the salaries of African American teachers were significantly less than those of their European American counterparts (Schultz, 1973). The African American schools were also found to be underfunded, and many courses offered by the European American schools did not exist at the African American schools (Schultz, 1973). This study also found that African American children were being deprived of the resources needed to achieve a quality education.

In 1844, more than one hundred years prior to the *Brown* decision, Thomas Dalton, along with 70 of his neighbors, led a protest demanding that their children be allowed to attend European American schools in the district. Benjamin Roberts tried to enroll his daughter in an all-European American primary school (Schultz, 1973). Sarah C. Roberts was a five-year-old African American girl who applied for admission to the public primary school nearest her home. Sarah walked past five other schools each day before she reached the school for African American children in Smith Court. A Boston city ordinance was passed in 1845, which stated that any child unlawfully excluded from the city's public schools could sue the city for damages. Sarah petitioned the all-European American school closest to her home for admission. The school rejected the plaintiff's application and sent her case to the Boston School Committee. The committee reaffirmed the school's decision. Although the committee denied admission to Sarah, she did not let this stand in her way. Sarah's parents attempted to enroll her in the school designated for European Americans. She was again rejected, and as a result of the school's actions, Sarah's father filed a suit claiming that the Boston School Committee had violated the Massachusetts statute, which stated that qualified children could not be excluded from public education. The trial court ruled in favor of the school district.

In response to this ruling, city reformers sued the city of Boston in the Massachusetts Supreme Court on behalf of an African American child, Sarah Roberts. In 1850, the Supreme Judicial Court ruled that the Boston School Committee had a right to maintain separate schools for African American and European American children (*Roberts v. City of Boston*, 1849). The Massachusetts Supreme Court ruled that Sarah Roberts had not been excluded from public education; however, her father had denied her admission by refusing to send her to the designated African American school. The parents of African American children did not give up, and in 1855, the Massachusetts General Assembly passed a law making segregation illegal.

Prior to the end of the Civil War, there were no public education systems for African Americans in the South. It was during the Reconstruction Era that public schools for African Americans were established in the South. The Southern states did not mandate the segregation of schools; however, only two states—South Carolina and Louisiana—had laws against segregated schools. Although these states forbade segregated schooling, it was generally the rule that African Americans and European Americans attended separate schools. Only the University of South Carolina and some elementary schools in Louisiana were desegregated. From 1880 to the early 1900s, state laws known as Black Codes were enacted in the South to keep the black man in his place (Barth, 1974, p. 26).

From 1865 to 1935, the school desegregation laws were challenged 37 times; however, only nine were successful. In each of these 37 cases, the "separate but equal" doctrine was upheld by the court (Bardolph, 1970). This became evident in 1899 in *Cummings v. Board of Education*. In this case, a school board in the state of Georgia decided to close a public high school and convert it into an elementary school for African American students. By converting the school to an elementary school, it left the African American students without a high school. The court decided that the fact that European American students were able to attend high school while their African American counterparts were left without a secondary school did not violate the equal protection clause of the 14th Amendment. Justice Harlan decided that closing the European American high school would only deprive European American students of an education and would not help the African American students at all.

In the 1930s, the NAACP devised a plan to legally dismantle segregation in the nation's public schools. Against the backdrop of the New Deal Era, the attorneys for the National Association for the Advancement of Colored People (NAACP) decided that the political climate in the country had become a bit more liberal and therefore the time was right to challenge the doctrine of "separate but equal." The Roosevelt Administration recognized the potential and actual political power of African Americans. The assumption was that the public would support public policies that sought equal access to educational opportunities; however, these same individuals would not support the social integration between African Americans and European Americans (Wexler, 1993). In 1933, Nathan Margold, a European American Harvard law school graduate, published a report that outlined legal strategies for challenging the application of the doctrine of "separate but equal" as it applied to public schools (Wexler, 1993). The lawyer's challenge was based upon the fact that the justices based their decisions on the ruling handed down in *Plessy v. Ferguson.*

The challenges to segregated schooling began in higher education. These cases signaled the beginning of a new activism by African Americans. The United States Supreme Court ruled in several decisions that the doctrine of "separate but equal" violated the equal protection clause of the 14th Amendment. These cases also had a direct influence on the 1954 *Brown* decision. In *Gaines v. Canada,* 1938 and *Sipuel v. Board of Regents,* 1948, the United States Supreme Court invalidated school desegregation because the facilities provided for African Americans were found to be unequal to those provided for European Americans. In 1950, the United States Supreme Court stipulated that the physical structures and other facets of a school program were not the only considerations in determining educational opportunity; the entire educational experience needed to be considered (Report of the United States Commission on Civil Rights, 1975).

The *Brown* decision resulted in the court ruling that legally compelled that segregation of students by race is a deprivation of the equal protection law as guaranteed by the 14th Amendment. Although the ruling in *Brown* was directed against legally sanctioned segregation, the language in the *Brown* decision supported a broader interpretation. The court recognized the inherent inequality of all segregation, noting only that the sanction of the law gives it greater effect.

This ruling reflected a concern for segregation resulting from factors other than legally mandated policies. *De jure* segregation refers to deliberate, official segregation of students on the basis of race, as in the school districts represented by the *Brown* decision and other school districts operating under state law requiring separation. *De facto* segregation refers to racial segregation that results from illegal actions of school officials—for example, through gerrymandering or attendance boundaries.

The May 17, 1954, *Brown* decision declared that segregation in public education was unconstitutional. This ruling was followed by the May 31, 1955, *Brown II* decision, which stated that "all provisions of federal, state or local law requiring or permitting segregation in public education must yield to the principle announced in the 1954 Decision." The 1954 *Brown* decision provided the avenue through which the public schools could begin to desegregate their districts voluntarily. One year after the *Brown* decision, strategies for the elimination of segregated schools were argued before the United States Supreme Court. The court established a standard for the implementation of desegregation. The 1954 *Brown II* decision required a "good faith" start in the transformation from a dual to a unitary education system, under the jurisdiction of district courts, "with all deliberate speed" (United States Commission on Civil Rights, 1975). The court also permitted limited delays in achieving complete desegregation if a school board could establish that such time was necessary in the public interest (350, U.S. 413, 1954).

During the early 1950s, United States Senator Harry F. Byrd was the most influential political figure in the state of Virginia. Senator Byrd was the chief supporter and developer of the state's massive resistance policy. He believed that the federal government had no right to interfere with state and local issues, and he utilized the 10th Amendment to the constitution to support his contentions. He referred to the 1954 *Brown* decision as "the most serious blow that has been struck against the rights of states" (Muse, 1961, p. 5). Byrd's position reflected an extremely Southern conservative view that African American and European American students should not be mixed; therefore, he strategically developed plans of massive resistance that would keep Virginia's public schools segregated.

On August 3, 1954, Governor Stanley of Virginia appointed state senator Garland Gray as chair of a 32-member committee charged with investigating the impact of the 1954 *Brown* decision on state-level education policy. This committee was asked to identify policy implications and make recommendations to the governor (Campbell, Bowerman, & Price, 1960). The committee, known as the Gray Committee, released its findings on November 11, 1955. The committee suggested that the governor should require: (1) public school districts that allow European American and African American students to attend school together to not receive any funding from the state of Virginia to support public education; (2) local school boards be allowed to transfer and utilize funds to award grants to students attending private nonsectarian schools; (3) the placement of students in the public schools and school attendance districts be determined by a special state board appointed by the governor; and (4) the state to mandate segregated public schooling, and any district attempting to desegregate be removed from the public school system (Muse, 1961). The state of Virginia began to develop and implement policies designed to avoid the United States Supreme Court's mandate in the 1954 *Brown* decision. The state developed a program that was described as "massive resistance."

The philosophy of the massive resistance program reflected the philosophy that racial segregation was socially desirable and should be perpetuated. As Campbell et al. (1960) noted, as soon as one plan of avoidance was successfully defeated, another plan was developed and implemented. Philosophically, the advocates of the resistance platform contended that the 1954 *Brown* decision violated the United States Constitution and was therefore void (Ely, 1976).

The 1956 session of the Virginia Assembly signaled the beginning of the Era of Massive Resistance in the state of Virginia. Norfolk was considered one of the most liberal cities in the South and was not viewed as a primary player in the massive resistance movement. However, the city would become an important player in the massive resistance struggle. In 1954, Norfolk was the most populated city in the state and about one-third of the population was associated with the Navy, home of the North Atlantic Treaty Organization (NATO). On August 18, 1958, the Norfolk school board met to consider the applications of 151 African American junior and senior high school students for admission to the public schools within the city. Prior to this time, no African American children were allowed to attend school with European American children. At the August 15, 1958, meeting, the school board rejected the applications of the African-American students (Muse, 1961). The school board cited the possibility of racial confrontations as the primary rationale for rejecting the applicants. United States District Judge Walter E. Hoffman rejected the validity of the school board's decision and ordered the students admitted. The Norfolk school board admitted 17 African American students to six all-European American junior and senior high schools (Campbell et al., 1960). The judge's actions presented what many contended was a conflict between state and federal law in the state of Virginia. The laws of the state of Virginia required the governor of the state to seize control and close any public schools that were required to admit African Americans. On September 28, 1958, Governor Almond closed Norfolk's six European American high schools, which had an aggregate enrollment of 10,000 students. These schools were closed in the pursuance of an act of the Virginia Legislature. More than 3,000 children were deprived of any schooling at all, and 4,000 attended tutorial classes (Muse, 1960, pp. 158–162). On January 19, 1959, the three-judge federal district court of Norfolk listed the school closing statutes and the governor's school closing order in violation of the 14th Amendment to the United States Constitution and therefore void (Muse, 1960, p. 182). The United States Supreme Court's decision on May 17, 1954, declared that the practice of segregating students in public school districts was unconstitutional.

In 1956, African-American parents in the city of Norfolk sued to integrate the schools. However, the city resisted, and the litigation continued until 1971 when a federal judge approved a desegregation plan that required cross-town busing between paired schools. Almost 50% of the students were transported to new schools. Busing eliminated the all-African American schools; however, the percentage of African American students in some of the schools was between 65% and 70%.

As a result of this decision, the Norfolk school district was required to desegregate. The court placed the primary responsibility for eliminating segregated schools on the local boards of education. The public schools in Norfolk did not desegregate until January 1970. The school district utilized clustering and pairing techniques as methods of desegregation. Busing was instituted to facilitate the integration of the public schools.In February 1975, the United States District Court of Virginia declared the district a unitary school system.

Given the hands-off approach to school desegregation from the federal government, the Norfolk school board met during the 1981–82 school year to consider a reduction in cross-town busing for integration. Numerous meetings were held with citizens throughout the city to discuss proposed plans. The primary issue concerned the status of African American children in the city of Norfolk who were assigned to all-African American schools. Many parents contended that African American children would suffer educationally and socially in these segregated schools. The school board members sought to eliminate such fears by proposing an expansion of pre-kindergarten programs to include four-year-olds from lower income homes; a program to increase parental involvement in schools attended primarily by African American children; a school effectiveness program to ensure that poor children would learn at the same rate as the more affluent students.

It is important to note that just before the desegregation of Norfolk public schools in 1970, 57% of the system's 56,830 students were white and 43% were African American. However, after more than 15 years of mandated busing for integration, enrollment dropped to 34,803 students. Of this number, 43% were White, and 58% were African American. As a result, they experienced a loss of more than 18,000 students. The Norfolk school board suggested a new approach to desegregation. The school board voted to abolish cross-town busing for elementary school children. The revised desegregation plan assigned students to neighborhood schools, creating 10 elementary schools that were more than 95% African American.

This new neighborhood school plan was challenged in the United States District Court for Virginia. On May 6, 1983, Paul Riddick, Jr., filed a suit on behalf of all the African American elementary students in the city of Norfolk. The Norfolk school board was named as defendant in the suit. The plaintiffs charged that the school board intentionally adopted an elementary school assignment plan that was unconstitutional and that discriminated against African American students because of their race. The plaintiffs demanded that the court declare the Norfolk public schools student assignment that was adopted on February 2, 1983 as unconstitutional.

In 1984, a Virginia district court ruled that the Norfolk public schools could end court-mandated cross-town busing of elementary students for the purpose of desegregation. The court held that the neighborhood school plan adopted by the Norfolk school board on February 2, 1983, did not discriminate against African American students because of their race. Additionally, the court ruled that the plaintiffs had failed to show that the school board's assignment plan was motivated by race.

Riddick et al. appealed the decision in the Fourth Circuit Court of Appeals. In 1986, the circuit court upheld the ruling of the district court. The Fourth Circuit Court of Appeals' rationale for the decision was that although the court originally ordered the district to utilize busing as a means of desegregating the public schools, it withdrew from the case in 1975. In 1975, the court ruled that the Norfolk public school system was unitary. However, the plaintiffs contended that the system had become more segregated since 1975. The court did not agree, and the judge ruled: "we do not think that this is a case which a school board upon obtaining judicial decision that is unitary, turns it back on its minority students. If such were the case, we would not approve Norfolk's new assignment plan. In 1986, the plaintiffs attempted to get the United States Supreme Court to review the circuit court's findings; however, the court refused to hear the case. The ruling of the Fourth Circuit Court of Appeals was left intact without approval or disapproval by the high court. The ruling in *Riddick* has had a significant impact on African American elementary students in the city of Norfolk. This ruling left many African American students in racially isolated schools.

PURPOSE OF STUDY

In 2002, Section 22.1-18 of the Code of Virginia was amended by the General Assembly (HB 884, Hamilton and SB 350, Howell). In essence, this code required all public schools in the state to list standards of quality along with a justification for each of the eight standards (Annual Report on the Condition and Needs of Public Education in Virginia, 2003). Standard 3 of this Code:

> ...authorizes the Board of Education to establish course and credit requirements for graduation, and to prescribe Standards of Learning (SOL) Assessments including end of courses and end of grade Standards of Learning tests for English, mathematics, science, history and social science. (p. 49)

The purpose of this Standards of Learning testing initiative was to improve the quality of instruction for children in the state of Virginia and to eliminate the achievement gap between disadvantaged and advantaged children. Therefore, the purpose of this study is to describe the trends in the mathematics and science achievement gaps that continue to exist between African American and European American students in the Norfolk Public schools.

RESEARCH QUESTION

What are the trends in the (science/mathematics) achievement gap between African American and European American students at the elementary, middle and high school levels?

SOURCES OF DATA

Data were obtained from the Norfolk Public Schools Department of Research, Testing and Statistics. Specifics relevant to Standards of Learning (SOL) test results were gathered from the Norfolk Public Schools Division Performance Report (February 9, 2006). The SOL testing program was adopted by the school district in June 1995. The Virginia Board of Education approved Standards of Learning testing in four core content areas: mathematics; science; English; history and the social sciences; and in computer technology. The 3rd, 5th, 8th and 11th grade SOL scores in science and mathematics were utilized in this study. The SOL achievement gap scores of African American and European American students in science and mathematics from 2000–2005 were analyzed.

FINDINGS

Figures 9.1, 9.2, and 9.3 summarize mathematics and science achievement gap trends (2000–2005) between African American and European American students in Grades 3, 5, 8, and 11. The Virginia SOL test results were utilized as the achievement measure. As indicated in Figure 9.1, the third-grade mathematics achievement gap between the two groups declined by 11 points between 2000 and 2005. The Grade 5 mathematics gap also continued to shrink and decreased from 21 in 2000 to 14 in 2005. A more extensive narrowing of the mathematics gap can be found at Grade 8 (–14 points); however, the mathematics (Algebra I) gap at the high school level only declined by 1 point between 2000 and 2005.

Trends in the science achievement gap between the two groups can be found in Figure 9.2. The Grade 3 science gap declined from 24 points to 12 points during the same five-year period. This 12-point decrease was significant; however, the achievement gap between Grade 5 African American and European American students was only 4 points during this same period. Achievement gap trends indicated that the decline remained constant at Grade 8 (4 points) and Grade 11 was unchanged at the end of the five-year period. (0.2 points).

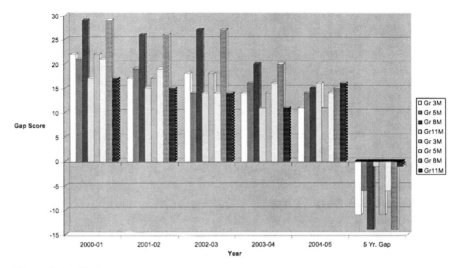

Figure 9.1 Math gap scores.

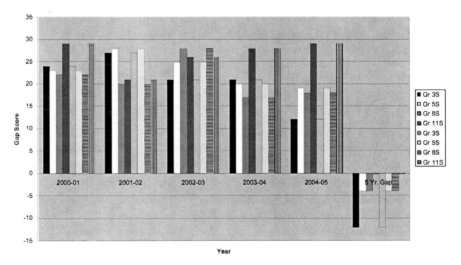

Figure 9.2 Science gap scores.

As indicated in Figure 9.3, the most significant decreases during this five-year period were noted in Grade 8 mathematics (14 points); Grade 3 science (12 points); and Grade 3 mathematics. The declines were less evident in Grade 11 mathematics (1 point) and Grade 11 science (0.2 points).

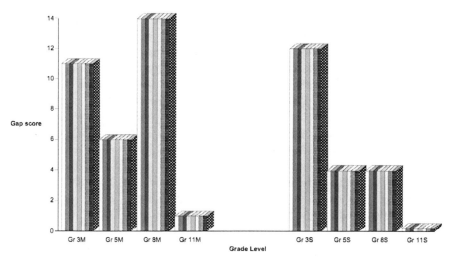

Figure 9.3   Five year gap trends.

SUMMARY

In 2004, 43% of all school age children were members of a racial or ethnic minority group. It is also interesting to note that the European American population has decreased from 78% in 1972 to 58% in 2004 (National Center for Educational Statistics, 2007). As the demographic composition of our schools change, educational institutions must be redefined and restructured. As is the case with many previously desegregated public schools, these shifts have resulted in resegregation. Although economically driven global and sociopolitical forces have impacted the demographic changes in our public schools, educators must realize that the 21st century school cannot survive and thrive if our children are not academically prepared. As is the case with many resegregated schools across the country, the Norfolk Public School District continues to develop strategies that will address the needs of increasingly diverse racial and ethnic minority students. The district has implemented accountability systems and continues to utilize data-driven decision-making to narrow achievement the science and mathematics achievement gaps.

The district's success in narrowing the achievement gap was recognized on September 23, 2005 when it was awarded the Broad Prize for urban education. This coveted prize is given annually to the urban school district that has made significant progress in reducing the achievement gaps between ethnic and racial minorities as well as economically stratified students. The Broad Foundation's charge is to assist districts in improving "K–12 urban public education through better governance, management, labor relations and competition" (Broad Foundation, 2007). The organization seeks to accomplish these goals by: training a broad, deep bench of current and aspiring school leaders in education; redefining the traditional roles, practices, and policies of school board members, superintendents, principals, and labor union leaders to better address contemporary challenges in education; attracting and retaining the highest quality talent to leadership roles in education; equipping school systems and their leaders with modern tools for effective management; providing tangible incentives for educators to advance academic performance; and honoring and showcasing success wherever it occurs in urban education. Prior to winning this award, the district was a finalist in 2002, 2003, and 2004. Results from the science and mathematics Standards of Learning Tests indicated that the district is meeting the challenge of narrowing the achievement gap between African American and European American students.

REFERENCES

Aptheker, H. (1969). *The history of the Negro people in the United States.* New York: International Publishers.

Annual Report on the Condition and Needs of Public Schools in Virginia. (2003, November 26) Virginia Board of Education, Richmond, VA.

Bardolph, R. (1970). The *civil rights record: Black Americans and the law.* New York: Thomas Crowell Co.

Barth, A. (1974). *Prophets with honor: Great dissents and great dissenters in the Supreme Court.* New York: Knopf.

Campbell, E. Q., Bowerman, C. E., & Price, D. O. (1960). *When a city closes its schools.* Chapel Hill: University of North Carolina Press.

Cubberly, E. (1947). *Public education in the United States.* Cambridge, MA: Houghton Mifflin Co.

Education Alliance. (2004). *Closing the achievement gap: Policy implications for teacher quality, curriculum and teacher expectations. 1866–31—4Kids.* Charleston, WV: Author.

Education Commission of the States. (2004). *Helping state leaders shape education-policy.* Denver, CO: Denver Department of Education.

Ely, J. (1976). *The crisis of massive resistance. Twentieth Century America Series.* Knoxville: University of Tennesee Press.

Haycock, K. (2002, March). *It takes more than testing: Closing the achievement gap.* Washington, DC. United States Department of Education.

Levy, L., & Phillips, H. (1951). The Roberts Case: Source of the "Separate but Equal" Doctrine. *American Historical Review, 56,* 510 –518.

Muse, B. (1961). *Virginia's massive resistance.* Bloomington: University of Indiana Press.

National Center for Educational Statistics. (2001). *NAEP, Summary Data Tables.* Washington, DC: United States Department of Education.

National Center for Educational Statistics. (2007). *NAEP, Summary Data Tables.* Washington, DC: United States Department of Education.

Report of the United States Commission on Civil Rights. (1977). *Reviewing a decade of school desegregation, 1966–1975: Survey of school superintendents.* Washington, DC: United States Commission on Civil Rights. CR1,2: SCH/21/966-75.

Riddick v. School Board City of Norfolk, 627Fsupp at 822, Aff'd, 784 F.2d 521 (4th Cir. 1986) cert. Denied, 479 U.S. 938 (1986).

Schools: Division Report (2006, December). Norfolk, VA: Norfolk Public Schools.

Schultz, S. K. (1973). *The culture factory: Boston Public Schools, 1789–1860.* New York: Oxford University Press.

Spellings, M. (2007, April 23). *Key policy letters signed by Education Secretary.* Washington, DC: United States Department of Education.

Wexler, S. (1993). *The civil rights movement.* New York: Facts on File.

Woodson, C. (1919). *The education of the Negro prior to 1861: A history of the colored people.* Whitefish, MT: Kessingler Publishers.

CHAPTER 10

EDUCATION POLICY AND STUDENT ACHIEVEMENT IN URBAN SCHOOLS

Assessing the P.A.T.H.S. Program

Diane Bowen-Lipscomb

The educational system in America is failing to educate all children in the United States. This is evidenced by the alarming disparity in achievement test scores in reading and mathematics between students who live in poverty and their middle class counterparts. "Additionally, one fourth or roughly 11 million children in the United States attend school in urban districts, while African-Americans, Latinos, and American Indians account for one third of the 54 million children in the nation's K–12 classrooms. Statisticians predict that these numbers will increase to two-thirds over the next 15 years" (Johnston & Viadero, 2000, p. 18).

School districts are trying many different school reforms to improve student achievement. Dr. David Grissmer, a senior researcher at the RAND Corporation, stated his findings plainly: "Where we have devoted additional resources, particularly to minority and disadvantaged children, we have

Policy, Leadership, and Student Achievement, pages 141–161
Copyright © 2008 by Information Age Publishing
141

gotten significant payoff in higher achievement" (CFE Reports, 2000, p. 1). He testified that targeting money to reduce class size in the elementary grades is the most effective way to improve student performance. Dr. Jeremy Finn, professor at the State University of New York at Buffalo and a national expert on class size demonstrated by the landmark STAR study in Tennessee, the most comprehensive study of class size ever, "that students placed in small classes from kindergarten to third grade, especially poor and minority students, show lasting gains in their educational achievement" (CFE Reports, 2000, p. 1).

Parents are aware that a good education is fundamental to financial, professional, and personal success. All parents want the best for their children, whether they are poor, middle class, or upper elite. In the large urban districts, there is a higher than average proportion of students living in poverty, students with poorly educated parents, students of immigrant parents and with limited English skills, students from unstable family settings, crime infested living conditions, and a high proportion of the social ills of society. The research clearly shows that children in urban districts perform most poorly of all students, while failing to meet the basic level of standards on national tests in reading and mathematics.

> On the 1994 National Assessment of Educational Progress (NAEP) reading test, only 23% of fourth graders in high-poverty urban schools achieved at the basic level or above as compared with 46% of students in high-poverty schools in non-urban areas. In non-poverty schools, 69% of fourth graders were ranked at the basic level and above. (Quality Counts, 1998)

Most of the children living in urban areas are minority and poor. *Savage Inequalities* by Jonathon Kozol notes that most of the urban schools that he visited were 95 to 99% non-White. In no school anywhere in the United States did he see non-White children in large numbers truly intermingled with White children (Kozol, 1991, p. 3). The public schools are extremely segregated, by race and economics. The wealthy are able to purchase homes in elite suburban school districts while the poor or non-affluent are trapped in inner city schools that are handicapped by limited resources, bureaucracy, politics, and ineffective school practices with no accountability.

In Kozol's book, the author also argued that the racially segregated schools were unequal due to the way schools were funded. Basically, this is due in part to the "inherited status" of the parents based primarily on race and their socioeconomic background. These contributing factors give wealthy schools an advantage. In addition, since schools are financed by property taxes, the homes of the wealthy are worth more, and the schools receive more revenue from the property taxes. In the December 1992-January 1993 issue of *Educational Leadership*, the article titled "On Savage Inequalities: A Conversation with Jonathan Kozol," Kozol stated, "To use the local property tax as even a portion of school funding is unjust because it always benefits the children of the privileged" (p. 6). In addition, the foundation formula that determines funding for schools presents a problem. Instead of using the richest district to determine the foundation level for funding most states use the low foundation level. This is set at such a low line that the poor districts never have enough money generated to compete with the richer districts. Consequently, the poorer districts are only able to meet the needs of their students and afford them a basic or minimum education (Kozol, 1991, p. 208). President Bush's plan, No Child Left Behind, intends to give a better-balanced field for educating all children, even if the urban schools receive the extra funds to have the resources to meet the students' needs.

Poverty, racism, high-unemployment, the continued decline in the influence of the family, and the media, all are factors contributing to violence in the cities which spill over into the schools and affect student performance. The National Urban League, the nation's oldest and largest community-based movement, is devoted to empowering African Americans. In its "Opportunity Agenda: A Blueprint for Success, April 2001" points noted are that, nationwide, roughly 6.3% of all workers in the United States live below the poverty line; the ratio for African American workers is nearly twice that at 11.7%. The ultimate goal of the Urban League movement is to level the playing field of opportunity and eliminate the "opportunity gaps" that separate African Americans from mainstream America: the achievement gap, the technology gap, the employment gap, the poverty gap, the healthcare gap, the home ownership gap, the entrepreneurship gap, and the criminal justice gap (National Urban League Institute, 2001, p. 3).

Data from the National Assessment of Education Progress (NAEP), a federally funded test program that provides the best state-by-state data on student performance show that students in urban areas perform at far lower levels on standardized tests than their peers in non-urban areas. "The states with the largest achievement gaps are the ones with the most socially and economically isolated central cities, such as Connecticut, Maryland, Massachusetts, Michigan, Missouri, New Jersey, and Pennsylvania" (Olson & Jerald, 1998b, p. 12). NAEP data indicate that 40% of fourth graders read below the minimum level. Nearly three-fourths of Illinois' third graders in 1996 were rated proficient on the state reading test, but fewer than half the third graders in East St. Louis and Chicago met the standard (Quality Counts 98). Christopher Jencks and Meredith Phillips (1998) note that African American kindergartners perform statistically significantly lower in math, reading, and vocabulary skills when compared to their European counterparts beginning in early elementary school and persisting throughout high school (*BASRC Newsletter*, 2002, p. 2). Even in wealthier schools, one-quarter of fourth graders are unable to reach NAEP's basic level. More than two-thirds of fourth graders in high poverty schools are unable to reach the basic level.

The Harrisburg City School District in Pennsylvania reflects the same issue findings as the NAEP report. As an urban district with a high poverty concentration per capita, the district has more than 7,500 students, mostly non-White and poor. The data show that more than 60% of its students are performing in the lowest quartile on the standardized Pennsylvania System of School Assessment (PSSA). Statewide, 53.8% of White students scored above the median on the PSSA test in 1999. They scored slightly above the expected norm that is set at 50 percent. "Only 29.2% of African American students and 40.2% of Hispanic students scored above the norm. Asian American students scored 62.3% above the median" (*Bucks County Courier Times*, 2002, p. 1).

On national and local levels, educators are being questioned about their action plans to improve student scores on standardized tests, especially in the urban districts. To help change public perception and improve achievement scores of reading and mathematics on standardized tests, school districts must ensure that all students are academically successful. Research-based social and emotional learning intervention curriculums may be the vehicles to increasing academic performance in schools that have a consistent history of low-level achievement scores on standardized tests. The PATHS (Providing Alternative Thinking Strategies) program represents such a curriculum and has been implemented in the Harrisburg City School District.

THE POLICY ISSUES

Extensive research has been conducted concerning students' poor performance in reading and mathematics on standardized tests. Currently, "more than half of all students in urban settings have repeated at least one grade level by the time they leave elementary school" (Slavin, Kraweit, & Wasik, 1994, p. 3). In his 1997 State of the Union address, former President Clinton stated that teaching students to read was a priority of his administration. According to President Clinton, "Forty percent of our eight-year-olds cannot read on their own. We must do more to help all our children read, to make sure every child can read independently by the end of the third grade" (p. 5). With the passage of the Goals 2000—Educate America Act, former United States Secretary of Education in the Clinton administration, Richard W. Riley, stated:

> The federal government must be an effective supportive partner with states in realizing the vision—which an education system is committed to produc-

ing real results, for all its students. . . . Are we a nation truly connected to its children, child-centered and committed to their futures when it allows one of every five children to grow up in poverty, and often with violence? (U.S. Department of Education, Goals 2000)

In 2001, President Bush issued his education reform policy, "No Child Left Behind Act," in which he stated that his administration was committed to improving achievement test scores in reading and mathematics for all students, regardless of socioeconomic status, gender, or race. President Bush seeks to make education across the board for *all* children a priority. This national commitment to reforming schools has implications for the entire nation. By increasing its focus for accountability on the state and local levels, the federal role in education is shifting to serve the children, not the system. Two of the key components, important for the purposes of this research paper, and which have implications in this research, are the proposals for closing the achievement gap and improving literacy by putting reading first. As the schools today serve students of diverse backgrounds, ability, and temperament, the challenge to teach and nurture these increasingly complex, dynamic student populations is imperative for the nation as a whole.

When a child enters kindergarten, one must keep in mind that the child has a working knowledge of language and his/her surroundings from home. Learning starts from infancy. From the time a child is born, his/her cyes see and hear all things that are around. As they grow older, they speak the language heard and eventually they learn to communicate by reading and writing their thoughts on paper. Students enter school at many different levels of readiness for reading and writing, including the obstacle of a language barrier in some students.

Reading is the key to academic achievement in every subject. Students who cannot read will experience little success in school or life. Urban schools which educate a vast number of the nation's children and have the most children of color, embrace the "No Child Left Behind Act." The National Black Caucus of State Legislators in its Education Report of 2001 notes that we need to provide funding for prevention-intervention initiatives that give students more concentrated time for learning and studying, including before and after school programs, summer learning programs and weekend academies. As a productive citizen, one must be able to read and write. "Frederick Douglass, the first crusader for universal literacy, freed himself from bondage but understood he was not fully free until he taught himself to read. He then realized he was still not free until the nation ended slavery and freed people knew how to read . . . too many people lack the literacy skills to actively participate in the economy or become engaged citizens" (National Black Caucus of State Legislators, 2001, p. 26).

Schools today are multiculturally diverse, making them quite different from the schools of yesterday. They are made up of students from all ethnicities, varied socioeconomic backgrounds and more language groups than ever before. The structure of today's family does not typically consist of two parents, a father, and mother. Single working parents need help with children's care. As parents' work hours are changing, the schools are providing more stability for students by extending the school day through before and after school programs. It is for these reasons that schools are viewed as the institution in the best position to address the needs of children and help them become successful, productive citizens. Thus, the urban schools have a greater challenge than the rural and suburban districts in terms of providing additional services and programs even though they have more financial restraints due to fewer funds.

"The earlier that children who are truly at-risk for adopting violent coping strategies can be identified, the better chances for an effective intervention. Because the large majority of children attend public schools, it is often more cost effective to deliver an intervention in the school setting" (Elliot, Hamburg, & Williams, 1998, p. 16). Due to the consistent low standardized test scores in reading and mathematics in December 1999, Pennsylvania's ex-Governor Tom Ridge declared the urban Harrisburg City School District, a district that needed to be empowered. In an effort to improve test scores, the district has implemented numerous innovative programs: however, these initiatives have not met with sustained success compared to the years before empowerment. In addition, there has been no research or nationally award winning programs that address the impact that these initiatives have on urban students in the Harrisburg City School District.

As a former school administrator in the Harrisburg City School District and a product of an inner city education, this research study has significance for the author both personally and professionally. Having attended inner city schools as a youngster, this author is committed to urban education and its students. Professionally, the author is interested in the body of scholarly research on urban education, curriculum and instruction, standardized tests, and research-based intervention programs.

In an effort to create a more positive school climate and to help students with their social coping skills, the Harrisburg City School District implemented the PATHS (Providing Alternative Thinking Strategies) curriculum in three controlled and three experimental schools. However, the impact and effectiveness of the PATHS program on standardized achievement test scores have not been measured or addressed. It is for this reason that this paper seeks to address this gap in research. Hopefully, school administrators, social scientists, and behaviorists, as well as local, state, and federal policymakers will find the results from this study useful as they develop and implement education policies for urban school reform.

STANDARDIZED TEST SCORES: THE POLICY CONTEXT

Educational achievement was the driving motive behind a "back to basics" movement in the 1970s and 1980s followed by a call for learning levels to exceed minimum competency. When the Soviet Union launched Sputnik in 1957, Americans fell to second place in the space race and looked to the nation's schools as having failed to educate and prepare students to their fullest potential. With the publication of A Nation at Risk, in 1983, it became apparent that as a nation, educationally, we needed to get beyond a minimal level of performance for our students and that the government was calling for a higher level of academic excellence. Accountability came to the forefront. Testing programs for school improvement proliferated in the 1980s including the trend to assess the quality of schools and teachers and the use of standardized tests. In the 1990s, legislators stressed the desired goal that all students attain high levels of academic achievement, which was expressed through the establishment of challenging national education goals and state academic standards. By 1999, a National Education Goals Panel was formed, and a standards-based reform movement was begun which resulted in 40 states adopting statewide standards in English, mathematics, science, and social studies.

> Against this backdrop, the National Assessment of Educational Progress (NAEP) has served as the nation's only ongoing monitor of student achievement across time. As a project of the National Center for Education Statistics (NCES) of the U.S. Department of Education, NAEP has regularly administered assessments in a variety of subject areas to nationally representative samples of students since 1969. Among the many components of the NAEP program, the long-term trend assessments have provided a gauge of student achievement over time by administering the same assessments periodically across NAEP's 30-year history. (Campbell et al., 2000, p. ix)

Standardized measurement incorporates the idea that writing ability, reasoning, critical thinking, and process are measured for the individual student through their answers on the tests. "The trend in mathematics skills development is characterized by declines in the 1970s, followed by increases during the 1980s and early 1990s, and mostly stable performance since then. Some gains are evident in reading skills development, but they are modest. Overall improvement across the assessment years is most evident in mathematics. Average mathematics scores for 9-year-olds increased in the 1980s after a period of stable performance in the 1970s. Additional modest gains were evident in the 1990s, and the 1999 average score was higher than that in 1973" (Campbell et al., 2000, p. x).

The average reading scores for 9-year-olds increased during the 1970s. Since 1980 there has been no further improvement in scores, however, the average score in 1999 was higher than that in 1971. "The racial/ethnic subgroups measured in the NAEP assessment were White, Black, and Hispanic students. Other racial/ethnic subgroups are not reported, as the sample collected was of insufficient size to analyze and report separately. Results for Hispanic students are not available for the first assessment year 1971 in reading" (p. xiii). "Among White students, gains in average reading scores are mostly evident across the assessment years for 9 and 13-year-olds. Between Black and Hispanic students, overall gains are evident at each age. In 1999, White students had higher average reading scores than their Black and Hispanic peers. The gap between White and Black students in reading narrowed between 1971 and 1999 in each group. Since 1988, it has widened somewhat at ages 13 and 17. The gap between White and Hispanic students narrowed between 1975 and 1999 at age 17 only" (Campbell et al., 2000, p. xiii).

The students in each racial/ethnic group and at all three ages 9, 13, and 17 showed gains in mathematics scores across the assessment years. In 1999, White students had higher average mathematics scores than their Black and Hispanic peers. The gap between White and Black students in mathematics narrowed between 1973 and 1999 in each age group. Some widening is evident since 1986 at age 13, and since 1990 at age 17. The gap between White and Hispanic 13 and 17-year-olds narrowed between 1973 and 1999 but has widened since 1982 among 9-year-olds (Campbell et al., 2000, p. xiii).

Significantly, the NAEP reports that:

- Among male students, overall gains in reading are evident across the assessment years for 9- and 13-year-olds. Among female students, only 13-year-olds show a significant increase between the first and last assessment year. In 1999, female students had higher average reading scores than male students in each age group. Among 9-year-olds, the gap between males and females narrowed between 1971 and 1999.
- Among male students, 9- and 13-year-olds show overall gains in mathematics between 1973 and 1999. Among female students, overall gains across the years are evident at each age. In 1999, the apparent difference between male and female students' average mathematics scores was not significant at any age. Among 17-year-olds, the scores gap that had favored male students in the 1970s ultimately disappeared, and by 1999 the difference was no longer statistically significant (Campbell et al., 2000, p. xiv).

The highest education level of either parent in each subject area was reported. Students who reported higher parental educational levels tended to have higher average scores.

- Among students with at least one parent who pursued education after high school, average reading scores in 1999 were lower than in 1971 for 17-year-olds. Among students whose parents' highest level of education was high school graduation, overall declines in performance are evident at ages 14 and 17. Among students whose parents did not graduate from high school, scores in 1999 were similar to those in 1971 at age 13, and the apparent increase at age 17 was not statistically significant.

- Among students at the highest level for mathematics scores, parents were college graduates, wherein the scores in 1999 were similar to those in 1978 at ages 13 and 17. Among students whose parents' highest education level was some education after high school, 13-year-olds show overall gains across the assessment years. Among students whose parents did not go beyond high school graduation, score increases across the years are evident for 17-year-olds. Among students whose parents did not complete high school, overall gains in mathematics are evident at ages 13 and 17. It should be noted that 9-year-olds reports of their parents' education level may not be as reliable as those of older students, therefore results for 9-year-olds were not included in this study (Campbell et al., 2000, p. xv).

The statistics show that poor minority youth are much less equipped for educational success than more affluent Whites. For every 100 White students who enter kindergarten, 88-graduate high school, 40 attend college, 12 earn an undergraduate degree, and two go on to some form of graduate school. For Blacks, only one-half as many reach the same level of education. These numbers are reinforced by student performance on standardized tests: while one in twelve White students achieve level one on the NAEP reading test, only one in fifty Black and Hispanic students reach this same measure. This achievement gap grows wider the longer young people are in school. In terms of reading achievement, the average 17-year-old Black or Hispanic student reads at the same level as the 13-year-old White student (Center for Education Reform, 2001, p.1).

The results of the Reading 2000 Report Card for 4th graders in the United States, summarized that between 1992 and 2000, the Black/White gap among average score results increased from 32 to 33; the Hispanic/White gap widened from 24 to 28 points; and the American Indian/White gap displayed a dramatic gap with a differential growing from 18 to 30 points. The Asian American population is the only group where the gap decreased: in fact, Asian/Pacific Islanders now score better than Whites by six points (p. 1).

Title 1 of the Elementary and Secondary Education Act implemented in 1965 provided financial assistance to state and local education agencies to meet the special needs of children who were educationally disadvantaged or from schools with concentrations of poverty. It has been extremely valuable for low socioeconomic schools. As the act's chief component and the federal government's largest education program, its mission was to spend $7.7 million in its inception year. "Since 1965, the federal government has poured more than $120 billion into Title 1 programs" (Heritage Foundation, 1999, p. 1). The federal funding supports a variety of supplemental services that share the collective purpose of improving educational opportunities and outcomes for low-achieving students from schools with concentrations of poverty. "Evaluation of Title 1 programs has usually been through a norm-referenced model based on achievement test result changes" (Borman & D'Agostino, 1995). The meta-analysis, which included 17 studies, considered whether program services had significantly affected student achievement. Evidence from the analysis indicated that Title I has not fulfilled its original expectation of closing the achievement gap between at-risk students and their more advantaged peers. The results did suggest that without the program it is likely that children served over the last 30 years would have fallen further behind academically. Evaluated from this perspective, Title I has been an invaluable supplement to schools serving lower socioeconomic children.

In poor neighborhoods, the deck is stacked against children from the moment they are born. The odds are higher that they will have lower-than-normal birth weights, lack access to regular medical care, live in a household headed by a single mother, become a victim of crime, have a parent who never finished high school, become pregnant before reaching adulthood, and possibly drop out of school. Urban schools are more likely than non-urban ones to have a high percentage of low-income students. Concentrated school poverty is consistently related to lower performance on every educational outcome measured.

The most recent evidence comes from the "Prospects Report," a congressionally mandated, four-year study of about 27,000 students served under Title 1. The report concluded that "school poverty depresses the scores of all students in schools where at least half of the students are eligible for subsidized lunch, and seriously depresses the scores when more than 75% of students live in low-income households" (Olson & Jerald, 1998a, p. 14). On the other hand, poor students who attend middle-class schools perform significantly better. A small but important number of successful schools in poor neighborhoods prove that children in concentrated areas of poverty can excel. It requires a greater commitment from educators and the public. Former Superintendent of Schools in Philadelphia, PA David W. Hornbeck noted that while poverty is not an excuse, thousands of urban children and urban teachers and principals and parents have a tougher time because of it. Any restructuring effort that does not aggressively respond to the impact of poverty is naïve (Olsen & Jerald, 1998a, p. 14).

Even if poverty is not the single most important cause of the minority-majority achievement gap, it is a major contributor. Data compiled for the College Board showed that in 1990, Hispanic children were twice as likely as White and Asian American children to be raised in low-income families. African Americans were nearly three times as likely to come from poor families. Growing up poor often means getting inadequate health care and nutrition, having fewer educational resources in the home and in the neighborhood, and moving frequently, all factors known to depress school performance on standardized tests. The legacy of poverty can last for generations. Even when two families have the same income levels, chances are the children from the family whose affluence began more recently is worse off educationally. David Grissmer, a senior management scientist in Washington for the RAND Corporation, a Santa Monica, California-based think tank states, "It's not only the education of your parents, it really depends on the education of your grandparents, because wealth does accumulate over time" (Viadero, 2000, p. 18).

The mobility of moving from school to school because of poor home conditions also slows the pace of instruction for students and accounts for low performance on tests. In one 1996 study of Chicago schools, researchers found that by 5th grade the level of instruction in those schools that had a high student turnover rate, was almost a year behind that of schools with more stable populations (Viadero, 2000, p. 19).

Kozol notes that reading and mathematics in America are graded not against an absolute standard but against a "norm" or "average." For some to be above the norm, others have to be below it. Preeminence, by definition, is a zero-sum matter. There is not an ever-expanding pie of "better-than-average" academic excellence. There cannot be. Two-thirds of American children can never score above average. Half the population has to score below the average and the average is determined not by local or state samples but by test results for all Americans. We are 16,000 districts when it comes to opportunity, but one nation when it comes to the determination of rewards. When affluent school districts tell their parents that the children in the district score "in the eightieth percentile," they are measuring local children against children everywhere (Kozol, 1991, p. 200). With the theory of the have and the have not, the academic achievement gap on standardized tests continues to widen in reading and mathematics.

AT-RISK STUDENTS' PERFORMANCE
ON STANDARDIZED TESTS

Historically, at-risk students were primarily those whose appearance, language, culture, values, communities, and family structures did not match those of the dominant White culture that schools were designed to serve and support. These students, primarily minorities, the poor, and immigrants, were considered culturally or educationally disadvantaged or deprived. As large numbers of these students were not achieving at minimally acceptable levels in school, it seemed natural and certainly easy to define the problem as arising from deficiencies in the students themselves (Goodlad & Keating, 1990, p. 1).

But children of color and poor youth are not the only children at-risk. Any child who lacks sufficient support may fail to develop adequate academic and social skills. Prenatal conditions, quality of health, family characteristics, peer influences, community climate, and social status may be affected by support networks and significantly influence a child's readiness to learn. Coupled with the conditions of living with one parent, being a member of a minority group or having limited English proficiency is defined as at-risk also. Statistically, the students in these categories are more likely to be among the lowest achievement groups in school.

In *Teaching Strategies for the Culturally Disadvantaged* by Hilda Taba and Deborah Elkins, the authors state that "... to engage students with an already weakened or nonexistent drive for learning, the use of experiences with strong emotional impact is an essential device" (1966, p. 74). The motivational patterns are markedly different for at-risk students and the middle-class child. Whereas the middle-class child if told he or she needs to redo a paper or that it is sloppy, responds by doing it again, the at-risk student may respond quite differently. The middle-class child understands that the reward of getting good grades constitutes a passport to success for entering college and finding a good job. For the at-risk student, grades may not be considered a value at home and besides what difference does it make. The student feels that it makes no difference how well or badly he or she does. A shrug of the shoulders and no push for the future or to improve in school is how a majority of at-risk students may respond.

When a student feels alienated from school, behavior and achievement decline precipitously. This sense of not belonging to the school contributes to alienation and a lack of interest in school activities (Mahan & Johnson, 1983; Eckstrom et al., 1986). It has been found that when a significant difference exists between the students' culture and the school's culture, teachers can easily misread students' aptitudes, intent, or abilities as a result of the difference in styles of language use and interactional patterns (Delpit, 1995). This cultural disconnect often places minority students in conflict with expected school norms, exacerbating alienation. Poor attitudes about school appear to correlate with low academic achievement and behavioral problems.

An article by Margarita Donnelly (1987), states that some researchers believe that the root of at-risk behavior begins in the elementary grades with low achievement patterns, high absenteeism, and low self-esteem (p. 1). An emerging body of research that looks at school factors as potential causes of at-risk behavior has identified school characteristics as hindering the academic achievement of many students. The characteristics are: narrow curricula; a priority focus on basic/lower-order skills; inappropriate, limited, and rigid instructional strategies; inappropriate texts and other instructional materials; over-reliance on standardized tests to make instructional and curricular decisions; tracking; isolated pullout programs; and teacher and administrators' beliefs and attitudes toward both students and their parents (Richardson & Colfer, 1990, p. 3).

PROGRAM EVALUATION: THE PATHS PROGRAM

Third grade students in an urban school district are not developing the reading and mathematics skills necessary to ensure their academic success. This study is designed to ascertain the answer to the following research question:

What are the effects of participating in the PATHS program on the reading and mathematics achievement test scores of third grade at-risk students and their counterparts who did not participate in the program?

This study is significant since the labor force projections indicate a severe decline in the number of blue-collar jobs and a substantial increase in jobs that require high levels of technical skill. Given this economic picture and the fact that "by the year 2010, African Americans and Hispanics will comprise approximately 30% of our population," (Kuykendall, 1991, foreword) we must as a nation for economic survival and the United States' leadership role around the world, ensure that educational opportunities exist for all students to succeed. As educators, superintendents, principals, legislators, and parents, we must work together to meet this challenge.

THE RESEARCH SETTING

The city of Harrisburg is located in the south-central region of Pennsylvania in Dauphin County. The total population of the county is approximately 252,000. Analysis of demographic characteristics from the U.S. Census 2000 indicates that approximately 121,000 of these individuals are male and 131,000 are female. The median age is 37.9 years. Approximately 24% of the county's population is under the age of 18, while 14% is over the age of 65. European Americans comprise 77% of the total population, 17% are African Americans, 0.2% are American Indian and Alaskan natives, 4.1% Hispanic, 2% Asian, and the remainder comprises other races. Approximately 39% of school-age children live in poverty. The per-capita income for the city of Harrisburg is $15,787 with a median family income of $29,556 with 24.6% of the population and 23.4% of families are below the poverty line. Out of the total people living in poverty, 34.9% are under the age of 18 and 16.6% are 65 or older (Harrisburg Statistics).

This research study will be conducted in the Harrisburg City School District (HSD). This culturally diverse urban school district is the thirteenth largest of the 501 public school districts in the state of Pennsylvania. The district consists of 11 schools that enroll students in grades K5–7, one intermediate school that houses grade 8, one high school—grades 9 through 12 and new this year, a partnership with a for-profit agency to handle alternative education at-risk students. An added component to the district in the 2001 school year was the placing in the schools of security resource officers, who are Harrisburg City police officers. At least one or two officers are assigned to each of the city schools to work with students, staff, and community to maintain a safe learning environment for all students.

District enrollment figures indicate that 9,228 students were enrolled during the 1994–95 school year. However, by the 2000–2001 school year, the student population declined to 7,600. The district is currently under the state's Education Empowerment Act. The Pennsylvania State House of Representatives passed the Education Empowerment Act in 2000. This Act gives extra funds to students in public schools in which 50% of the students in grades 5, 8, and 11 scored in the lowest quartile on the standardized test, Pennsylvania System of School Assessment (PSSA), for two consecutive years in reading and mathematics. The funds are to be used to improve academic performance. The Harrisburg City School District is currently the only district in the state that qualifies for a special category of empowerment districts. "With the district having at least 60% of its students' achievement scores in the lowest quartile, the district is under the control of a mayor-appointed Board of Control for a minimum of five years" (HSD Empowerment Team, 2001, p. 1). The city is also the capital seat for the state government. Although the Governor at the time of the district empowerment was a Republican, the city's Democratic mayor is currently serving his sixth term in office and is also at the helm of the Harrisburg City Schools.

Former Governor Tom Ridge of Pennsylvania echoed what many politicians and educators have said for years, "that children and young adults who cannot read or write don't stand a chance in today's world. Starting today, we refuse to accept the unacceptable. The Educational Empowerment Act will give our most vulnerable schools the tools they need to innovate and improve—and to provide a quality education to our kids" (Commonwealth of Pennsylvania, 2000, p. 1). The mayor and a 17-member council govern both the city of Harrisburg and the county of Dauphin. Surrounded by independent boroughs and townships, Harrisburg tried and was unable to expand its boundaries after 1950 and due to slum clearance and reduced housing, lost populations to the suburbs. Today, the city of Harrisburg has a population of 48,950 and a metropolitan area population of 616,900, which includes Harrisburg-Lebanon-Carlisle (Harrisburg Profile).

RESEARCH DESIGN

This $2 \times 2 \times 2 \times 2 \times 2$ quasi-experimental design has both a control and experimental group of students. The experimental design as shown in Table 10.1 shows that each of the five classification variables has two levels, which was utilized for this study. The control group includes students enrolled in three schools not utilizing the intervention model program, PATHS. The three experimental group schools received the PATHS curriculum. Both sets of participating schools were randomly selected by the district's central office Academic Services Department to pilot for the program.

The dependent variable in the study is the reading and mathematics achievement test scores on the Stanford Achievement Test 9 of third grade at-risk students in the Harrisburg City School District (HSD). The primary independent variable investigated was student participation in the PATHS program. The program curriculum includes training for classroom teachers and is conducted twice weekly by Penn State instructors, or the social/counseling firm, Hempfield Associates. The other independent variables considered for investigation were individual characteristics of the students: gender, race, and academic status.

TABLE 10.1 Class Level Information

Class	Levels	Values
Group	2	Control Group, PATHS Group
Gender	2	Male, Female
StatusCol	2	Regular Ed, All Other
RaceCol	2	Black, Non-Black
Time	2	PreTest, PostTest

Goodrich and St. Pierre (1979) estimate that 20% attrition of students per year is a realistic level for planning (p. 230). As this study focused for the two school years, 1998–99 and 1999–00, student mobility (transience) was a critical point to note as students movement from school to school or from the district showed they did not take all the SAT 9 standardized tests.

Data were collected beginning with the PATHS program, which started in 1998. The 1998 reading and mathematics scaled composite test scores from the Stanford Achievement Test 9 was used as the pretest measure. The 3rd graders took the SAT 9 primary test in the spring of 1999. In the spring of 2000, the students took the SAT 9 intermediate test. Even though the SAT 9 primary test was administered to students as the pretest and the SAT 9 intermediate test was administered to students as the posttest, this did not pose a problem. The students in the research received the same pretest (primary SAT 9) and the same students received the same post-test (intermediate SAT 9). The students in the control and experimental (PATHS) groups were being compared at the beginning of the experiment on the same test (primary test) and at the end of the research on the same test (intermediate test). The appropriate method utilized for studying the relationship between the dependent variable SAT 9 reading and SAT 9 math scores and the independent variables are the repeated-measurements analysis of variance.

The researcher used this method because the dependent variables, SAT 9 scaled composite reading scores and SAT 9 scaled composite math scores, were administered to students repeatedly (twice), at the beginning of the treatment, when the primary version of the test was administered, and at the end, when the intermediate version was administered. Repeated-measurements analysis of variance is frequently used by researchers because it can greatly increase the chance that the sought after phenomenon will be discovered. Comparing students directly with themselves is much "cleaner" and much less subject to extraneous "noise" than comparing students with others. In performing the repeated-measurements analysis of variance, the Type 2 method was used as it is considered by researchers to be more powerful than the Type 3 method.

The statistical tests were conducted to determine if there was a statistically significant difference ($p = .05$) between the control and PATHS groups. The results and empirical findings are presented in a manner designed to answer the hypothesis put forth in the study.

Hypothesis: *Participation in the PATHS program has no statistically significant effects on the reading and mathematics achievement test scores of third grade at-risk students in the Harrisburg City School District.*

Population and Sample

The targeted population, which includes all the members of a real or hypothetical set of people, events, or objects to which researchers wish to generalize the results of their research (Gall, Borg, & Gall, 1996, p. 220), was the third grade students in the Harrisburg City School District (HSD). The accessible sample population were the students who were in the third grade during the academic years 1998–99 and fourth graders in 1999–00, from the three experimental schools, which participated in the PATHS program, and the three controlled schools that did not participate in the PATHS program, as shown in Table 10.2.

Summary

The major purpose of this study was to ascertain whether there was an effect on the sampled 208 third grade at-risk urban students standardized academic tests of reading and mathematics from their participation and exposure to the PATHS curriculum, a proactive intervention social program designed to promote the development of self-control, emotional awareness, and interpersonal problem-solving skills. The methodology and research design of the study included (1) to identify the two populations that were studied, (2) to gather and code the data pertaining to the sample population's academic standardized Stanford Achievement Test 9 scores in reading and mathematics, and (3) to analyze and report the findings.

Findings revealed that there is no significant evidence of the PATHS program having an effect on the standardized reading test scores of 3rd grade at-risk students. The moderate increase on the pre and posttest scores in mathematics for the experimental group is inconsistent with the null hypothesis. Thus, the findings did not find evidence of the effectiveness of the PATHS program on students reading and math test scores. The null hypothesis cannot be rejected.

TABLE 10.2 The Frequency Procedure of the Variable of Group

Group	Frequency	Percent
Control group	103	51.24
PATHS group	98	48.76
Frequency missing = 7		

IMPLICATIONS FOR RESEARCH

The implications of the findings of this research represent a paradox for educational policy makers in this district. The findings cannot be generalized insofar as the sample population should be much larger than the 208 students in this study. The grouping of students by regular education and all other should be further investigated with a larger sample of students evenly categorized among special education, behavioral, emotional and chronic behavioral students. Also, it is important to remember that the study only represents students in 6 of the districts 11 elementary schools and that the analysis related to the students in the district's pilot program. In order to ensure the validity and reliability now and in the future, further research should be conducted.

The implications of the research were nevertheless surprising to this researcher, and essentially demand further inquiry into the PATHS curriculum program. The findings would support the present administration's initiative for having the PATHS program in all the K–8 schools along with the fact that "the Nation's Report Card for 2003 revealed that Pennsylvania has one of the largest racial achievement gaps in the nation. The NAEP results have the largest gap between scores of Black and White fourth-graders, except for the District of Columbia" (Chute, 2003, p.1). Also, social skills are as important in preparing for kindergarten as are thinking and language skills (Bales, 2001, p. 3).

IMPLICATIONS FOR POLICY

This study provides the school district with some real opportunities for positive change in terms of school district policy initiatives, programs, projects, and research studies. Faced with a window of opportunity to address the widening gap that exists in standardized achievement test scores of students, and the fact that in most urban settings, the urban student entering school is not fully equipped with the literacy skills needed to succeed, it would be very fitting to expand this research study and do a longitudinal study and have all the Harrisburg schools participate rather than the initial six. Other possible next steps may include:

- To replicate the study with a much larger sample population;
- To replicate the study with a qualitative paradigm to get a better understanding of the independent relationship between parental perception and standardized tests in the education of children in an urban setting;
- To examine the effects of transience on individual schools;

- To re-evaluate these same students in a longitudinal study for 5th, 8th, and 11th grade standardized scaled test scores in reading and mathematics.

REFERENCES

Bales, D. (2001, Fall). What do we really know about childcare and aggression? *Child-Care Concepts,* No. 21.

Bay Area School Reform Collaborative Newsletter (BASRC). (2002, March). *The achievement gap: What does color have to do with how we teach reading?* Retrieved January 10, 2004 from http://www.basrc.org/Pubs&Docs/Idliteracy2002.pdf

Borman, G. D., & D'Agostino, J. V. (1995), *Title 1 & student achievement: A meta-analysis of thirty years of test results.* [Abstract]. Paper presented at the annual meeting of the American Education Research Association, San Francisco, CA. [Abstract]. (ERIC Document Preproduction Service No. ED393888)

Bucks County Courier Times. (2002). *Data shows racial divide in Pennsylvania schools.* Calkins Media, Inc. Retrieved March 17, 2002 from wysiwyg://294://www. phillyburbs.com/couriertimes/news/news/1008paschools. htm

Campaign for Fiscal Equity (CFE). (2000, Winter). *Fight for fair school funding moves to court,* vol. 4(1). Retrieved January 10, 2004 from http://www.edpriorities. org/Pubs/Pubs/Archive/pubs_00Win.Fight.html

Campbell, J. R., Hombo, C. M., & Mazzeo, J. (2000). *NAEP 1999 trends in academic progress: Three decades of student performance in reading 1971 to 1999; science 1969 to 1999; mathematics 1973 to 1999.* (Report No. NCES 2000-469). Washington, DC: U.S. Department of Education. Office of Educational Research and Improvement.

Center for Education Reform (CER). (2001, April 6). *Reading results: The learning gap widens: Results from the reading 2000 report card,* (p. 1). Retrieved January 28, 2002 from http://www.edreform.com/index.cfm?fuseaction=document&do cumentID=622&s ectionID=55

Chute, E. (2003, June 20). *State pupils ahead of average on national reading test.* Post-Gazette. Retrieved November 23, 2003 from http://www.post-gazette.com/ localnews/20030620readingr6.asp

Clinton, W. J. (1997, Feb). *4th State of the union address.* Retrieved January 10, 2004 from http://www.geocities.com/americanpresidencynet/1997.htm

Commonwealth of Pennsylvania: 2000. (News Release, May 3). *Gov. Ridge hails House passage of Education Empowerment Act.* Retrieved January 9, 2002 from http:// findarticles.com/cf_dis/m4prn/2000_may_3/61875992/pl/article/jhtml

Delpit, L. (1995). *Other people's children: Cultural conflict in the classroom.* New York: The New Press.

Donnelly, M. (1987).At-Risk students. *ERIC Digest* Series Number 21. ED 292172. Retrieved February 20, 2002 from http://www.ericfacility.net/ericdigests/ ed292172.html

Eckstrom, R. B., Goertz, M. E., Pollack, J. M., & Rock, D. A. (1986). Who drops out of school and why? Findings from a national study. In L. Magdol (Ed.), *Factors for adolescent academic achievement.* Retrieved December 20, 2003 from http://www.cyfernet.org/research/youthful3.html

Elliott, D. S., Hamburg, B. A., & Williams, K. R. (1998). *Violence in American schools.* Melbourne: Cambridge University Press.

Gall, M. D., Borg, W. R., & Gall, J. P. (1996). *Educational research: An introduction* (6th. Ed.). White Plains, NY: Longman Publishers.

Goodlad, J., & Keating, P. (1990). Access to knowledge: An agenda for our nation's schools. In J. Hixson & M. B. Tinzmann (Eds.), *Who are the "at-risk" students of the 1990s?* Oak Brook, IL: NCREL.

Goodrich, R. L., & Pierre, R. G. (1979). Opportunities for studying later effects of follow through. In M. Gall, W. Borg, & J. Gall (Eds.), *Educational research: An introduction* (6th ed.). White Plains, NY: Longman

Harrisburg Profile. Retrieved January 10, 2004 from http://www.harrisburgpa.gov/econprofile/facts.html

Harrisburg School District. (1998, June). *Demographic DataBook.* Harrisburg, PA: Harrisburg School District, Department of Pupil Services. http://www.nebulasearch.com/encyclopedia/article/Harrisburg,_Pennsylvania.html

Harrisburg School District. (2001, June 19). *Establishing a culture of excellence. School District Improvement Plan.* Harrisburg, PA: Harrisburg School District, HSD Empowerment Team

Harrisburg Statistics. Retrieved January 10, 2004 from, http://www.nebulasearch.com/encyclopedia/article/Harrisburg, Pennsylvania.html.

Heritage Foundation. (1999, April 13). *Largest federal education program has failed to close achievement gap between rich and poor children, analyst says.* Retrieved June 22, 2000 from http://www.heritage.org/news/99/nr041399.html

Jencks, C., & Phillips, M. (1998, September 30). The Black-White test score gap. *Education Week,* p. 1–51. Retrieved February 20, 2001 from http://www.edweek.org/ew/vol-18/04jencks.h18

Johnston, R. C., & Viadero, D. (2000, March 15). Unmet promise: Raising minority achievement. *Education Week, 19*(27), p.1, 18–19. Retrieved January 20, 2003 from http://www.edweek.org/ew/ewstory.cfm?slug=27gapintro.h19&keywords=unmet%20promise

Kozol, J. (1991). *Savage inequalities: Children in America's schools.* New York: Crown Publishers.

Kuykendall, C. A. (1989/91). *Improving black student achievement by enhancing student's self-image.* Retrieved January 23, 2003 from http://www.maec.org/achieve/achieve.html

Mahan, G., & Johnson, C. (1983). Portrait of a dropout: Dealing with academic, social, and emotional problems. In L. Magdol (Ed.), *Factors for adolescent academic achievement.* Retrieved December 20, 2003 from http://www.eyfernet.org/research/youthful13.html

National Black Caucus of State Legislators. (2001, November). *Education Report: Closing the achievement gap.* Education Symposium in Gulfport, Mississippi.

National Urban League Institute. (2001, April). *Opportunity agenda: A blueprint for Success, "How President George W. Bush can eradicate the major inequities confronting Black America during his Presidency.* Funded by Nationwide Insurance Company.

Olson, L., & Jerald, C. D. (1998a, January 8). Concentrated poverty. *Education Week, 17*(17), p. 14–15.

Olson, L., & Jerald, C. D. (1998b, January 8). The achievement gap. *Education Week, 17*(17), p. 10–13. Washington, DC. In *Quality Counts 98: The Achievement Gap.* Retrieved June 22, 2000 from http://www.edweek.org/sreports/qc98/challenges/achieve/ac-n.htm

Quality Counts '98: The Urban Challenge (series). (1998). *Education Week.*

Richardson, V., & Colfer, P. (1990). Being at-risk in school. In J. Hixson & M. B. Tinzmann (Eds.), *Who are the "at-risk" students of the 1990s?* Oak Brook, IL: NCREL.

Slavin, R., Karweit, N., & Wasik, B. (1994). *Preventing early school failure: Research, policy, and practices.* Needham Heights, MA: Allyn & Bacon.

Taba, H., & Elkins, D. (1966). *Teaching strategies for the culturally disadvantaged.* Chicago: Rand McNally & Company.

U.S. Department of Education, Goals 2000, Educate America. (1994, March). *America's moral urgency to reconnect children and schools.* No.11.

U.S. Department of Education. Office of Educational Research and Improvement. National Center for Education Statistics. (2000). *The Nation's Report Card: Fourth Grade Reading 2000,* NCES 2001-499, by P.L. Donahue, R.J. Finnegan, A.D. Lutkus, N.L. Allen, and J.R. Campbell. Washington, DC: 2001.

Viadero, D. (2000, March 22). Lags in minority achievement defy traditional explanations. *Education Week.* 18–19, 28. From http://www.edweek.org/we/newstory.cfm?slug=28causes.h19.

PART 4

EDUCATION POLICY, REFORM, AND STUDENT PERFORMANCE

CHAPTER 11

SUPPLEMENTAL EDUCATIONAL SERVICES IN PENNSYLVANIA

Policy Perspectives, Effects, and Challenges

Charlyene C. Pinckney

This chapter will examine the implementation and success of the Supplemental Educational Services (SES) provision of the No Child Left Behind Act of 2001 (NCLB) in Pennsylvania. After a discussion of theoretical frameworks, inherent policy tensions, and policy effects, a discussion of Pennsylvania's implementation of the federal policy and its results will ensue. A review of federal education policy is included and contrasted with current levels of involvement and policy approaches. National effects of the federal SES policy are examined. Recommendations for needed changes to the NCLB-SES policy are reviewed and considered in order to improve program implementation and student success.

Policy, Leadership, and Student Achievement, pages 165–181
Copyright © 2008 by Information Age Publishing
All rights of reproduction in any form reserved.

The SES portion of the most recent reauthorization of the Elementary and Secondary Education Act (i.e., NCLB of 2002) requires that individual schools and school districts (local education agencies or LEAs) that haven't made adequate yearly progress (AYP) for three or more consecutive years provide academic interventions to eligible low-income students outside of the regular school day. Eligible students are those who: (1) attend Title I schools that have not made AYP for three consecutive years and (2) opt to stay at their current school rather than enroll in another one under the school choice provision of NCLB. The SES may be provided by the district (if it is not underperforming), or a state-approved provider such as a for-profit company, or a community-based organization. Districts must set aside 20% of their Title I funds to provide school choice-related transportation and SES for eligible students.

There are a series of requirements that both state education agencies (SEAs) and LEAs must negotiate together in order to affect this part of the NCLB policy (USDE, 2006a). The U.S. Department of Education oversees SES implementation nationwide and provides guidance and technical assistance. Among the major state and local responsibilities are: notifying students/parents of their eligibility, SES provider selection criteria, approval process, monitoring and evaluation, list generation, contracting for services, assurances of SES program quality, consistency with state academic standards, the demonstration of a research-based program, and proof of resulting increases in student academic achievement. These extensive administrative, enforcement, evaluative, and monitoring requirements were not supported with additional federal funding or staffing. Many districts and states alike have been left to devise means of achieving the goals of the law while managing the inherent and extant challenges of implementation of the SES policy (Sunderman & Kim, 2004).

ANALYTICAL FRAMEWORKS

It is important to point out that NCLB is principally a regulatory policy employing mostly mandates and system change as its instruments of choice. Such policies generally take the form of laws or rules that explicitly require and/or prohibit certain behavior and assign penalties for failure to comply. Fowler (2000) clearly states that the choice of such vectors for achieving success creates an atmosphere of conflict, volatility, competition, and distrust among policy actors. Distributive and redistributive policies are generally more widely accepted, although not without drawbacks of their own. She also describes a major change by NCLB policy developers in departing from a type of educational policymaking, which usually included the recommendations of "experts"—educators and administrators—and provided for their contribution to the design process. Add to this the increased activity in recent years of the alliance of policy elites (corporations, foundations and wealthy individuals) clearly exercising a significant amount of influence on the policy process in education. All three combine to intensify the challenges faced by local authorities responsible for the actual implementation of the programs.

The Advocacy Coalition Framework as defined by Heck (2004) focuses on the impact of large wealthy policy actors in setting the national education agenda, from issue definition, to disbursing technical information, to influencing public opinion and the legislative process itself. Studies and position papers released by universities, think tanks, and other research organizations hold sway within educational communities and their voice is strengthened by this influence beyond what their considerable resources are able to promote independently. This perspective applies generally to the standards-based educational accountability movement and specifically in the NCLB Supplemental Educational Services (SES) provision in particular. For example, Bracey (2005) documents serious concerns with the number of SES providers who are private, and with the estimated sum of public dollars moving from the public schools into the hands of nonpublic providers. He makes the case that private contractors (standardized testing, tutoring services providers, etc.) are direct benefactors of the SES policy under the guise (value) of choice and competition. Worse yet, these entities are absolved from the very same quality standards that public schools and their teachers are required to adhere to and demonstrate as a rule. This glaring example of preferential treatment also lends to a hostile policy environment especially for school districts disqualified from offering the services to students themselves. An August 2006 report by the U.S. Government Accountability Office pointed out additional problems: lack of provider availability in some geographical areas, coordination issues for SES implementation, inadequate parent notification processes, unclear guidance across federal education offices, inadequate capacity at the state level to monitor and evaluate provider performance and SES costs outpacing the designated Title I set-aside. This mix of strained cultural issues, powerful policy players (and benefactors), local implementation and funding problems, and the punitive qualities of the statute itself all combine to heighten naturally existing, competing values. The question is whether a policy derived and administered amid such an atmosphere can truly have its desired effects under such adversarial circumstances.

The overall design of the NCLB policy also makes a strong case for the presence and effects of cultural and ideological differences. Heck (2004) describes yet another means of analyzing policy as one with a focus on the movement of ideas over time as well as their development, gains in support and influence with time. It incorporates a means to understand ideology and values, especially of the dominant culture, and how power is wielded to translate those ideas and values into policy. Heck states that the sources of conflict are always rooted in differences in ideology, i.e., difference in beliefs about the way social, economic and political systems should be organized and operate. Of the three cultural typologies noted (traditional, moralistic, and individualistic), Pennsylvania exhibits a mostly traditional typology. While there are localized areas of cultural difference and contrast overall, the state is largely conservative, even regressive in its policies regarding taxation and educational funding. Its legislative leadership largely espouses moralistic ideals, but enacts few progressive policies. Its citizenry, only recently galvanized by indignation over a controversial midterm legislative and judicial pay raise, is generally plagued by apathy toward these same goals, a factor derived at least in part from their assortment of distant, splintered, and highly localized units of control in education (e.g., 501 school districts). This splintering of communities has also been found regarding implementation problems, perception of the law, and the effects of the law. The core policy values for education in the Commonwealth focus on quality (high academic standards, rigorous teacher certification rules, extensive candidate testing, etc.) and efficiency (tight economic control, accountability measures, authoritarian structure, etc.). Equity (poor equal opportunity record, no level funding formula for public schools) is last as a value. This remains a major problem for the state's poorest communities. Urban, poor, and high-minority areas of the state are disproportionately affected by these features. This reality further strains working relationships among school communities, and between the state and local education agencies.

The education policy culture in Pennsylvania has changed for the better under the leadership of Governor Edward G. Rendell. The Accountability Block Grant Program (ABG) was initially enacted by the PA Legislature for the 2004–05 school year, and continues to represent an integral part of Governor Rendell's long-term plan to revitalize Pennsylvania's education system and to ensure an equitable system of support and accountability for student academic and personal success (PDE, 2005a). The $200 million plus in state funds appropriated each year since then have been employed by 500 school districts to balance their local decision-making with investments in proven educational practices, such as full day kindergarten, quality professional development opportunities, lower class sizes, tutoring assistance, and technology integration into classroom settings. Districts may use their allocated ABG funds to establish, maintain, or expand any of 11 quality program types to meet the specific learning needs of their students. Through both individual and compiled reports, the Accountability Block Grant program has demonstrated its effectiveness in helping districts to meet the needs of their respective school communities, as well as state and federal demands for increased student performance and school improvement. Also, Pennsylvania instituted the landmark Educational Assistance Program, providing $66 million in 2006–07 to districts to aid struggling students via earmarked funds for tutoring programs. Many districts choose to aid their Supplemental Education Services program via one or both sources of funds. Importantly, both programs also require strategic local program administration and evaluation of student progress so that proposals are carefully integrated into larger school and district plans for student achievement via improvements in curriculum and instruction, high academic standards, provisions for technology and materials, ancillary student services, teacher quality, early childhood education investments and programs targeting special populations (special needs, English language learners, etc.). This has been a very successful education policy approach in PA, deftly combining policy types, engaging policy actors and securing the support of the public and educational experts alike. Other states could likely benefit from such an exemplary model to assisting school and LEAs toward improving student achievement and meeting the goals of NCLB.

OVERVIEW OF THE PENNSYLVANIA SUPPLEMENTAL EDUCATION SERVICES POLICY

It is interesting to note that Pennsylvania's culturally derived focus on regulation and structure may actually be helping it to perform its requirements under the SES provision of NCLB fairly well, despite the reports of low student participation and program success nationwide (Saulny, 2006). The department has an entire Web page devoted to SES including listing of approved providers, sample evaluations, contracts etc., all designed to assist schools and districts alike (Pennsylvania Department of Education, 2005b). They represent the relative roles and responsibilities as follows:

- Responsibilities of PDE—provider selection criteria; monitoring.
- Responsibilities of the LEA—parent notice, contracts, background checks.
- Responsibilities of the School—notification, coordinate PTP meetings.
- Responsibilities of the Supplemental Services Provider—approval, attendance and progress documentation.
- Expectations of the Parent—return forms, communications, ensure student participation.

As noted previously, there are also two major state funding initiatives provided to help districts meet the SES goals. The Educational Assistance Program (EAP) is a subsidy that provides direct financial assistance by the

Commonwealth to school districts to operate effective tutoring programs as required by NCLB. The Accountability Block Grant Program (ABG) is another source of direct financial assistance to school districts to implement any of 11 proven programs to assist student achievement; one option is Tutoring Services. These distributive policies have been well received by districts. The state has also engaged in a series of programming and organizational efforts to help districts implement the SES provision. The SES Web site contains the following:

- SES Toolkit Web Posting (PDE, 2005c).
- Responsibilities.
- Samples: parent letters, provider selection form, contract components, individual learning plan, data tracking forms, report forms—individual students, report forms—compiled results.
- Provider Application.
- Approved provider list.
- Financial Policy.
- Provider Checklist.
- Approved Models in Math and Reading.
- Title I Buildings/Per pupil Amounts.
- USDE Guidance.

As NCLB itself calls only for basic requirements for providers, it requires states to develop and apply objective criteria for selection and evaluation. Pennsylvania employs a relatively rigorous provider selection process. Providers must supply an online application, fiscal documentation, and original background check forms, as well as attend a PDE sponsored annual meeting and use an approved evidence-based model aligned with state academic standards. Pennsylvania also employs a scoring rubric for application approval (alignment, communication, program qualities (duration, tutor-student ratio, intensity), student assessment, accessibility, evidence basis of a program, staff qualifications (clearances only), effectiveness, financial and organizational stability, assurances (federal, state, & local: facilities, safety, civil rights, IDEA/ADA, etc.). The rating scale includes the categories "no evidence," "limited evidence," and "substantial evidence." Finally, PA provides an SES Provider Accountability Plan. Its components are:

- Announced and unannounced visits.
- Regular updates on student progress and attendance rates.
- Parent survey.
- School district checklist of concerns.
- If fewer than 80% of students tutored fail to make "significant progress" over a two-year period, the provider is removed from the list.

Some of the expanded elements of the PA program were developed subsequent to additional guidance and support from the US Department of Education amid criticism that it was not addressing local and state needs for additional assistance (NEA, 2006a). Regional education labs and professional educators' organizations have been helpful in explicating the policy, influencing changes, and providing assistance as well (NWREL, 2004; Schwartzbeck, 2005; NEA, 2006b).

The one clear drawback to Pennsylvania's efforts is that staffing at the state level is not adequate to conduct thorough monitoring and evaluation or providers. Some concerns also exist regarding the definition of significant progress. It is clearly understood however, to be different (lower) from those standards applied to schools and districts. Currently in PA, 250 schools (8%) and 27 districts (5%) are required to offer SES (PDE, 2005a). But similar to the nationwide findings, most of the troubled districts in this state are in urban, poor, and ethnically diverse areas struggling to meet the needs of many low-income and low-performing students.

NCLB-SES POLICY TENSIONS

An explication of the existence and enduring conflicts surrounding values and ideology in our society has been well documented by several authors (Fowler, 2000; Winch & Gongell, 2004; Heck, 2004). All explain the cornerstone values expressed by our founding fathers and the fact that even upon our earliest efforts to "form a more perfect union," value conflicts have been at the heart of the difficulty involved in policy formulation. The NCLB statute states that its central public values are choice and excellence. The positive aspects of the law are its flexibility in permitting states and districts to meet their obligations under the law. The import and role of adequacy, efficiency, and equity, however, were de-emphasized and/or delegated to the state and local education agencies to manage. Likewise, the federal policy instrument of choice was principally via mandates and sanctions. The capacity building and inducements options again were ceded to SEAs and LEAs. This selection of policy vehicles and line-up of competing values has created very clear tensions among the three levels of government concerning this federal education policy from the outset. SEAs and LEAs argue that they support academic excellence and flexibility (with perhaps somewhat less exuberance for choice), but that they need far more federal attention to and support for the values of adequacy, efficiency, and capacity building to reach the stated goals. The issuance of additional federal guidance over the past two years of the law has addressed some of the concerns voiced by the states and LEAs, but most agree that more is needed.

Another source of overall increased tensions, especially within the educational community, stems from reports of increasing dropout rates and the ever-increasing academic proficiency requirements. The fact that the number of schools/districts not making AYP each year is increasing, is also a major factor. The impending approach of the harshest sanctions (school reconstitution, third-party management, and closure) further complicates and escalates the tensions.

FEDERAL INTERVENTION AND FUNDING OF PUBLIC EDUCATION PRIOR TO NCLB

According to the United States Department of Education, public education is a federal concern, but primarily a state responsibility and a local function (USDE, 2006a). Other than the "general welfare" clause, the U.S. Constitution contains no specific reference to public education. All functions not specifically mentioned in the document to be federal in nature, are by default, the responsibility of the states. The Articles of Confederation (via Northwest Ordinance) contained a federal law requiring certain lands to be set aside for schools, generally for higher education purposes. While new states were required to establish free systems of public education, they did so largely without much intervention from any federal requirements, mandates or funding (Oravitz, 1993).

As noted previously, Winch and Gongell (2004) states that conflict over public values and ideology have existed since the founding of our nation. The Federalist position, championed by John Adams, was that more government control of individuals was needed to ensure peace and stability. This group of early framers did not support extensive individual rights, yet the Bill of Rights (first 10 Amendments to the U.S. Constitution) was added to the document to ensure that every American was granted just that. The Federalists did not extend this application of government control and power to financial markets. In this instance, the "free economic hand of individuals" should be protected from the freewill of the populace. Their belief was that highest good would result from individuals pursuing their own self-interests. At the other end of the spectrum were the Jeffersonians (named for their champion, Thomas Jefferson), who believed an educated populace was best for the success of the new republic. This group believed that people would employ their greater responsibility and freedom to achieve peace, stability, and the greatest good. Community was important to preserving democracy and an educated populace would place the welfare of society above self-interest. Essentially, these same tensions exist today, and evidence themselves throughout the policymaking process in every aspect of government, especially education. NCLB can indeed be thought of as a trend toward a federalist approach after 35 years of a more populist approach concerning the role of government with regard to federal education policy.

What follows is a partial listing of federal interventions and investments in public education over the past 240 years (Oravitz, 1993). It shows that the federal government has intervened several times in the past to promote public education in response to external and internal social economic and competitive global factors. NCLB marks a significant shift away from supporting public schools as simply a "common good" function to one with an economic, free-market, and accountability focus. A key question is whether such an approach produces real gains in student achievement, supports school environments where children can learn and grow, and/or prepares them for postsecondary scholarship or high-skilled trades, citizenship, and participation in a global, technologically expanding economy.

FEDERAL INTERVENTIONS AND INVESTMENTS IN PUBLIC EDUCATION

- First federal education agency was formed in 1867 to collect information on schools and teaching.
  - Gradual emergence of other functions over the years, many in response to world events, politics, and socioeconomic changes.
- Second Morrill Act (1890)
  - Support for original land grant colleges and universities.
- Smith-Hughes Act (1917)
  - Agricultural, industrial, and home economics training for high school students.
- World War II—period of great expansion.
  - Lanham Act 1941 and Impact Aid laws of 1950—eased the burden on communities effected by military and other federal lands by making payments to local school districts.
  - "GI Bill"—authorized postsecondary assistance to nearly 8 million veterans for college education.
- Cold War period—another expansion via comprehensive education legislation National Defense Education Act of 1958 (NDEA).
  - Response to the launch of Sputnik.
  - Ensure Americans were highly trained in science and technology to compete with the Soviet Union.
  - Included loans for undergraduate college students, graduate fellowships, and vocational training initiatives as well as improvements in instruction in math, science, and foreign languages in elementary and secondary schools.

- Antipoverty and Civil Rights Laws of 1960s and 1970s.
  - Response to social/economic pressure to fulfill its equal access mission; prohibited entrenched, longstanding discrimination across the nation.
  - Title VI of the Civil Rights Act of 1964 (race)
  - Title IX of the Education Amendments of 1972 (sex)
  - Section 504 of the Rehabilitation Act of 1973 (disability)
- Elementary and Secondary Education Act of 1965.
  - Federal aid to disadvantaged children in poor urban and rural areas.
- Higher Education Act.
  - Assistance for disadvantaged postsecondary education students (loans, work study, grants).
- Congress established the Department of Education as a cabinet-level agency in 1980; Operates 175 programs across all levels of education.
  - Elementary and Secondary Programs.
  - Annually serves 50 million students in more than 85,000 public schools in 15,000 school districts, and 26,000 private schools nationwide.
  - Higher Education Programs.
  - Annually serves 8 million postsecondary students.

RECENT TRENDS IN FEDERAL EDUCATION SPENDING

In FY 2004–05, the U.S. Department of Education reported that of the more than $900 billion spent on public education by all government levels combined, 90% comes from state, local and private sources. Of the remaining 10% spent by the federal government, 20% (or about $18 billion) is used to support related programs from other agencies such as Head Start (Department of Health and Human Services) and the School Lunch Program (Department of Agriculture). The balance (approximately $72 billion) was appropriated specifically for expenditures and programs via the U.S. Department of Education. This amounted to only 8% of total education spending across government levels, and represented less than 3% of the federal government's $2.5 trillion budget in FY 2005 (USDE, 2006a).

President Bush's proposed general budget for FY 2006–07 (announced in February of 2006) was $2.77 trillion. It called for cuts in the education budget by 3.5 billion, level funding for Title I programs, and sought the elimination of 42 other established programs, including vocational education grants, Perkins Loans for low-income students, and the Even Start program for poor families (Peterson, 2006). If approved, it would have been the largest spending cut in the 26-year history of the Department.

Fortunately, Congress restored programs and funding for many of the proposed eliminations and cuts via its appropriation in October 2006. The notion that federal spending on education has spiraled out of control is not supported by these facts. Indeed, they instead appear to support the need for increased federal investment given the types of access, equality, professional training, and response to global pressures the federal government should be addressing and must continue to address. Although there exists an inherent tension between values, the current law, in the absence of adequate funding, creates a gross imbalance that threatens to do more damage to public schools and their students than good. It is also important to recall the ultimate consequences of not meeting the AYP requirements of the law: forfeiture of all Title I funds to the school, LEA, and state (USDE, 2006a). This can hardly be thought to be a satisfactory solution to the plight of the nation's poorest children for whom Title I of the ESEA of 1965 was originally conceived to assist. There must be a way to advance the ideals of excellence, equity, flexibility, and adequacy without abandoning disadvantaged youth and their communities.

RECENT TRENDS IN FEDERAL PROGRAM MODIFICATIONS AND NCLB-SES PROVISION

In general, the past 10–15 years have seen the repeal or consolidation of 144 duplicative or narrowly focused programs via federal education block grants (PSBA, 2001). The selling point of such policy action is that it provides for increased flexibility to states by eliminating administrative restraints. While proponents state that funds can be used for general aid versus categorical funding, which requires specific adherence to program criteria, opponents argue that block grants cut/dilute federal commitment to K–12 program funding and eliminate targeted federal dollars to serve districts and children with inadequate resources to provide a high-quality education. The reauthorization of the ESEA in 2002 (NCLB) threatens to further reduce the federal government's commitment to K–12 public schooling via inadequate funding and provisions that place the entire responsibility for student improvement on LEAs and SEAs, while completely ignoring pre-existing factors or progress made to this point.

NCLB's four basic reform principles are stated as stronger accountability for results, increased flexibility and local control, expanded options for parents, and an emphasis on teaching methods proven to work (USDE, 2006a). NCLB also calls for "stronger accountability" for results via a focus on repeated, cross-sectional standardized test performance in Grades 3–11. Proponents state that test scores will have a motivating effect on students, teachers, and administrators alike and encourage them to improve school and individual test performance. The law's proponents also frequently cite lack of effort, ability, and focus by students, teachers, and administrators as reasons for deficits. Other assumptions are that test scores are the only direct outcome of standardized testing; the law ignores other factors known to influence student and school performance (funding, quality of student teacher interactions, class size, poverty, etc.). It further ignores the possibility of other testing effects to individual students (decreased motivation toward schooling, increased dropout rates), to school staff (low morale, increased turnover) or entire school communities (effects of labeling, instability, school reconstitution or closure). It does not address the availability or conditions of school structures, resources, and/or finances to support supplemental educational services. Research studies have supported these assertions. Urdan and Paris (1994) found that high external control of school curriculum tends to be related to decreased staff morale and school climate. Likewise, Newmann, King, and Rigdon (1997) found that high external accountability was related to decrease internal school capacity. Amrein and Berliner (2003) reported that student motivation is adversely affected by high-stakes testing environments, and Roderick and Engel (2001) determined that this finding was particularly true for low achieving, at risk students. One of the most subtle, yet deceptive underlying assumptions of the law is that schools and districts making AYP have no educational issues worth addressing, and prescribes no challenges to their existing academic status other than maintaining it. This is unacceptable from the standpoint that all students should be appropriately challenged and supported to succeed academically and personally. The NCLB-SES provision, while perhaps imparting some benefit to individual students receiving assistance, seems inadequate to counteract the pervasive, school and community-wide negative effects of the other provisions and omissions of the law and its lack of funding.

POLICY DECISION-MAKING AND MULTIPLE POLICY EFFECTS OF NCLB-SES

A major criticism of the NCLB-SES policy in particular is that the research on the effects of tutoring outside of the school day is mixed. A review by Cosden et al. (2004) found that after-school academic tutoring or homework assistance may not result in an improvement in academic performance, but instead prevent a decline in performance evidenced by at-risk youth in particular. The programs seemed most helpful for English language learners and least beneficial for average students. Interestingly, they also reported that extracurricular activities that were nonacademic in nature decreased dropout rates and improved academic achievement among at-risk students in particular. Programs geared toward increasing student competence, self-esteem, social networks, and connectedness to their schools also had positive effects on academic achievement. In fact, the article warned against a wholesale replacement of nonacademic extracurricular programs with academic ones for these very reasons. Other concerns were the replacement of parents as academic role models, integration with regular schoolwork, and program quality. This evidence at best supports an experimental, optional, and varied SES policy rather than one in which localities are required to contract with unknown agents, using unproven strategies.

A detailed report by Sunderman and Kim (2004) noted serious deficiencies of the SES provision in general. They noted that most school districts reported major capacity issues in implementing the requirements from an administrative, contract, and facilities standpoint. States also identified complicating capacity issues that were administrative in nature, especially regarding the monitoring and evaluation of providers. A major drawback to the policy is that it decreased Title I operating funds by 20% each year due to the set-aside requirement in order to pay for choice and SES options under NCLB. The report noted that districts found this to be a serious impediment to operating function during the year and it interfered with existing school-wide programming efforts. Another major criticism is that the policy shifts the improvement goal from school improvement to individual student improvement. This is not as effective an approach when working in impoverished communities. The study also noted that there has been a reduction in the number of districts serving as providers from 37% to 27%. This has occurred mostly in the country's urban areas. Yet another criticism is that while certified teachers may be hired by providers, there is no objective criteria required for SES teachers and tutors unless they are established individually by the provider. This report also noted great concern with the redistribution of public funds to private parties. Approximately $2 billion per year went to tutoring services providers last year, most being for-profit enterprises. These same entities also saw a five to tenfold increase in enrollments and profits. One positive commentary about SES is that it serves more students than the choice option; only about 1% of eligible students opt to transfer schools. That said, only about 20% of students eligible for SES participate. This also indicates that it will be ineffective for overall school improvement needed for significant AYP improvements.

These findings were disappointing, but not so much as finding out that they were not, or should not, have come as a surprise. Several researchers have documented that similar results were evidenced from the implementation of precursor policies in Texas (Haney, 2000; Darling-Hammond, 2004; Bracey, 2005; Sunderman & Kim, 2004). Key findings of several recent studies call into question the positive effects of high-stakes testing policies in general. Linda Darling-Hammond (2004) and others have clearly shown that imposing high academic standards alone is not enough to produce large-scale improvements in academic achievement. She does point to several factors that do work to increase student achievement: professional development, redesigning school structures, school-wide and classroom assessments, and targeted supports and services to needy students. Other researchers have reported the same (Wang, Haertel, & Walberg, 1993). The current NCLB-SES policy does not sufficiently address any of these issues.

RECOMMENDED CHANGES TO THE FEDERAL AND STATE SUPPLEMENTAL SERVICES POLICY

In 2006, the US Government Accountability Office made a series of recommendations for the NCLB SES provision. Many of the research papers read for this report however, promote the elimination of the SES program altogether (Bracey, 2005; Sunderman & Kim, 2004). Based on these considerations, it seems prudent for policymakers to seriously review the SES provision in time for the next NCLB reauthorization process, and plan to institute an aggressive set of changes including:

1. Significantly increase Title I funding to more fully support local and state costs for providing supplemental educational services to all eligible students.
2. Repeal the diversion of existing Title I funds to pay for the program.
3. Provide increased staffing and consulting supports to states and districts for the capacity to conduct effective selection, monitoring, and evaluation of providers and programming.
4. Re-evaluate the likely contribution of SES to the academic achievement of students if participation remains at approximately 20% of those qualifying for the service or find ways to significantly increase eligible student participation.
5. Hold providers to the same level of accountability as teachers, schools, and districts for participation and results.

CONCLUSION

The Supplemental Educational Services provision of the No Child Left Behind Act of 2001 has seen some positive results in the state of Pennsylvania due largely to the efforts of local and state level policy makers, administrators, and educators. Whatever the stated intent of the NCLB ES provision, many of its direct effects are making public education and operations within the most challenged districts more difficult to create, sustain, and augment academic achievement. States already challenged by fulfilling their original obligation of providing for a thorough and efficient system of public education are burdened by the added mandates of the attendant and unfunded federal law and program. The law intensifies existing competition for scarce public dollars and competing public values. It uses principally compliance, enforcement, and penalty policy measures to accomplish goals that could just as likely be achieved through other instruments. At the same time, private enterprises, unfettered by the restrictions and mandates placed upon the public institutions and actors, are benefitting from the redirection of public dollars with weak evidence of their ability to impact achievement or accountability for student results. The educational environment at all levels has become highly charged, frustrating, distrusting, and extremely counterproductive for promoting student academic achievement and personal success. All of our school communities deserve better.

While Pennsylvania in this instance provides an example of how improvements can be made to an existing funding and education accountability system, it is insufficient to assert that successful policy implementation and outcomes lie solely with states and local school boards as the primary decision-makers of education policy. Federal policy developers should request, accept, and act upon feedback from the other two levels in order to remove obstacles, facilitate improvements, and obtain authentic results from their policies. It should also provide the financial supports necessary to reinforce our commitment to public schooling, especially for disadvantaged students from impoverished areas. It has done so before, and that, after all, is the original intent of Title I funding (ESEA, 1965). Federal education policy can exert its guiding and supportive role in public education, informed and confident in its financial and human resource investment in our institutions necessary to do the job of educating all of our youth for the challenges of a global, technologically advancing, modern society.

REFERENCES

Amrein, A. T., & Berliner, D. C. (2003). The effects of high stakes testing on student motivation and learning. *Educational Leadership, 60*(5), 32–38.

Bracey, G. W. (2005, June). No Child Left Behind: Where does the money go? *Education Policy Research Unit.* Tempe: Arizona State University.

Cosden, M., Morrison, G., Gutierrez, L., & Brown, M. (2004). The effects of homework programs and after-school activities on school success. *Theory Into Practice, 43*(3), 220–226.

Darling-Hammond, L. (2004). Standards, accountability, and school reform. *Teachers College Record, 106*(6), 1047–1985.

Elementary and Secondary Education Act. (1965). Washington, DC: United States Department of Education. Available at: http://www.ed.gov/policy/elsec.

Fowler, F. C. (2000). *Policy studies for educational leaders: An introduction.* New York: Merrill.

Haney, W. (2000). The myth of the Texas miracle in education. *Education Analysis Policy Archives, 8*(41). [Online]. Available: http://epaa.asu.edu/epaa/v8n41

Heck, R. H. (2004). *Studying educational and social policy: Theoretical concepts and research methods.* Mahwah, NJ: Lawrence Earlbaum Associates.

Keller, J. M. (1987). Strategies for stimulating the motivation to learn. *Performance and Instruction Journal,* 1–7.

National Education Association. (2006a). *Nine changes help NCLB but more needs to be done.* [Online]. Available: http://www.nea.org/esea/rules-changes.html

National Education Association. (2006b). *NEA: No Child Left Behind policy position statement.* [Online]. Available: http://www.nea.org/esea/policy.html

Newman, F. M., King, M. B., & Rigdon, M. (1997). Accountability and school performance: Implications from restructuring schools. *Harvard Educational Review, 67*(1), 41–67.

Northwest Regional Educational Laboratory. (2004, February). *Evaluating supplemental educational service providers: Issues and challenges.* Portland, OR: NWREL Office of Planning and Service Coordination.

Oravitz, J. V., (1993). *Understanding school finance: A basic guide for Pennsylvania school directors.* Harrisburg: Pennsylvania School Boards Association.

Pennsylvania Department of Education. (2005a). *Academic achievement report 2004–05.*[Online]. Available: http://www.paayp.com/

Pennsylvania Department of Education. (2005b). *Supplemental Educational Services. Main resource page.* [Online]. Available: http://www.pde.state.pa.us/nclb/cwp/view.asp?a=3&Q=82596&nclbNav=|6375|&nclbNav=|

Pennsylvania Department of Education. (2005c). *Supplemental Educational Services: PA schools, districts, and providers toolkit.*[Online]. Available: http://www.pde.state.pa.us/nclb/lib/nclb/PA_Toolkit.doc

Pennsylvania School Boards Association. (2001). *Understanding school finance: Federal funding.* Mechanicsburg, PA: PSBA.

Peterson, K. (2006, Feb. 6). *Bush budget cuts education.* Stateline.org [Online]. Available: http://www.stateline.org/live/ViewPage.action?siteNodeId=136&languageId=1&contentId=86486.

Roderick, M., & Engel, M. (2001). The grasshopper and the ant: Motivational responses of low-achieving students to high stakes testing. *Educational Evaluation and Policy Analysis, 23*(3), 197–227.

Saulny, S. (2006, February 12). Tutor program offered by law is going unused. *The New York Times.*

Schwartzbeck, T. D. (2005, May). *Understanding Supplemental Education Services.* American Association of School Administrators. [Online]. Available: www.aasa.org

Sunderman, G. L., & Kim, J. (February 2004). *Increasing bureaucracy or increasing opportunities? School district experience with Supplemental Educational Services.* Cambridge, MA: The Civil Rights Project at Harvard University.

Sweetland, S. R., & Hoy, W. K. (2000, December). School characteristics and educationaloutcomes: Toward an organizational model of student achievement in middle schools. *Education Administration Quarterly, 36*(5), 703–729.

United States Department of Education. (2006a). *Elementary and Secondary Education Act.* Washington, DC: USDE. [Online]. Available: http://www.ed.gov/about/offices/list/oese/index.html

United States Department of Education. (2006b). *The No Child Left Behind Act of 2001.*Washington, DC: USDE. [Online]. Available: http://www.ed.gov/admins/lead/account/nclbreference/index.html?src=rt

United States Government Accountability Office. (August 2006). *No Child Left Behind Act: Education Actions Needed to Improve Local Implementation and State Evaluation of Supplemental Educational Services.* Washington, DC: GAO.

Urdan, T. C., & Paris, S.G. (1994). Teachers' perceptions of standardized achievement test. *Educational Policy, 8,* 137–156.

Wang, M., Haertel, G., & Walberg, H. (1993). What helps students learn? *Educational Leadership,* 74–79.

Winch, C. & Gongell, J. (2004). *Philosophy and educational policy: A critical introduction.* New York: Routledge Falmer.

CHAPTER 12

ALTERNATIVE CERTIFICATION

Does It Lend Itself as a Form of Viable Policy to Be Included as a Factor in Teacher Preparation and Certification?

Debra Johnson

INTRODUCTION

The process of obtaining a teacher certification in most states has only one focus, meaning that the method, which includes coursework taken at a college or university, a teaching practicum and the passing of a national or state teacher's exam or both, is believed to be the one best way for obtaining a teaching certification. The practice of teacher certification encompasses values that the education community believes and accepts (http://www.teaching.state.pa.us/teaching/cwp/view, 2004). Policy pertaining to what makes a teacher a professional educator includes a teacher's knowledge base as to how a teacher was prepared, the conduct and performance of a teacher, and how a teacher is considered competent.

Policy, Leadership, and Student Achievement, pages 183–206
Copyright © 2008 by Information Age Publishing
183

These elements are encompassed in the act of traditional teacher certification. These elements are also encompassed in the act of alternative teacher certification. Alternative certification for teachers is not new. The actual certification itself is based on programs, study, and experience, as defined by individual states. Obtaining an alternative certification may or may not involve passing the Praxis series exam, formerly the National Teacher Exam (NTE), and may or may not involve institutions of higher education (Hawley, 1990). In some states, the alternative license converts to a regular teacher's certification within two years ("Who should be a teacher?," *Denver Rocky Mountain News*, 1999 January 18, p. 49A, editorial). From the early 1970s through the present, alternative teacher certification as it relates to the preparation of teaching staff has been regarded with both disdain and hope. By 1997, 41 states including the District of Columbia had instituted alternative teacher certification programs for individuals who hold degrees and want to teach (Feistritzer, 1998). Various states reported 117 additional alternative certification programs sponsored by colleges and universities (Bradshaw, 1998). Out of the 117, 30 alternative certification programs have renewal requirements for university course work that could lead toward a full certification (McKibbin, 1988). Thirty-seven states have alternative certification programs in which districts hire uncertified teachers who then undergo on-the-job training (Jelmberg, 1996).

American society has its foundation in the four societal values of equity, efficiency, efficacy (liberty), and excellence (Sergiovanni et al., 1992; Bierlein, 1995). It is from these values that policy processes and products are formed, interpreted, and applied (Bierlein, 1995). Dvora Yanow (2000) further explains that to find what various policies mean, one must first understand that the promises and implications are not easily seen, nor is the language necessarily clear when it comes down to policies. According to Michael Fullan (1999), the policy process is not linear even though it appears to be so on paper. Therefore, conclusions are most likely reached with the same material; however, they are interpreted differently.

There are different interpretations of the term "alternative teacher certification" (Feistritzer, 2001); people interpret meanings that are created by others (Yanow, 1996). The types of people who come through an alternative route have the tendency to be older, people of color, male, and have degrees in other areas and experiences in other occupations. However, experts claim that those who have not gone through a teacher preparation program in a college or university approved by a state's Department of Education are not qualified to teach. These criticisms are mostly due to the lack of a clear-cut definition as to what alternative certification actually is, faulty data, and bias (Feistritzer, 2001).

According to Anne Lockwood (2002), there are two distinct interpretations that concern teacher education practice and preparation relating to professional teaching standards and the teacher certification process. There are individuals with a traditional point of view who believe that how a teacher is prepared to teach, pertaining to qualifications, is closely linked to teacher education programs offered and standards set by colleges and universities. However, those individuals, referred to as nontraditionalists, believe that alternative certification could open new paths to the teaching profession without the coursework in education, thus accommodating more of those with baccalaureate degrees in other subjects.

Stoddart and Floden (1995) explain that candidates who enter teaching by way of alternative routes may have gone through programs that placed different emphases on preparation on subject matter, pedagogical knowledge, and the role of personal experience in learning to teach. Thus, when traveling different routes of becoming certified there is likely to be teachers with different levels of competency. There are tensions concerning the overall concept of alternative certification. Linda Darling-Hammond (1990) informs us that from policy issues, there is a possibility of underlying political agendas. These agendas are often unspoken yet inclusive within the statements and actions of the proponents of a particular agenda as well as the opponents. The aspect of credentialing takes on an integral role within various contentions and apprehensions as to the validity of a certification obtained by alternative means and its influence on professional standards for teachers in the field, including the teacher certification process.

In essence, alternative certification is difficult to define (Travers, 2004). The problem is—and why policy is so different from state to state in regard to alternative certification—that different definitions describe the same concept. According to Willis D. Hawley, alternative certification is alternative licensure. It provides a means for a person who has a degree in a subject other than in education to become the teacher of record (Hawley, 1990). Another definition is that alternative certification is a term used for nontraditional avenues leading to teacher licensure. A more complete definition is that policies in relation to alternative certification describe it as involving innovative programs put into practice in order to bring quality individuals into the teaching profession. These individuals have at least a baccalaureate degree, a core body of knowledge in a particular subject, and practical life experiences that they bring to the profession without going through traditional teacher preparation (Travers, 2004; Cook, 2002; Mayesky, 1989). Therefore, we find policies, which govern this type of teacher certification, address this issue as programs that are very similar to traditional programs in form and discipline. However, there are still policies that address alternative certification as not being a real certification.

CHANGES IN EDUCATIONAL REFORM THAT LED
TO ALTERNATIVE CERTIFICATION

In the United States, alternative certification was originally introduced as a component of educational reform in the Higher Education Act of 1965 (Public Law 89-329, Sec. 102 & Sec. 501). As the act was written, alternative certification was alluded to as a community service program to assist in solutions to community problems in urban, rural, and suburban areas.

> For the purposes of this title, the term "community service program" means an educational program, activity, or service, including a research program and a university, extension, or continuing education offering, which is designed to assist in the solution of community problems in rural, urban, or suburban areas, with particular emphasis on urban and suburban problems, where the institution offering such a program, activity, or service determines (1) that the proposed program, activity, or service is not otherwise available and (2) that the conduct of the program or performance of activity or service is consistent with the institution's overall educational program and is of such a nature as is appropriate competencies of its faculty. (Public Law 89-329, Sec. 102)

> The Commissioner shall establish an Office of Education and Advisory Council on Quality Teacher Preparation for the purpose of reviewing the administration and operation of the programs carried out under this title and of all other Federal programs for complementary purposes. This review shall pay particular attention to the effectiveness of these programs in attracting, preparing, and retaining highly qualified elementary and secondary school teachers, and it shall include recommendations for the improvement of these programs. (Public Law 89-329, Sec. 501)

STUDIES ABOUT ALTERNATIVE CERTIFICATION

Concerning research on alternative certification, the concept of professional standards for teachers emerges through the research of Michael Fullan and Andy Hargreaves (1992), whose frameworks look at how the professionalization of education relies partly on willingness and how much freedom individuals have in order to develop professionally and personally. Research on professional standards and how they influence the teacher certification process also has its basis in the work of Christopher Lucas (1997), who takes the historical path of explaining how particular professional standards came to pass and how some still stand in the present.

According to Willis Hawley (1990), there are limitations to research on alternative teacher certification programs, and therefore to how they can influence educational policy in the field. A small number of studies have attempted to compare traditional programs to alternative programs; however, the samples were very small and the findings have been limited.

John Miller, Michael McKenna, and Beverly McKenna's (1998) study compared alternatively prepared teachers with those who had been traditionally prepared. In this study, the effectiveness of an alternative certification program for middle grade teachers at a southeastern university was investigated, since the researchers wanted to answer questions about the strengths and weaknesses of the program. The results were interesting in that there was an examination of behavioral differences in teachers in relation to training differences. Some of the findings were that certification programs did not affect a teacher's performance after the individual was working and there was mentoring support for the initial year.

In a study written by Naomi Schaefer (1999) for the Thomas B. Fordham Foundation, comparisons between alternative certification and traditional certification were outlined. This study makes a point concerning alternative certification and elementary education: alternative certification for individuals interested in elementary education is not generally a choice for those interested in certification. Schaefer (1999) elaborated with the following three reasons for this phenomenon. The first pertained to the knowledge of pedagogy (instructional skills), which she stated is considered to be even more important at the elementary level than at the secondary level. Second, specialized academic expertise seems to matter less because a wide range of subjects are taught, all at a lower level. Last, teacher shortages are not comprehensive at elementary level, so there is less incentive for a state to allow candidates to bypass traditional requirements.

As far as making judgments on how effective alternative teacher certification programs are, Hawley outlines various criteria for assessing their practicality and credibility. Issues remain as to whether or not alternative teacher certification credentials can reduce emergency certificates. Temporary and emergency certificates serve as a present strategy for building a pool of teachers. From a philosophical point of view, Hawley also explains that the justification for alternative certification also reflects on traditional certification. What he means here is that alternative certification has the ability to attract individuals who are academically able in traditional academic subjects such as math, science, and history. Hawley contends that because these individuals are academically able, they are also able to convey the subject matter in a classroom. He also expresses beliefs that pre-service preparations in traditional teacher certification programs essentially go beyond what is actually required in order to teach in the field.

Hawley raises more points in his research as to why people pursue alternative teacher certification. One issue concerns the aspect of altruism within the system of education reform, as in whether those who pursue an alternative certification see themselves as rescuers within the system.

From these concerns, we can see different needs mixed with different expectations. Linda Darling-Hammond (1990) and Karen Zumwalt (1991) take up points of dispute concerning how alternative teacher certification influences professional teaching standards and disagree with Hawley on the point that if people know a subject very well, they also can convey it in a classroom. According to Darling-Hammond (1990), the preparation in education coursework has a profound influence on how a teacher performs in the classroom and pedagogical knowledge is the foundation for the professionalization of the field of education. Darling-Hammond goes on to say that there is a direct positive relationship between the influence of education coursework on a teacher and how that teacher performs in the classroom. Thus, the individual is able to apply various teaching strategies in order to reach a wider range of student levels of understanding in a given subject.

Zumwalt is in agreement with Darling-Hammond, but from a different perspective based on possible policy implications of alternative teacher certification versus traditional or college-based teacher certification. Zumwalt writes that both types of certification are quality-driven. However, in order for both to be enhanced, there must be a realization that there is not one best way to prepare a teacher for the classroom. Even though there are well-known alternative credential programs for teachers who do not have degrees in education, but major assumptions are generated by the argument pertaining to the level of professionalism. One of the assumptions has to do with addressing how alternative certification programs measure alongside more traditional teacher credential programs. Another assumption deals with addressing how policy contributes to increasing teaching excellence or keeps the status quo concerning teacher preparation.

POLICY: THE VALIDATION OF A CERTIFICATION

When hiring an individual, administrators must consider the relationship of a person's certification to other school activities or the possibility of teaching other grade levels or both. This point raises concerns as to what makes a teaching certification a certification that has a standard of professionalism.

In the state rules and regulations for private schools, requirements are expressed in the following general, though explicit, terms in section 22PA Code 51.34 and 24PA Cons. Stat. S 13-1327(b).

> Only teachers holding a valid Pennsylvania professional certificate under Chapter 49 (relating to professional personnel), a private academic teaching certificate, or a private academic temporary approval certificate may teach in a licensed private school.

When this section of the document is read in conjunction with Article XII of the Public School Code of 1949, there is clarity with respect to those who are seeking employment in private academic schools; they have more avenues of becoming certified than indicated in the rules and regulations for public schools.

Dissenting reaction to the rules and regulations in Title 22 was based upon responses from public comment concerning alternative means of becoming certified. The response was considerable regarding permitting equivalent education and experience to take the place of formal teacher preparation and policies of an alternative program for entry into the teaching profession. Because of the dissenting comments, 49.13(b)(12) was formally removed. The fear was that the proposed policy would have allowed the Secretary of Education to have the responsibility of establishing levels of equivalencies and experience for all areas requiring a certification. Therefore, the language of the policy reflected changes in the requirement policies of all areas concerning certification.

The opinions of commentators, legislators, and the Independent Regulatory Review Commission (IRRC) gave statements that the equivalencies were questionable based upon the current statutes in teacher certification law. Therefore, opposition to the equivalencies (they did not mention experience) was based on the following reasons:

- The equivalencies undermine the teaching profession.
- The belief that the equivalencies undermine other revisions that are being proposed for strengthening the criteria for entry into the teaching profession.
- There was no justification as far as need due to the projections for the number of certified teachers (p. 2).

The goal was to encourage institutions to develop programs for the purpose of attracting individuals who initially did not decide on education as careers. The vision was that as an experimental program, it would provide avenues to certify those prospective teachers who might not meet course requirements in educational methods or pedagogy but had academic preparation and experience either in industry or in a specialized area. Therefore, the linkages of the subject matter referred to in section 49.15, as well as indications of the methods used in order to communicate the subject matter, link to what a teacher needs to know in order to teach a subject to students.

Policy is not translated directly into action (Mills & Hyle, 2001; Yanow, 1996; Smith, 1973). Van Meter and Van Horn (1975) give a very clear explanation of how a policy is implemented and thus influences other factors. They spell out that implementation consists of actions by an individual or groups of individuals whose focus is to achieve objectives set forth by an existing policy decision. The purpose of implementation is to transform those objectives set forth by a policy decision into systems for operating as well as making an effort to achieve small and large changes, which are also set forth by policy decisions.

Dvora Yanow (1996) explains that there is the possibility of having "gaps" between the intent of a policy and what actually happens when it is in motion. The reasons she gives for this may include vagueness of language and lack of incentive to induce cooperation from different parties involved with the policy at various levels. The reasons may also include poor organization on the part of the parties involved in the implementation process and the lack of, or a blockage in, the communication network between important parties at different levels and possibly between different demographic areas. In the context of education, the influence of policy either indirectly or intangibly affects individuals. How a policy is implemented also bears on how and what it influences in practice. When it concerns the professionalization of teaching, policy influence is an attempt to change the present system of how teachers are prepared in form (methods) and content (subject matter) (Hargreaves, 1994).

CREDENTIALING: CERTIFICATION OR LICENSURE

According to Dvora Yanow (1996), a certification is an artifact or a symbol of competency. Therefore, it carries with it a level of value, significance, and respect. A policy can convey many varied meanings to us in ways it is worded, how it is presented, and to whom the policy is presented. Therefore, individuals and groups may interpret the same symbol differently or place a different value on various aspects that revolve around that symbol (Yanow, 1996). Within the context of credentialing, there is a need to be clear about what constitutes a certification or a license. In the state of Pennsylvania, for example, to be a certified teacher means that an individual has met the minimum standards or requirements to be able to teach in public schools. Clarification of the terms licensure and certification is needed within the context of this discussion, because they are two subtly different frames of thought.

In the state of Pennsylvania, the terms license, certificate, and certification are sometimes used synonymously, which can lead to the belief they have the same meaning and can be used interchangeably. This can lead to different interpretations as to who is or is not certified or certifiable.

Gary Fenstermacher (1990) explains the difference between licensure and certification. He states that licensure is a function of a state acting on its authority to protect and promote the general welfare of those who depend on public education. He does not include information concerning those teaching in private schools. Fenstermacher adds that the act of certification is the function of the profession itself acting to acknowledge those with advanced capabilities. As far as alternative certification, Fenstermacher contends that having this type of certification is the same as having a license, because, in most cases, it is awarded at the beginning of a person's teaching career.

Traditionally, certification is the process by which a person goes through four years of course work at an institution of higher learning and pass the Praxis series exams, formerly the National Teachers Examination (NTE). Within this framework of teacher preparation, the state also requires participation in a supervised practicum or internship before recognizing a person as qualified to become a teacher. (http://www.edweek.org/context/glossary/tecertif.htm, 2000).

Historically, the design of the traditional route toward a teaching degree and eventual certification included graduating from teacher preparation programs that were primarily for undergraduate education majors (Feistritzer, 2001). The emphasis in traditional teacher preparation programs was placed on college course work, participating in a practicum or an internship, and passing a national exam in addition to probable exams required by a particular school district or school.

THE PURPOSE FOR TEACHER CERTIFICATION

Historical, cultural, and political perspectives influence educational policies (Sergiovanni et al., 1992). Because the field of education is value-laden, it, in turn, reflects the perceptions and beliefs of individuals and organizations that have strong opinions as to the definition of a teacher and how a person becomes a teacher. Within the context of educational history, the appropriate way to attempt to examine the purpose for teacher certification is to discuss how college-based or traditional certification programs compare to state-sponsored alternative programs. In these two areas, research takes a significant role.

Some of the setbacks that Hawley acknowledges concerning the research involving alternative certification have been focused on education theory as it relates to educational practice. He points out that theory is the vehicle that motivates practice, which, in turn, affects the implementation and influence of educational policies.

Hawley maintains that there are six primary weaknesses in the research concerning alternative certification. The first is that comparisons of teachers with alternative certifications from a given school district or a particular demographic area were not made with teachers possessing traditional certifications from the same school district or demographic area. Usually, comparisons of individuals with alternative teacher certification statewide or nationally are taken from another jurisdiction that has a very different type of population from the school district being studied.

A second point suggests that alternatively certified teachers usually have higher test scores, grade point averages, and solid knowledge of their chosen subject matter; however, these criteria are used more as a way to screen out applicants. Therefore, we can surmise that different requirements for entry into alternative certification programs result in different kinds of applicants. This could justify the possibility for tougher admission standards for alternative certification and traditional certification.

The criteria for measuring performance are the third factors limiting the research. Hawley explains that measurement of teaching performance and conduct is often administered by the principals of particular schools where alternative certification candidates have been assigned. He stresses that data records from these measures may contain bias. The reason for this bias is likely due to the principals at these particular schools having a stake in seeing alternative certification teachers succeed. Another area of bias is due to the principals' setting aside resources and devoting mentoring support for this very purpose. When it comes to mentoring, the individuals who mentor are also involved in the evaluation of the candidates. Therefore, when teachers with alternative certifications and teachers with traditional certifications are evaluated, there is a possibility for more non-objectivity due to possible value judgments the mentors may have in regard to both types of certifications.

The fourth factor as a cause for limited research or unreliable research is the focus on the assessment of low-level procedural skills when comparing the two types of certification (traditional and alternative) using state requirements. State requirements nationally, are varied for traditional and alternative teacher certification. A fifth factor is that the completed studies involved very small numbers of people; therefore, questions arise as to the validity of these studies. This, in turn, leads to a sixth factor, which is whether these studies really reflect actual alternative certifications from actual programs or simply different models for teacher preparation.

As for making judgments on how effective alternative certification programs are, Hawley outlines various criteria for assessing their effectiveness. Issues remain as to whether alternative certifications can reduce the issuance of temporary or emergency certificates. Temporary and emergency certificates serve as a present strategy for building a pool of teachers. This is just one of the assessment factors that Hawley believes is possible. In Pennsylvania, the state education authority views an emergency certificate, which is a form of alternative certification, as temporary until an individual reaches the point to qualify for an Instructional I Certificate. According to reports from the National Center for Alternative Certification (NCAC), in 2000, the state of Pennsylvania issued 3,045 emergency certificates and awarded 296 certificates to individuals who have gone through alternative routes (http://www.teach-now.org, 2004).

Hawley concurs with Darling-Hammond (1990) and Zumwalt (1991) that wide variations in alternative certification programs are primarily due to the curricula and mentoring support. It is because of these two components that designers of these programs need to be more cautious about equating background in a given discipline with the type of employment; this also includes additional up-to-date knowledge.

Additional study of the subject matter of teachers who have an alternative certification is also necessary. In order to do this, there is a possibility that research could be conducted on more selective alternative certification programs compared to more selective traditional certification programs. Teachers and administrators make assessments of performance and conduct as they occur in the context of teaching. Within the context of professional teaching is how policies can influence levels of professional teaching standards. More contentions arise as to whether alternative certification programs can ascertain if a person will be a good teacher and whether or not alternative certification programs can institute more effective mechanisms for screening out prospective individuals for the teaching profession than traditional certification programs.

Hawley raises more points in his writings as to why people pursue alternative certification. One issue concerns the aspect of altruism within the system of education reform, as to whether those who pursue an alternative certification see themselves as rescuers within the system. From these concerns, we can see different needs mixed with different expectations. Traditional certification teachers receive instruction on how to apply different teaching strategies. One perspective of teachers with traditional certifications is the point of view that they are more responsive to students' needs and more capable of working through misunderstandings when it comes to subject matter (Darling-Hammond, 1990). Therefore, there is a need for research to look further into what types of courses alternative certification teachers are taught within their programs compared to traditional certification teachers. The purpose of this would be to see what strategies would be effective in helping the alternative certification teacher bring forth the subject matter on the level that the student can understand.

Therefore, the purpose for a teacher certification lies in how traditional and alternative programs view what is needed for a teacher to enter the classroom. The purpose of research in these circumstances is to bring any bias to light based on types of certification.

POLICY AND STANDARDS—INTERPRETATIONS
OF ACTION PLANS AND PROFESSIONAL STANDARDS
FOR TEACHER PREPARATION

Throughout American history teachers have had very limited and sporadic success in achieving position and status that other professional groups take pride in having (Profy, 1992). Therefore, tensions that have evolved and still help to shape educational reform and policy extend from how teachers received preparation in the past and how they are currently being prepared for the classroom.

Prior to explaining or illustrating a concept of professional standards, there is a need to establish definitions as to what it means to be a professional, and what the terms professionalism and professionalization mean. According to Robin Barrow and Geoffrey Milburn (1990), the general terminology of what constitutes a professional when applied in the field of education is primarily used to distinguish certain forms of conduct and attitudes from others. It is also used to distinguish some fields of study from others based upon the competencies in those other fields and the activities that a person engages in order to acquire them (Ginsburg, 1988).

In defining professionalism in such a way that it could be applied to the overall field of education, Fromberg (1997) presents six characteristics that separate a profession form an occupation (craft) or amateur practice. When examining how policy relates to the professionalization of a field, it is important to se how the term "profession" is defined.

> A profession, as distinct from an occupation or amateur practice, connotes six distinct characteristics: (1) ethical performance that is fair and disinterested; (2) a high level of expertise and skill that "must be essential to the functioning of a society, suggesting that the absence of its knowledge and techniques would weaken the society in some areas" (Katz, 1987, p. 3); (3) a body of knowledge and skills that laypeople do not possess (Wise & Liebbrand, 1993, p. 135); (4) considerable autonomy in its practice and control of entry into the profession; (5) commensurate compensation; and (6) a professional organization. (p. 190)

Much of the controversy surrounding alternative teacher certification pertains to the policies that govern this type of certification, their programs, their criteria for awarding alternative certification, and their effect on professional teaching standards. Discussions concerning teacher certification and its importance within the structure of professional teaching standards have been going on for the last 30 years (Augus, 2001).

Various strategies instituted from policies evolve from the concepts of what counts as professionalism and what is considered craftsmanship, which in turn connect to alternative teacher certification. After understanding what counts as being a professional and what is considered craftsmanship, then other policy areas relating to how a certification influences other matters—such as teacher performance and conduct, the type of training received from an institution or through a professional organization, pedagogical knowledge, and state monitoring of institutions of higher education—can be further examined.

In 1987, L. S. Shulman stated that the present knowledge base for teaching does not indicate what a teacher should know and be able to do. In order to integrate a knowledge base into what students need and how teachers are to meet the other demands that may arise in the classroom, Shulman presented the following elements of teaching knowledge, which he classified as establishing the criteria for meeting professional teaching standards.

The Criteria for Meeting Professional Teaching Standards

- Content knowledge.
- General pedagogical knowledge, including principles and strategies for classroom organization and management.
- Curriculum knowledge, including materials and programs.
- Pedagogical content knowledge, an amalgam of content and pedagogy that is a teacher's form of professional understanding.
- Knowledge of learners and their characteristics.
- Knowledge of education contexts, including the characteristics of classrooms, schools, communities, and cultures.
- Knowledge of educational ends, purposes, and values and their philosophical and historical grounds (Shulman, 1987, p. 8).

Included in the professional standards concerning alternative teacher certification are the standards of competency pertaining to teacher performance and conduct. According to Laczko-Kerr and Berliner (2003), these are the elements where teachers apply their beliefs and values regarding what should take place in the educational environment in light of student learning.

Standards of Competency

- Should act on the belief that all students can learn.
- Should have deep subject-matter knowledge about the subject and structure of their disciplines.
- Need to manage and monitor students, identify learning goals, and choose from teaching styles to meet those goals.

- Need to be reflective about their teaching and evaluate their decisions and experiences to make adjustments in their teaching.
- Must be a part of a larger community consisting of school staff, parents, and broader nonparent community coordination (Shulman, 1987, p. 8).

Rossi and Shlay (1982) and Smith (1973) recommend modifying research to give more attention to malleable or dependent variables. In the case of Pennsylvania, policy research could reflect more descriptions of the types of individuals who apply for alternative certification, taking into account their experience, education, and what aspects of alternative certification are attractive to them. To see how a policy affects a community, individual school environments in rural/small town, suburban, and urban communities should be examined and described. An examination of how various school districts, school boards, principals, and directors implement the policies of alternative certification as they apply to professional teaching standards needs to take place.

To cite examples in reference to the state of Pennsylvania's alternative certification educational policies, large portions of past and current research essentially focus on three aspects concerning alternative certification. One aspect is that the research essentially concentrates on how individuals navigate through the requirements in order to obtain an alternative certification as outlined by the state. The second aspect is that opponents and proponents of alternative certification generally make comparisons with traditional certification. The third aspect is that there is such a concentration of legal issues on various matters brought forth by opponents and proponents that discussion of how individuals fare in the actual education environments is lost.

LEGISLATIVE AND EDUCATIONAL HISTORY

Historical, cultural, and political perspectives influence educational policies (Sergiovanni et al., 1992). Because the field of education is value-laden, it, in turn, reflects the perceptions and beliefs of individuals and organizations that have strong opinions as to the definition of a teacher and how a person becomes a teacher.

The term professionalism leads the way to reflect on the literature of teacher education reform and educational practice. Christopher Lucas (1997) explains that different historical traditions shape present thinking concerning teacher preparation. He begins with the premise that even though teachers are not merely salaried employees in American society, there are points of view that teachers are not true professionals. Lucas explains that the foundation for this type of reasoning lies in history.

Based upon the legislative and educational history of alternative certification in the state of Pennsylvania, six policy areas emerge. These areas relate to: (1) professionalism; (2) teacher performance and conduct; (3) pedagogical knowledge; (4) type of institution, agency, or professional organization from which an individual received professional instruction; (5) performance on a teacher's exam, as well as an internship or a teaching practicum; and (6) the extent to which the state of Pennsylvania monitors institutions of higher education, accrediting agencies, and other alternative teacher certification programs that credential teachers in early education in private as well as public educational environments.

Up until the middle of the 1800s, the notion that teachers even needed formal education was considered out of the question. During that time, America was becoming more industrialized, and trades and occupations pertaining largely to agriculture were thought to be more important to pursue.

Primary education, especially during the 17th and 18th centuries, was mostly a private undertaking by housewives, widows, and spinsters who for the most part had very little education and earned income through charging a minimal tuition and working out of their kitchens. All they needed was an acquaintance with the common subjects. In essence, teaching was viewed as a part-time occupation for obtaining supplemental income (Lucas, 1997; Profy, 1992).

In South Carolina and Virginia, private ventures known as field schools received funding from plantation owners to provide some education for their children and sometimes other local children. In the North, the state of Massachusetts is an early example of a state that was committed to maintaining publicly supported schools since the 1640s; even so, during 1642–1689, primary or lower school instructors were not viewed as professional. There were no professional organizations and no standards for preparation (Butts & Cremin, 1953). In rural Pennsylvania, for example, the expectation of a schoolmaster was merely to teach reading, writing, and arithmetic (Butts & Cremin, 1953).

The term professionalization is a relatively new term and implies a considerable amount of freedom for individuals to pursue personal and professional development (Hickcox, 1996). Professionalization also extends to various discussions, study, and experimentation in the field of education. Throughout American history teachers have had very limited and sporadic success in achieving position and status that other professional groups take pride in having (Profy, 1992). Therefore, tensions that have evolved and still help to shape educational reform extend from how teachers received preparation in the past and how they are currently being prepared for the classroom.

Linda Darling-Hammond, Arthur Wise, and Steven Klein (1995), present the legal aspects of teacher licensing by defining what teachers should know and be able to do. This was after the National Council for Accreditation for Teacher Education released results from an opinion poll, which stated that most members of the public continue to think that professional training requirements for teachers are weaker than requirements for other professions.

Descriptions of past and current teacher education policies explain that the type of education an individual receives while attending a college or university results in traditional teaching credentials. The belief is that traditional credentials reflect more structure in the teaching (course work) and practice (methods) components that authorities view as needed to upgrade the status and quality of teacher performance (Hawley, 1990). On the other hand, there are also scholars who believe alternative teacher certification applies more to the concept of "craft," which in turn pays close attention to the uniqueness of teacher performance (Porter, 1981). Therefore, there is a need to be able to make professional decisions to the extent that policy will dictate while keeping in mind the professional weight of an individual's credentials.

Historically, the design of the traditional route toward a teaching degree and eventual certification included graduating from teacher preparation programs that were primarily for undergraduate education majors (Feistritzer, 2001). The emphasis in traditional teacher preparation programs was placed on college course work, participating in a practicum or an internship, and passing a national exam in addition to probable exams required by a particular school district or school.

In examining the mission and goals of teacher credentials in the context of legislative and educational history, the appropriate way is to discuss how college-based or traditional teacher certification programs compare to state-sponsored alternative teacher certification programs. In these two areas, research occupies a significant role.

Policymakers in various states felt there was a need for alternative teacher certification for primarily four reasons: (1) Demographics—shortages in areas (rural and urban), (2) Demographics—Colleges of education—the makeup of the population going into teaching is changing, (3) Demographics— attract highly competent people who hold at least a bachelor's degree most likely with a major in the subject matter to be taught, (4) Demographics— attract more minority candidates.

Naomi Schaefer (1999) discusses in one of her studies that alternative means of certification as another path for obtaining a teacher certification have raised the bar and helped to move forward careers for teachers. Policies that govern alternative teacher preparation and certification have provided opportunities for those who have a desire to teach (Feistritzer,

1998). Therefore, alternative certification gives attention to increasing opportunities in the educational profession as it pertains to the act of teaching (Johnson, 2005).

Policy at the federal, state, and local governing levels and accrediting agencies is a force in educational reform (Hall & Loucks, 1981). Where it concerns teacher education, and professional development, policy supports regulation in the field by identifying stipulations for meeting designated requirements and awarding credentials for meeting those requirements in order to teach. In most states, teacher certification is described in general terms when applied to school law. These descriptions pertain to what is involved concerning the act of certification (Heddinger & Russell, 1983). In other words, it is the law that all public school teachers are required to have a certification. It is also the law that a person must have a baccalaureate degree to meet the minimum requirements for teacher certification. However, the acts of obtaining a certification consist of policies, not laws. Policies are more explicit, unlike laws or statutes, which are worded in general terms as to how and where to put the act of certification into practice (Fowler, 2000). Policies explain the how by outlining the certification rules, regulations, and guidelines (Fowler, 2000).

The No Child Left Behind Act of 2001 as a federal initiative has directly influenced the number of individuals currently seeking alternative certification. State departments of education and legislatures began reviewing laws and policies that regulate teacher education programs, licensure, initial certification, and recertification of teachers (Ruhland & Bremer, 2003). At the present time, the act states that individuals who participate in alternative certification programs who hold at least a baccalaureate degree, pass a state test demonstrating subject knowledge, or demonstrate specific skills, would be considered to be highly qualified.

Theoretical Frame

Theoretical frames in regard to policy have evolved by conducting research. Six policy themes emerged from the literature: (1) professionalism; (2) teacher performance and conduct; (3) pedagogical knowledge or core body of knowledge; (4) type of educational institution, agency, or professional organization from which an individual has received training; (5) an individual's performance on a national teacher's exam, as well as completion of an internship or a teaching practicum; and (6) the extent to which a state monitors institutions of higher education, accrediting agencies, and other teacher programs that credential teachers in early education.

The analysis of each area includes an examination through the lenses of four change components and four elements. The theoretical frame for examining these change components and elements has its base in the research of T. B. Smith (1973) and D. S. Van Meter and C. E. Van Horn (1975). J. A. Maxwell explains, "The most productive ways of constructing a conceptual context are often those that integrate different approaches, lines of investigation, or theories that no one had previously connected" (Maxwell, 1996, p. 26).

T. B. Smith identifies four sources of tensions, which represent the change components. In education, these components are the policy itself; the organization of an institution; the target group, which for this study are early educators and educational environments, such as the culture of a school; and where the school is located, whether rural/small town, suburban, or urban area. The identification of these tensions in this study is to show how they function from each policy area.

The four change components represent the point of view that change due to various tensions concerning implementation means new contexts transforming old contexts, but designed to produce changes in patterns of interactions. The four change components in turn influence four elements. The four elements identified in this study are: (1) administration, which include the administration in educational facilities and the school districts; (2) subject matter content knowledge and subject matter methods; (3) teacher quality and effectiveness; and (4) demographics, which include the surrounding communities where the educational facilities are located. These four elements act as catalysts or sounding boards for feedback (Van Meter & Van Horn, 1975).

According to Yanow (1996), "The world as we know it is perceived and understood through theoretical constructs" (p. 15). Within these exchanges of information, the lines of communication represent possible courses of action that can lead to interpretive decision-making that moves beyond the strict regulation of the state.

The act of interpreting a policy can lead to different levels of understanding and opinions. Therefore, model building helps in order to begin to see what a policy means and for whom does it have meaning (Yanow, 2000). The theoretical frame represents exchange patterns of information or a communications theory.

CONCLUSION

What emerges as commentary returns to focus on the mission and goals of teacher certification. It also raises a question for further study: Why are all teacher certifications not created equal? In part, it has much to do with total teacher preparation, mentoring support, and continued professional development. Research has shown us what standards can be formed and where they are implemented in order to meet missions and goals. Standards have also shown us that teachers need to develop throughout their careers; this is to ensure that well-educated teachers are available to all children whether in the suburbs, urban, or rural areas.

Within the educational system of Pennsylvania, there are organizational disagreements concerning teacher certification in general. What this means is that the linkages between the schools, the school districts, the state and higher education institutions are loose. What this indicates is that no one institution has that much control over the other, thus causing the concept of tension within the structure of educational policy. Therefore, what is required for certification and what is expected on the job are not very well connected.

An assertion is that the real problem lies in state regulations that give colleges of education most of the authority on teacher training. It is because of this fact that there is a need to use constant comparisons when referring to alternative certification. The constant comparisons pertain to the various programs that are on the fringe of the teacher certification process in Pennsylvania, such as the Passport to Teaching program and Teach for America. The reason for this is not everyone thinks similarly about certification due to various understandings of what a certification is, and what it symbolizes professionally is construed differently by people in that reality.

Alternative certification is viewed as a fast and inexpensive way for a person to enter the classroom. In the state of Pennsylvania, the main point of dispute involving this type of certification is how best to prepare a teacher for the classroom. How alternative certification is implemented in a school district depends on supply and demand, which means the demand for teachers is quite geographic and subject matter-specific. The tensions that have evolved stems from how teachers received preparation in the past, and how they currently are being prepared for the classroom.

One of the problems with alternative certification in Pennsylvania is that it has not been fully defined in and of itself. For the state of Pennsylvania, it has been defined as an emergency or intern certificate, both of which are provisional. The individual who possesses one of these must eventually navigate through the traditional certification process in order to receive an Instructional I certificate.

There are points of view that teachers who work with young children are thought of as people who are providing a service rather than a professional. Therefore, how and where a person is prepared to become a teacher is stated in policies and is evidenced through the teacher credential process. These points formed the foundation in this study in order to analyze perceptions and beliefs of administrators of primary level educational facilities pertaining to alternative certification.

Concerning those in early education: based upon an indicated number of coursework credits, workshop instruction and practical experience, a person ought to be able to acquire a teaching credential (whether a certificate or a license) that would be legitimate for an indicated number of years. Certification and testing requirements are rarely uniform since each state has its criteria for obtaining a teacher's certification. Pertaining to pedagogical knowledge, the inclusion of the nontraditional teacher in an institution leads to the possible recognition of other types of degrees and credentials. Whether administrators believe other types of degrees and credentials are creditable can lead to increasing opportunities for those who want to teach.

As of 2004, based on reports from the National Center for Alternative Certification (NCAC), the Pennsylvania Department of Education no longer has what one would term an alternative certification program (http://www.teach-now.org, 2004). In 1999, Pennsylvania had an alternative certification program that was classified as a type "D" program. After various revisions in the state's educational policy, it is now classified as a type "I" program, which is a classification that indicates there is no alternative teacher certification being offered in this state (http://www.teach-now.org, 2004). However, the department still has the intern program, still issues emergency certificates, recognizes individuals who have gone through Passport to Teaching and allows school districts to recruit from Teach for America if a school district has the need for more teachers, and still awards an N–3 Certification, which still does not require individuals to take and pass the Praxis series exam. Why the alternative certification program was discontinued in Pennsylvania, reflects on the degree to which the department is unwilling to work with institutions of higher education and what changes are necessary in legislation.

Research needs to continue to develop ways to adequately assess these kinds of programs pertaining to teacher preparation and improve definitions as to what an alternative certification actually is. This is vital in order to cultivate better understanding of this type of certification, so the credentials attained from them will have credibility, and the policymakers in this state will be more inclined to reduce barriers.

RECOMMENDATIONS FOR POLICY

Alternative certification in relation to educational policy in Pennsylvania ought to take the shape of collaboration on different features within the teacher certification possess. Policy collaboration ought to include the Department of Education, the school districts and the schools, the institutions of higher education, and intermediate units that have locations in each county, as well as develop a partnership with the Pennsylvania Department of Public Welfare in order to establish pathways that are more congruent for those who are seeking teacher certification.

There are seven areas recommended that the state of Pennsylvania should view when structuring alternative certification programs. Four of these recommendations have to do with how teachers as well as school administrators are prepared when they are involved with the hiring of teachers or being recruited as a teacher; these areas include having a clear philosophy and design in delivery of instruction, curriculum, and practicum and/or internships. The remaining three points have to do with recruitment and ongoing assessment. Where recruitment is involved, there should be a focus on developing a more diverse pool of teachers to include not only more minorities, but more males, and recruitment should include individuals more sensitive to the needs of all children.

Where continued assessment is involved, there should be a clear path for professional development that includes a system that resists redundancy in the taking of various courses and to have the courses count toward either another degree and/or certification. Included in ongoing assessment, there should be clear program evaluation based on how the teacher actually performs in the field. These assessments should go beyond evaluations that occurred during a student practicum or internship.

REFERENCES

Angus, D. L. (2001). *Professionalism and the public good: A brief history of teacher certification,* J. Mirel (Ed.). Thomas B. Fordham Foundation, National Center for Alternative Certification. Retrieved July 2, 2004 from http://www.teach-now.org.

Barrow, R., & Milburn, G. (1990). *A critical dictionary of educational concepts: An appraisal of selected ideas and issues in education theory and practice.* New York: Harvester-Wheatsheaf.

Bierlien, L. A. (1993). *Controversial issues in educational policy.* Newbury, MA Sage Publications.

Bradshaw, L. (1998). *Policy, politics and contradictions of alternative certification* (ERIC Documentation Reproduction Service No. ED 422 388). Washington, DC.

Butts, R. F., & Cremin, L.A. (1953). *A history of education in American culture.* New York: Holt, Rinehart & Winston.

Capital report: New teacher certification unveiled. (1999, May 5). *Pennsylvania Law Weekly,* p. 9.

Commonwealth of Pennsylvania, State Board of Education. (1984). *Regulations of the state board of education, chapter 49: Certification of professional personnel.* Harrisburg, PA: Department of Education.

Cook, T. M. (2002). The relationship between teacher certification and the use of developmentally appropriate practices in kindergarten classroom in northeast Tennessee (Doctoral dissertation, East Tennessee State University). *Dissertation Abstracts International*, 63/02a, 492.

Darling-Hammond, L. (1990). Teaching and knowledge: Policy issues posed by alternate certification for teachers. *The Peabody Journal of Education, 67*(3), 123–154.

Darling-Hammond, L., Wise, A. E., & Klein, S. P. (1995). *A license to teach: building a profession for 21st century schools.* Boulder, CO: Westview Press.

Feistritzer, C. E. (1998). *Alternative certification: An overview.* Washington, DC: National Center for Education Information. (http://www.ncei.org).

Feistritzer, C. E. (2001). *Alternative routes to teaching.* Washington, DC: National Center for Education Information.

Fenstermacher, G. D. (1990). The place of alternative certification in the education of teachers. *The Peabody Journal of Education, 67*(3), 155–183.

Fowler, F. C. (2000). *Policy studies for educational leaders: An introduction.* Upper Saddle River, NJ: Merrill.

Fromberg, D. P. (1997). The professional and the social status of the early childhood educator. In J. P. Isenberg & M. R. Jalongo (Eds.), *Major trends and issues in early childhood education: Challenges, controversies and insights.* New York: Teachers College Press.

Fullan, M. (1999). *Change forces: The sequel.* Philadelphia: Falmer Press.

Fullan, M., & Hargreaves, A. (1992). *Teacher development and educational change.* New York: Falmer Press.

Ginsburg, M. B. (1988). *Contradictions in teacher education and society: A critical analysis.* Philadelphia: Falmer Press.

Hall, G. F., & Loucks, S.F. (1981). Bridging the gap: Policy research rooted in practice. In A. Lieberman & M. W. McLaughlin (Eds.)., *Policy making in education: Eighty-first yearbook of the national society for the study of education.* Chicago: University of Chicago Press.

Hargreaves, A. (1994). *Changing teachers, changing times: Teacher's work and culture in the postmodern age.* New York: Teacher's College Press.

Hawley, W. D. (1990). The theory and practice of alternative certification: Implications for the improvement of teaching. *The Peabody Journal of Education, 67*(3), 3–34.

Heddinger, F. M., & Russell, S. S. (Ed). (1983). *Pennsylvania school law.* Harrisburg: Pennsylvania School Board Association.

Hickcox, E. (1996). *School administration: Persistent dilemmas in preparation and practice.* Westport, CT: Praeger.

Jelmberg, J. (1996). College-based teacher education versus state- sponsored alternative programs. *Journal of Teacher Education, 47*(1), 60–67.

Johnson, D. L. (2005). Perceptions and beliefs of primary school administrators concerning the influence of alternative certification (Doctoral dissertation, Temple University.) *Dissertation Abstracts International*, 2005-DISS E 2005 J646.

Katz, L. G. (1987). The nature of professions: Where is early childhood education? In L. G. Katz & K. Steiner (Eds.), *Current topics in early childhood education* (Vol. 7, pp. 1–16). Norwood, NJ: Ablex.

Klein, P. S., & Hoogenboom, A. (1980). *A history of Pennsylvania.* University Park: Pennsylvania State University Press.

Kramer, R. (1991). *Ed school follies: The miseducation of America's teachers.* New York: The Free Press.

Laczko-Kerr, I., & Berliner, D. C. (2003). The effectiveness of "Teach for America" and other under-certified teachers on student academic achievement: A case of harmful public policy. *Education Policy Analysis Archives, 10*(37). (2002, 6 September). From http://www.epaa.asu.edu/epaa/v10n37.

Lockwood, A. T. (2002). *Who prepares your teachers? The debate over alternative certification.* Arlington, VA: American Association of School Administrators.

Lucas, C. J. (1997). *Teacher education in America: Reform agendas for the 21st century.* New York: St. Martin's Press.

Maxwell, J. A. (1996). *Qualitative research design: An interactive approach.* Thousand Oaks, CA: Sage.

Mayesky, M. E. (1989). *Innovative teacher certification program for teachers of young children—Duke University.* (ERIC Document Reproduction Service No. ED 319 536). Washington, DC.

McKibbin, M. (1988). Alternative certification programs. *Educational Leadership, 46*(3), 32–35.

Merriam, S. B. (1988). *Case study research in education: A qualitative approach.* San Francisco: Jossey-Bass.

Miller, J. W., McKenna, M. C., & McKenna, B. A. (1998). A comparison of alternatively and traditionally prepared teachers. *Journal of Teacher Education, 49* (3), 165–176.

Mills, M. R., & Hyle, A. E. (2001). No rookies on rookies: Compliance and opportunism in policy implementation. *The Journal of Higher Education, 72*(4), 453–477.

National Commission on Excellence in Education (1983). *A nation at risk: The Imperative for educational reform.* Washington, DC: U.S. Government Printing Office.

Porter, C. J. (1981). *Professionalization and day care: Friend or foe* (ERIC Document Reproduction Service No. ED 012 572). Washington, DC.

Profy, V. (1992). The influence of political culture on educational policy making during the 1989–1990 sessions of the Pennsylvania general assembly (Doctoral dissertation, Temple University, 1992). *Dissertation Abstracts International, 53-09A,* 3073.

Rein, M. (1976). *Social science and public policy.* New York: Penguin Education.

Rossi, P. H., & Shlay, A. B. (1982). Residential mobility and public policy issues: "Why families move" revisited. *Journal of Social Sciences, 38*(3), 21–34.

Ruhland, S. K., & Bremer, C. D. (2003). Perceptions of traditionally and Alternatively certified career and technical education teachers. *Journal of Vocational Education Research, 28*(3), 1–2. Retrieved May 1, 2004 from http://www.scholar.lib.vt.edu/ejournals/JVER/v28n3/ruhland.html.

Schaefer, N. (1999). *Good teachers through the backdoor.* Washington, DC: American Enterprise.

Seastrom, M., Gruber, K. J., Henke, R., McGrath, D. J., & Cohen, B.A. (2002). *US Department of Education, National Center for Education Statistics. Qualifications of the public school teacher workforce: Prevalence of out of field teaching, 1987–1988 to 1999–2000,* NCES 2002-603. Washington, DC: Government Printing Office.

Sergiovanni, T. J., Burlingame, M., Coombs, F. S., & Thurston, P. W. (1992). *Educational governance and administration*. Boston: Allyn-Bacon.

Shulman, L. S. (1987). Knowledge and teaching: Foundations of the new reform. *Harvard Educational Review, 57*(1), 1–22.

Smith, T. B. (1973). The policy implementation process. *Policy Sciences 4*, 197–209.

Stoddart, T,. & Floden, R. E. (1995). *Traditional and alternate routes to teacher certification: Issues, assumptions, and misconceptions*. East Lansing, MI: The National Center for Research in Teacher Learning.

Teacher's union, colleges sue to stop educator certification plan. (1999, July 14) *Pennsylvania Law Weekly*, p. 1.

Travers, P. (n.d.). *Some issues related to alternative teacher certification* Retrieved August 15, 2004 from: http://members@aol.com/jopheoo/travers.htm

U. S. Department of Education. (1991, March 28). *Alternative certification for teachers: A new career for you*. ED1.2.C33.

Van Meter, D. S., & Van Horn, C. E. (1975). The policy implementation process: A conceptual framework. *Administration and Society, 6*(5), 445–488.

Who should be a teacher? Teacher education in Colorado, fewer ed-courses, more time in real classrooms [editorial]. (1999, January 18) *Denver Rocky Mountain News*, p. A49.

Wise, A., & Liebrand, J. (1993). Accreditation, and the creation of a profession of teaching. *Phi Delta Kappan, 75*(2), 133–136, 154–157.

Yanow, D. (2000). *Conducting interpretive policy analysis*. Thousand Oaks, CA: Sage.

Yanow, D. (1996). *How does a policy mean? Interpreting policy and organizational actions*. Washington, DC: Georgetown University Press.

Zumwalt, K. (1991). Alternate routes to teaching. *Journal of Teacher Education, 42*(2), 83–92.

CHAPTER 13

DECONSTRUCTING SPECIAL AND GIFTED EDUCATION POLICY AND PRACTICE

A Paradigm of Ethical Leadership in Residentially Segregated Schools and Communities

York Williams

Over the last thirty years urban school district enrollment has increased. This increase is related to the Civil Rights Act (1964) and the educational climate of desegregation since Brown v. Board of Education. This increase has affected the diversity that exists in America's public school systems. The increase in diversity has led to a gap in achievement levels between the two groups because of funding/enrollment size in urban districts. African American students attending mostly large urban school districts, and those who are not students of color and attend suburban or private schools. There are critical problems with the rate of identification of African American students in both gifted and special education programs. African American

Policy, Leadership, and Student Achievement, pages 207–219
Copyright © 2008 by Information Age Publishing
All rights of reproduction in any form reserved.

students are underrepresented in gifted education programs and overrepresented in special education programs (Baldwin & Reis, 2004; Booth & Stanley, 2004; Gallagher, 2005; Grantham, 2004a). The former carries with it an identification and label of a bright and advanced student in need of acceleration, a more tightly structured curriculum, and an individualized academic program linked to strengths. The latter carries with it an identification of a "special needs" learner with severe to moderate learning problems linked to an individualized education program based on the student's learning disability and needs. Contemporary education research identifies weaknesses and flaws inherent within each program that prove detrimental for African American students (Booth & Stanley, 2004; Dixon, Reeves, & Mains, 1996; Ford, 2005; Gallagher, 2005; Grantham, 2003; Grant, 1992; Jordan, 2005; Steele, Perry, & Hilliard, 2003). Further, the success or failure of each program can be linked to the sociopolitical context and demographic characteristics of the school districts where they operate. Ethical and proper leadership and decision-making from administrators, supervisors, and educators can inform current practices and reform the current failure rate of such programs.

The first part of this paper examines the sociopolitical background of residentially segregated communities typical of the kinds of communities where most urban school students of color live. The second part of this paper identifies issues related to both gifted and special education programs. Finally, the intersection of residentially segregated school communities and their relationship to gifted and special education programs is analyzed with recommendations for reform through the theoretical and practical lens of ethical educational leadership. I argue that in order for reform to take place within these school contexts, leadership interwoven with social justice at all levels and coupled with "cultural critiques" of the public education school system is integral.

URBAN PUBLIC SCHOOL CONTEXTS
AND RESIDENTIAL SEGREGATION

Since school desegregation and the development of trends in Black and White achievement gaps (Crane & Mahard, 1978; Ikpa, 1994, 2004; Orfield, 1993) public schools have become so different and context-dependent that they can be viewed as either black or white in the strictest terms. Urban school districts have become increasingly "black" while suburban ones have maintained their majority "white" student bodies. Additionally, income has impacted the scope and delivery of such programs as gifted and special education. Although special education falls under the Individual Disability Education Act (IDEA) (1997), a federally mandated right for students with disabilities, urban schools have traditionally experienced struggles with funding. It was not until the implementation of the No Child Left Behind Act (NCLB) (2001) that suburban school districts began to experience and articulate on a national level their struggles with funding for gifted and special education programs. However, the urban environment has also exacerbated the effectiveness of delivering these programs to African American students, many who live in residentially segregated communities (Massey & Denton, 1993, 1988; Orfield, 2003; Wilson, 1987, 1997).

According to Massey and Denton (1988), residential segregation is a multidimensional phenomenon that varies along five distinct axes of measurement: evenness, exposure, concentration, centralization, and clustering. The authors maintain that not every city must meet each measurement exactly in order to be considered residentially segregated. However, most urban cities and their school districts located in the Rust Belt of the Northeast meet all five indices examined and identified by Massey and Denton. The authors maintain that residential segregation is a global construct that subsumes five underlying dimensions of measurement, each corresponding to a different aspect of spatial variation. They also contend that each dimension listed here represents a different facet of what researchers have called "segregation." The implications for schooling and how effective the delivery of gifted and special education programs these school districts become, merit discussion. First, the environment impacts how students see themselves and constitutes a conflict with the way they interact at home versus the way they interact in the school and community. Second, students identified as exceptional—either as gifted or under special education—are in need of additional supports to help retain them, provide them enrichment, and deliver instruction at their level of need. The aforementioned often meets with conflict and turbulence within the urban schools that are as outlined here, and are already segregated and confronted with illegal drugs, unemployment, crime, violence, gangs, and other social ills. Researchers and educators often look to the home and at the classroom teacher to reduce conflicts within urban public schools. However, ignoring problems and conflicts that occur outside the schools erroneously displaces the problems and any possible solutions, as well as how those problems affect students in specific educational programs. Further, by narrowly focusing on the issue that takes place within classroom contexts, educators fail to account for the impact that students' environments have on their motivation, achievement, and ability to learn. The latter are complicated for students identified as either special education and/or gifted. Unfortunately, dually exceptionally identified students—those who are both gifted and possess a learning disability in specific areas of academic achievement—are usually overlooked altogether.

GIFTED EDUCATION, SCHOOL LEADERS, AND URBAN EDUCATION

Gifted education, unlike special education, is not a federally mandated or protected right for every child. However, some states have taken measures to assure that every child identified as gifted using various testing instruments and criteria has access to academic acceleration and enrichment. Unfortunately, both the latter fall short in urban school districts and communities coping with issues mentioned here, especially those districts meeting the criteria of residential segregation. In addition to issues involving the curriculum, budgets, and location of gifted services, there are nationwide problems with the under representation of African American and Language-diverse students (Ford, 2005; Grantham, 2003). large urban school districts are confronted with issues of how to meet their gifted students' needs, train their teachers for gifted instruction, and find resources to supplement the curriculum coupled with training.

Urban schools already deal with low school budgets, high incidents of school violence, and other social and political problems that tend to complicate teaching and learning for their students. However, the rights of gifted children who need quality teachers who can work with them as their case manager, manage their gifted GIEPs, and provide accelerated, compacted curriculum and enrichment often go unmet. Additionally, these same schools also experience problems with access to nonbiased and culturally diverse testing instruments and usually lack culturally diverse eligibility criteria for students to gain entrance into their programs.

Ford and Naglieri maintain (Ford, 2005; Naglieri, 2005) that traditional testing instruments often exclude students of color and ones who speak English as a second language. This exclusion often results in under representation of students of color and who are language-diverse. The implications are far-reaching as our nation's urban and suburban schools, which educate extreme polar opposite races and classes of students, are already stratified by the achievement gap (Ferguson, 1998; Ikpa, 2004; Lee, 2002; Oakes, 1985; Schofield, 1991; Wells & Grain, 1994). Now, identification of gifted students as an already underrepresented nationwide program is experiencing both a gap and deficit in identifying potentially gifted ethnically and language-diverse students. The problems are compounded in urban districts already struggling to meet average students' needs who fall under the guise of NCLB (Boaler, 2003). Gifted students often go overlooked in urban public schools, while school leaders and administrators usually focus on students with special needs who are identified under IDEA. Although the latter merits worthy and important considerations, students who are in need of acceleration, compacted curriculums, and academic enrichment must take a back seat to students who are classified as general education under NCLB and special education under IDEA. Additionally, issues with crime, drugs, lack of parental involvement, and funding shift focus away from the needs of African American and minority gifted students who are already underrepresented in public schools. Additional training, professional development, and a paradigm that enable school leaders and administrators to understand the nuances involved with gifted programs is required to address issues with under representation and low-performing gifted programs.

SPECIAL EDUCATION, SCHOOL LEADERS, AND URBAN EDUCATION

Special education is a federally protected right administered by IDEA (1997). Students are identified using a psychological testing instrument that diagnoses the problems the student is having that interfere with learning. The federal government allows specific categories to fall under the disability code of IDEA. Disabilities range from Speech and Language Processing to Auditory Processing to Attention Deficit Hyperactive Disorder, which can also fall under Section 504 or under the title of Other Health Impairment (OHI) in IDEA. Given the complexities involved with specific learning disabilities, school districts and school leaders are also confronted with the challenge of finding a balance between making financial and curriculum decisions, which are many times complicated by the problems students experience living in residentially segregated communities. Certified special education staff members, the delivery of special education services, and overrepresentation of African American special education students paints a grim and yet troubling picture of the effectiveness of special education programs as they play out in urban schools (Gilbert & Gay, 1985; Grant, 1992; Hilliard, 1980).

Federally mandated funding for special education programs is already under scrutiny due to conflicts with NCLB and financial supports required for remedial instruction when students fail to meet adequate yearly progress (AYP). The consequences for failing to meet AYP place schools and sometimes entire districts on a "needs improvement list," which brings with it a negative reputation. However, a large majority of African American students and many urban schools are already familiar with a history of challenges in meeting the needs of regular education students. With the emphasis placed on meeting AYP, special education students are tested ad nauseam and educators fail to understand the complexities of their day-to-day lives as experienced through their living in communities in "chaos" that are also underserved and segregated. The issue of locating certified special education teachers has also complicated this dilemma.

Special education teachers who are effective at meeting the needs of students who live in residentially high-need communities are difficult to find. Some school districts have turned to alternative teaching certification routes as a way to address this shortage of highly qualified and competent teachers. However, the attrition rate of these teachers, who come from programs such as Teach for America and the New Teachers Project, is troubling. Many of these highly qualified candidates experience difficulty transitioning into these school positions, and as a result, leave the field after only a few years of teaching (Baines, 2006; Farber, 1991, 2000; Darling-Hammonds & Sykes, 2003). This once again leaves a gap in the field and repeats a loss in the lives of these special education students. Additionally, as a result of this chaos, schoolteachers erroneously resort to an over reliance on the special education identification process to effectively address the achievement gap as well as student behavior issues. The aforementioned results in the overrepresentation of African American special education students.

The instruments used to evaluate the learning and behavior characteristics of special education students usually unintentionally identify modes of learning styles adopted by culturally diverse students who are primarily African American (Ford, 1998; 2005; Ford & Grantham, 1998; Grantham, 2003). However, these learning styles are viewed negatively. Ford identifies traits of culturally diverse learners that are not usually taken into consideration as learning styles, but are instead mistaken by the evaluator as deficits. Ford suggests that educators move from deficit thinking to dynamic thinking in order to close the achievement gap that exists in troubling proportions within both special and gifted education programs (Ford, 2005). In order for the latter to be accomplished, administrators and school leaders will need to revisit the fundamental and ethical ideas of education, which will lead to equity and social justice.

ETHICAL LEADERSHIP AND SOCIAL JUSTICE

The idea of ethical leadership is interwoven with concepts outlined in Table 13.1. The scope of these concepts is quite broad, but takes on critical importance within urban schools. The school leader must utilize the concepts within this table in order to be guided by the principles of the ethics of care (Beck, 1994; Gilligan, 1982; Williams, 2007b). The ethic of care extends the necessary and required understanding that is essential for school leaders to deconstruct the longstanding issues that surround gifted and special education programs in urban schools and communities. The school leader who acts out of care works within a multiple ethical paradigm (Shapiro, 2006). Shapiro and Stefkovich (2001) maintain that the field of education and the profession of school leadership are incomplete by failing to adopt a frame-

TABLE 13.1

Human Rights	Conflict of Interest
Freedom	Loyalty
Responsibility & Authority	Prudence
Duty	Critique
Justice	Professional
Equity	Instructional Leader
Character, Commitment, and Formality	Ethics of Care

Note: Adopted from Lunenburg & Irby, 2006

work that underlies our teaching and scholarship. The authors outline the ethics of justice, care, critique, and profession as the basic concepts that serve as scaffolding for the conceptual framework of the ethical paradigm.

The urban school leader who is guided by the ethic of justice will undoubtedly work to diminish the inequity that persists for students in these schools and use the ethic to develop a cultural and social justice critique of how students are identified. Hence, the school leader must identify and develop an understanding of some of the most important social and cultural needs of identified students. Next, the urban school leader who is guided by the ethic of critique will develop a professional relationship with the school district administrators who oversee such programs in order to offer changes and introduce pedagogy and curriculum that are in line with the school and community. Finally, the school leader who adopts an ethic of care to drive the school mission will become culturally aware and develop a philosophical stance that unites students' experiences in their residentially segregated community, family, and church with the broad goals and aims of the educational programs. I combine three of the philosophical concepts here under one conceptual framework to show their inextricable relationship to school leadership within urban and residentially segregated schools. Gross, whose work is joined with the concepts of ethical leadership (Gross, 1998; Gross & Shapiro, 2007), maintains that different levels of turbulence exist within schools and communities. The degrees of this turbulence range from light to extreme According to Gross, an understanding of turbulence theory gives individuals the ability to more easily navigate leadership choices when severe issues occur. When understood and applied together, the urban school leader is armed with the knowledge and ability to promote change within both school and community.

The ethic of justice focuses on the urban school leader's role as an advocate for justice. Historically, the ethics of justice have been confined to philosophy, law, and criminal justice. However, on this view, school leaders can build upon the work of Rawls, Aristotle, Fontaine, and King in order to promote equity and recognition of human rights in an inequitable public school system. For example, the school leader who adopts the view of the ethic of justice when confronted by the inequity existing within the identification of gifted programs will no doubt introduce a nonbiased evaluation instrument that takes into account the diverse students' community, language strengths, weaknesses, socioeconomic status, and risks coupled with their potential to excel (Naglieri, 2005). Achievement indicators are not used as the be-all and end-all of the decision-making process. Likewise, the urban school leader guided by principles of the ethics of justice will evaluate the school's special education student population and make sure that each student's Individualized Education Plan (IEP) is in line with their social emotional and affective needs, and not just standardized goals and objectives that fall under NCLB. Turbulence occurs when the latter in both instances are overlooked. This can range from light turbulence, when the student does not respond, to severe turbulence, when the student's needs are overlooked long enough that they go underserved or unserved. As Gross (1998) maintains, turbulence adds the emotional response to the issue when it becomes a large-scale problem that must be managed. However, urban school leaders who are guided by concepts interwoven within an ethical paradigm will be able to confront such issues before they disrupt the school environment and become ruinous to the student. The school leader must also develop a professional relationship with the school district administrators who oversee such programs in order to offer changes and introduce pedagogy and curriculum that are in line with the school and community.

In line with the ethic of critique, Shapiro and Stefkovich maintain that the ethic of critique calls for scholars and educators to challenge the status quo and deal with inconsistencies that tend to stifle students' learning. On this view, the ethic of critique can allow the urban school leader to challenge the long-standing practices of gifted identification and special education which result in the under identification of minority students in gifted programs and overrepresentation of African American students in special education programs. The ethic of critique applied liberally within this urban context would challenge and reexamine concepts such as democracy, privilege, power, culture, and equity. On further examination, educators might deconstruct the evaluation procedures used to identify students for acceptance into gifted and special education programs. This would make certain that gifted and special education student eligibility criteria line up with appropriate services to be delivered, educational goals, and objectives alongside the curriculums. Additionally, the urban school leader who applies the ethic of critique will assure that there exists educational congruence with the student's school, community, family, and other possibilities. The urban school leader's application and analysis of the ethical paradigm are not limited in scope, but allow the urban school leader to become sensitive to the conflicts within the public education system that become complicated by residential segregation, coupled with the needs of students. Lastly, through the ethic of care, the school leader must adopt a culturally aware philosophical stance that attempts to unite students' experiences in their residentially segregated community with the broad goals and aims of their education program.

The ethic of care, as one of the primary guides for the urban school leader, helps to guide moral and equitable decisions based on the needs of the student. Urban school leaders will need to understand the community, the impact of crime and unemployment on schools, illegal drugs and violence, and how the students are directly affected by it all. This understanding, guided by the ethic of care, will further the urban school leader's conceptual framework of understanding and can help to align the goals of both gifted and special education programs. It can also improve how school leaders and administrators interact with students in general education courses and programs. Unfortunately, not just minority gifted and special education students suffer in the achievement gap, but key ethical principals can provide restoration as needed. Hence, on this view, the urban school leader develops and critiques rules and policies that support achievement, while also developing a deeper understanding of the life challenges and sociocultural needs of the school's students. The student who has potential to place in gifted education, but is experiencing issues with underachievement in a particular academic area, can be supported in enrichment activities and tutoring to make them excel and to prevent boredom with the curriculum in later stages of their education (Harmon, 2002; Morris, 2002). Additionally, the special education student who is experiencing bouts of anger and tantrums in school, but has the potential to experience success with just a bit more teaching support and periodic check-ins, can be granted such by the urban school leader. Both students' families are invited to stay involved by the urban school leader, and a team of teachers are developed to strengthen the family connections, and act as outreach for them, while other staff members are appointed similar roles on a rotating basis, and their school duty roles are decreased or eliminated altogether (Williams, 2007a). Within this framework of ethical leaders and policy making, students and families are most important as viewed by urban school leaders, not tests. Additionally, the students' and the communities' needs inform NCLB and IDEA, not the other way around.

SUMMARY AND CONCLUSIONS

If we are to level the educational landscape and make equity exist within urban schools and communities, we must begin with each individual.

However, as school leaders and administrators, we have the responsibility to make sure that teachers, students, families, and others within the school community share or at least understand the problems that exist and can become partners in solving the problems. One first step toward solving the problems is to adopt an advanced ethical stance that can be applied liberally and at will when issues with gifted and special education programs arise. However, we should not limit the scope of this ethical leadership paradigm in its application to special and gifted education programs. We must apply this framework liberally and broadly so as to include the needs of the community, parents, and others so that change can begin. If school leaders and administrators, school supervisors, superintendents, and other school personnel fail to adopt aspects of the ethical leadership framework, then we are further dividing the quality of education experienced by urban and suburban students, and thus adding to the ever-growing Black and White achievement gap.

REFERENCES

Baldwin, A., & Reis, S. (Eds.). (2004). *Culturally diverse and underserved populations of gifted students.* Thousand Oaks, CA: Corwin.

Baines, L. (2006). Deconstructing teacher certification. *Phi Delta Kappan, 88*(4), 326–328.

Beck, L. G. (1994). *Reclaiming educational administration as a caring profession.* New York: Teachers College Press.

Boaler, J. (2003). When learning no longer matters: Standardized testing and the creation of inequality. *Phi Delta Kappan, 84*(7), 502–506.

Booth, D., & Stanley, J. (Eds). (2004). *In the eyes of the beholder: Critical issues for diversity in gifted education.* Waco, TX: Prufrock.

Boyd, B., & Correa, V. I. (2005). Developing a framework for reducing the cultural clash between African American parents and the special education system. *Multicultural Perspectives, 7*(2), 3–11.

Brenal, E. (2002). Three ways to achieve a more equitable representation of cultural and linguistic different students in gifted and talented programs. *Roeper Review, 24*(2), 477–490.

Castellano, J. A., & Diaz, E. (2001). *Reaching new horizons: Gifted and talented education for culturally and linguistically diverse students.* Boston: Allyn & Bacon.

Clark, E. R. (1998). Voices and voces: Cultural and linguistic dimensions of giftedness. *Educational Horizons, 77*(1), 41–47.

Crain, R., & Mahard, R. (1978). School racial Compositions and black college Attendance and achievement test performance. *Sociology of Education, 51*(2), 81–101.

Cropper, C. (1998). Fostering parental involvement in the education of the gifted minority student. *Gifted Child Today, 21*(1), 20–24.

Darling-Hammond, L., & Sykes, G. (2003). Wanted: A national teacher supply policy for education: The right way to meet the "highly qualified teacher" challenge. *Education Policy Analysis Archives, 11*(22). Retrieved April 37, 2007 from http://epaa.asu.edu/epaa/v11n33.

Dixon, C., Reeves, M., & Mains, L. (1996). *Gifted and at risk.* Bloomington, IN: PDK Educational Foundation.

Farber, B. (1991). *Crisis in education: Stress and burnout in the American teacher.* San Francisco: Jossey-Bass.

Farber, B. A. (2000). Understanding and treating burnout in a changing culture. *Journal of Clinical Psychology, 56*(5), 675–689.

Ferguson, R. F. (1998). Teacher's perceptions and expectations and Black-White test score gap. In C. Jenks & M. Phillips (Eds.), *Blacks, science and American education.* New Brunswick, NJ: Rutgers University Press.

Ford, D. Y. (2005). Beyond cultureblindness: A model of culture with implications for gifted education. *Roeper Review, 27*(2), 97–103.

Ford, D., & Grantham, C. T. (1998). A case study of the social needs of Danisha: An underachieving gifted African-American female. *Roeper Review, 21.*

Fries-Britt, S. (1998). Moving beyond black achiever isolation: Experiences of gifted black collegians. *Journal of Higher Education, 69.*

Gallagher, J. J. (2005). The role of race in gifted education. *Roeper Review, 27*(3), 135.

Garibaldi, A. (1997). Four decades of progress...and decline: An assessment of African American educational attainment. *The Journal of Negro Education, 66*(2), 105–120.

Gilbert, S., & Gay, G. (1985). Improving the success in school of poor black children. *Phi Delta Kappan, 67,* 133–138.

Gilligan, C. (1982). *In a different voice.* Cambridge, MA: Harvard University Press.

Grantham, T. C. (2004a). Multicultural mentoring to increase black male representation in gifted programs. *Gifted Child Quarterly, 48*(3), 232–45.

Grantham, T. C. (2004b). Rocky Jones: Case study of a high-achieving black male's motivation to participate in gifted classes. *Roeper Review, 26*(4), 208–215.

Grantham, T. C. (2003). Increasing black student enrollment in gifted programs. *Gifted Child Quarterly, 47*(1), 46–65.

Grantham, T. C., & Ford, D. (2003). Beyond self-concept and self-esteem: Racial identity and gifted African American students. *The High School Journal, 87*(1), 18–29.

Grant, P. (1992). Using special education to destroy Black boys. *The Negro Educational Review, 63*(1), 7–21.

Gross, S. J. (1998). *Staying centered: Curriculum leadership in a turbulent era Staying centered: Curriculum leadership in a turbulent era.* Alexandria, VA: Association for Supervision and Curriculum Development

Harmon, D. A. (2002). They won't teach me: The onus of gifted African American inner-city students. *Roeper Review, 24*(2), 68–75.

Hebert, T. P., & Beardsley, T. M. (2001). Jermaine: A critical case study of a gifted black child living in rural poverty. *Gifted Child Quarterly, 45*(2), 85–103.

Hilliard, A. (1980). Cultural diversity and special education. *Exceptional Children, 46,* 584–590.

Holcomb-McCoy, C. (2007). *School counseling to close the achievement gap: A social justice framework for success.* Thousand Oaks, CA: Corwin Press.

Hrabowski, F., Maton, K., Green, M., & Grief, G. (2002). *Overcoming the odds: Raising academically successful African-American women.* Oxford: Oxford University.

Ikpa, V. (2003). A longitudinal analysis of the achievement gap between African Americans and European American students in the Norfolk Public Schools District. *Education Research Quarterly, 24*(4), 38–47.

Ikpa, V. (2004). Leaving children behind: the racial/ethnic achievement gap. *Research for Education Reform, 9*(2), 3–13.

Ikpa, V. (1994). The effects of school desegregation policies upon the achievement gap between African American and white students in Norfolk Public Schools. *Journal of Instructional Psychology, 21*(1), 49–58.

Individual Disabilities Education Act (IDEA). (2007). Retrieved May 13, 2007 from http://www.copaa.org/pdf/IDEA2004.pdf.

Johnson, C., & Kritsonis, W. (2006). The achievement gap in mathematics: A significant problem for African American students. *DOCTORAL FORUM: National Journal for Publishing and Mentoring Doctoral Student Research, 3*(1), www.nationalforum.com.

Jordan, K. A. (2005). Discourse of difference and the overrepresentation of black students in special education. *Journal of African American History, 90*(1/2), 128–149.

Lee, J. (2002). Racial and ethnic achievement gap trends: Reversing the progress towards equity? *Education Researcher, 31*(1), 3–12.

Lunenburg, F. C., & Irby, B. J. (2006). *The principal ship: Visions to action.* Houston, TX: Thomson Wadsworth.

Lynch, J. (2004). Gifted bilingual students. *Roeper Review, 26*(2), 112.

Massey, D., & Denton, N. (1993). *American apartheid: Segregation and the making of the underclass.* Cambridge, MA: Harvard University Press.

Massey, D. & Denton, N. (1988). The dimensions of residential segregation. *Social Forces, 67*(2), 281–315.

McCray, E. (2004). Young, gifted and black. *Urban Education, 39*(1), 108–113.

Morris, J. E. (2002). African American students and gifted education: The politics of race and culture. *Roeper Review, 24*(2), 59–62.

Naglieri, J. A. (2005). Increasing minority children's participation in gifted classes using NNAT: A response to Loham. *Gifted Child Quarterly, 49*(1), 29–36.

National Research Council. (Eds.) (2002). *Strategy for equity: Minority children in special and gifted education.* Washington, DC: National Academy Press.

No Child Left Behind Act. (2001). Retrieved November 10, 2004 from http://www.nochildleftbehind.gov.

Oaks, J. (1985). *How schools structure inequality.* New Haven, CT: Yale University Press.

Orfield, G. (2003). *The growth of segregation in American schools: Changing patterns of separation and poverty since 1968. A report on the Harvard Project on School Desegregation to the National School Boards Association.* Cambridge, MA: Harvard University Press.

Reis, S. (2005). Understanding resilience in diverse, talented students in an urban high school. *Roeper Review, 25*(4), 154–157.

Schofield, J. (1991). School desegregation and intergroup relations. *Review of Research in Education, 6*(17), 335–409.

Shapiro, J. P., & Gross, S. J. (2007 forthcoming), *Ethical educational leadership in turbulent times: (Re)solving moral dilemmas.* New York: Routledge.

Shapiro, J. A. (2006). Ethical decision making in turbulent times: Bridging theory with practice to prepare authentic educational leaders. *Values and Ethics in Educational Administration, 4*(2), 1–7.

Shapiro, J. A., & Stefkovich, J. A. (2001). *Ethical leadership and decision making in education: Applying theoretical perspectives to complex dilemmas.* Mahwah, NJ: Lawrence Erlbaum Associates.

Shealey, M. W., & Lue, M.S. (2006). Why are all the black kids in special education? Revisiting the issue of disproportionate representation. *Multicultural Perspectives, 8*(2), 3–9.

Steele, C., & Perry, T., & Hillard, A. (2003). *Young, gifted, and black: Promoting high achievement among African-American students.* New York: Beacon.

Valdes, G. (2003). *Expanding definitions of giftedness: Young interpreters of immigrant backgrounds.* New York: Erlbaum Associates.

Vanderslice, R. (1998). Hispanic children and giftedness: Why the difficulty in identification? *The Delta Kappa Gamma Bulletin, 64*(3), 18–23.

Weis, L., & Fine, M. (1993). *Beyond silenced voices: Class, race, and gender in United States schools.* Buffalo, NY: SUNY.

Wells, A., & Grain, R. (1994). Perpetuation theory and the long-term effects of school desegregation. *Review of Education Research, 64*(13), 53–76.

Williams, Y. (2007a)). *Charter school reform as rational choice: An analysis of African American parents' perceptions of a charter school located in a residentially segregated community.* Philadelphia: Temple University.

Williams, Y. (2007b). *Gifted education and the inclusion of African American male middle school students: It takes a village.* Paper presented at the Pennsylvania Association of Gifted Education Conference, Pittsburgh, PA.

Wilson, J. (1987). *The truly disadvantaged.* Chicago: The University of Chicago.

Wilson, J. (1997). *When work disappears: The world of the new urban poor.* Thousand Oaks, CA: Sage.

Young, M. I. (1990). *Justice & the politics of difference.* Princeton, NJ: Princeton University Press.

Young, M. I. (1999). Residential segregation and differentiated citizenship. *Citizenship Studies, 3*(2), 77–94.

Zirkel, S. (2002). Is there a place for me? Role models and academic identity among white students and students of color. *Teachers College Record, 104*, 357–376.

PART 5

THE K–12 URBAN CONTEXT:
IMPROVING STUDENT ACHIEVEMENT

CHAPTER 14

REFORMING
URBAN SCHOOLS

Five Years from Despair to Hope

Donald J. Anticoli

In July 2002, amidst some hostility and opposition, Edison Schools Inc. became the educational management partner for 20 public schools in the School District of Philadelphia (Philadelphia Inquirer, August 2002). This was part of a larger reform effort, initiated by former governor Tom Ridge, who had since February 2002 been serving as Homeland Security Administration director in the first term of President George W. Bush. The 20 schools were part of a larger initiative involving a total of 45 schools that became managed by either of the following:

1. For-profit educational management organizations (EMO) such as Edison, Victory Schools, Chancellor Beacon, or Universal.
2. Not-for profit EMOs such as foundations.
3. University partners such as Temple University & University of Pennsylvania (Education Notebook, Fall 2002).

Policy, Leadership, and Student Achievement, pages 223–231
Copyright © 2008 by Information Age Publishing
223

The schools for the reform effort were selected by the School Reform Commission (SRC), a five-member governmental body created to oversee all of the SDP schools. This SRC replaced the previous body of the Philadelphia School Board, a nine-member body representing the areas and regions of the City of Philadelphia. The SRC included three state appointees and two city appointees. It has been chaired by Mr. James Nevels, a Swarthmore businessman, since its inception in 2002.

WHY REFORM?

The SDP, since the inception of the Pennsylvania System of School Assessment (PSSA) in 1996, had scored well below state averages through 2001. Yet, each year the SDP—during the superintendencies of David Hornbeck (1994–2000) and Deirdre Farmby (2001–2002)—had run large deficits of 25 to 200 million dollars. About half of the district's current 2-billion-dollar budget comes from direct state funding, 40% from city taxes, 7% from the United States Department of Education (USDOE) in the form of Title I dollars, and 3% from direct city funding with an additional 1% from state and federal grants. While the SDP budget continually ran a deficit and the PSSA scores lagged behind state averages, Harrisburg became increasingly reluctant to raise the funding they provided.

Also, the city population was both declining numerically and becoming increasingly socioeconomically needy; thus, tax revenue was not showing any gains. Mayor Ed Rendell (1992–2000), who would become governor of Pennsylvania in 2003, and current Mayor John Street (2000–2008) found it increasingly difficult to raise SDP funding.

Therefore, amidst this scenario, Governor Ridge commissioned Edison Schools, Incorporated, founder and president Chris Whittle, John Chubb (Edison Chief Education Officer) to conduct a study of SDP operations and educational functions. Edison was also given the task of making recommendations on the future management and academic structure of the SDP. To avoid implications of being self-serving, Edison carried out the study by subcontracting individual components of the analysis to organizations such as McKinsey Consulting, Merrill Lynch, Harris Interactive, and others. The results of the study recommended that the entire school district be run by an EMO and that Edison directly manage as many as 60 schools. This created great controversy.

As the study was progressing, the events of September 11, 2001 occurred. Governor Ridge became Homeland Security Administration (HSA) director in February 2002 and Lieutenant Governor Schweiker took the helm of Pennsylvania. The city leaders opposed the schools outright takeover, with Mayor Street going so far as to move his office to SDP's historic headquarters at 21st and Winter Streets to stave off the takeover. Edison was vilified in the local press (*Philadelphia Inquirer, Daily News,* and *Philadelphia Tribune*) as an evil for-profit entity intent on ruling all of Philadelphia's public schools Governor Schweiker and the Pennsylvania Legislature crafted a compromise that created the SRC to oversee the schools. The SRC granted Edison 20 middle and elementary schools, which were among the lowest performing SDP schools on the PSSA through the 2000–01 school year. The SRC also hired Paul Vallas as the Chief Executive Officer in July 2002. Mr. Vallas had successfully engineered both a fiscal and academic turnaround of the Chicago Public Schools in the 1990s.

THE CONTEXT

The balance of this piece will focus on the academic results attained at one of the Edison-managed middle schools: Penn Treaty Middle School (PTMS), located in the Fishtown section of Philadelphia encompassing the entire square block of Berks, Thompson, Montgomery, and Moyer Streets. Constructed in 1927, it consists of five stories and six levels. The main entrance is topped by a stained glass window. The interior design includes a two-level terrazzo-tiled marble atrium, with a lantern-style hanging lamp.

The school was originally a junior high school serving grades 7–9 from the surrounding working-class White neighborhood. Courses offered included the standard English, math, science, and history as well as home economics, metal/electric/wood shop, sewing, art, music, physical education, and health. By 2002, the grade configuration was grades 5–8 and the population had changed to 48% Latino, 25% African American, 22% Anglo, 5% Asian/Other. The home economics and shop/sewing areas were converted to computer labs, one existing and one brought by Edison for electronic benchmark testing. Currently a former cooking area is in the process of conversion to a science lab, courtesy of Comcast Inc., who has also provided funds for 24 new computers in the general computer lab.

Edison became the school's management partner in the 2002–03 school year. Also, this writer arrived as a new principal at the school through the partnership of Edison & SDP. For the first time in many years, a core curriculum aligned with state standards and tied to the PSSA was implemented. The Edison/SDP partnership provided the following core curricula:

Grades 5–6: Everyday Math
Success for All Reading
BSCS Science
History Alive & Cultural Geography
Grades 6–8: Transitions Math
Choices in Literature
Science Plus
U.S. History

Currently 139 of our 711 students are provided special education, and 114 are in the English Language Learning (ELL) Program of studies. This means that approximately 37% of our student population is provided with either special education or ELL programs.

The special education program practices responsible inclusion, with up to 40% of the students educated in regular education settings. Steck-Vaughn and American Guidance Services curricula supplement the common core curriculum for special education. The ELL program is provided and overseen by SDP. Highpoints and Moving into English are the crux of the ELL curriculum. Also, we use Prentice Hall Math as a Grades 6–8 supplement, and we are part of a two-year Language Study for Grades 7 and 8.

The following figures and tables provided by Tung Le of Edison Schools, show the progress of Penn Treaty's fifth and eighth-grade students in Reading and Math for the 2003–2006 test administrations.

TREND ANALYSIS

As can be seen in Figures 14.1 and 14.2, Penn Treaty Middle School has shown rather steady growth in almost all demographic/programmatic areas

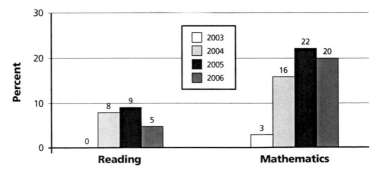

Figure 14.1 Penn Treaty Middle School Pennsylvania State School Assessment (PSSA) Grade 5. Percent students proficient and advanced (2003–2006).

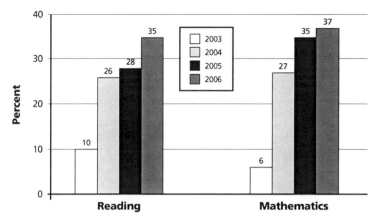

Figure 14.1 Penn Treaty Middle School Pennsylvania State School Assessment (PSSA) Grade 8. Percent students proficient and advanced (2003–2006).

TABLE 14.1 PSSA Data (Overall Performance)

	2002–2003	2003–2004	2004–2005	2005–2006
Grade 5		*Proficient and Advanced*		
Reading	0%	8%	9%	6%
Math	3%	16%	22%	20%
Grade 6		*Proficient and Advanced*		
Reading				17%
Math				40%
Grade 7		*Proficient and Advanced*		
Reading				29%
Math				35%
Grade 8		*Proficient and Advanced*		
Reading	10%	26%	28%	35%
Math	16%	26%	35%	37%
Special Education (Overall performance)				
Reading		0%	0%	3%
Math		6.5%	6.5%	4.4%

TABLE 14.2 ELL (Overall Performance)

	2003–2004	2004–2005	2005–2006
Reading	5%	N/A	11.4%
Math	21%	N/A	23%

TABLE 14.3   Total (Overall Performance)

	2003–2004	2004–2005	2005–2006
Reading	20%	22%	22%
Math	24%	31%	30%

TABLE 14.4   Ethnic Subgroups (Overall Performance)

	2003–2004	2004–2005	2005–2006
Caucasian			
Reading	29%	42%	37%
Math	32%	46%	45%
African American			
Reading	13%	25%	22%
Math	15%	25%	20%
Latino			
Reading	20%	18%	16%
Math	19%	25%	24.5%

TABLE 14.5   PSSA Proficiency Goals for 2006–2007

	2005–2006	2006–2007	# of students needed to reach goal %
Reading (Overall)	22%	30%	212
Math (Overall)	30%	38%	268
Special Education—Reading	3%	12%	14
Special Education—Math	4.4%	15%	21
ELL—Reading	11.5%	20%	30
ELL—Math	23%	31%	45
Caucasian—Reading	38%	46%	72
Caucasian—Math	45%	52%	81
African American—Reading	22%	30%	54
African American—Math	20%	28%	50
Latino—Reading	16%	25%	89
Latino—Math	25%	33%	117

TABLE 14.6   Terra Nova Data

Grade 5	National Percentile Rank Fall 2005 (4th Grade)		
Reading	29		
Language Arts	29		
Math	39		

Grade 6	National Percentile Rank		
	Spring 2005 (5th Grade)	Fall 2005 (6th Grade)	Change
Reading	21	34	+13
Language Arts	30	36	+6
Math	21	37	+16

Grade 7	National Percentile Rank		
	Spring 2005 (6th Grade)	Fall 2005 (7th Grade)	Change
Reading	27	35	+8
Language Arts	24	32	+8
Math	24	39	+15

Grade 8	National Percentile Rank		
	Spring 2005 (7th Grade)	Fall 2005 (8th Grade)	Change
Reading	36	39	+3
Language Arts	40	42	+2
Math	45	40	−5

in reading and math, Grades 5 and 8, from 2003–06. In spring 2007 all the grades that Penn Treaty Middle School encompasses (Grades 5–8) will be included in the PSSA and counted toward AYP (Adequate Yearly Progress) and AMO (Annual Measureable Objectives). For 2007, we anticipate continued success, since in the trial year of 2006 our Grade 6 students scored on average 10% higher in proficiency than Grade 5. Also Grade 7 scores were comparable to Grade 8 in both reading and math.

All of this success nearly did not happen. When Edison was first coming on board the mother ship, "USS" SDP, the original proposal called for 1,500 additional dollars for each student in the Edison Schools. At the last moment, the per-pupil allocation was reduced to $750, and Edison made the tough decision to stay in Philadelphia and make a courageous stand. The students and families of Penn Treaty, and across the Edison spectrum in Philadelphia, have certainly benefitted.

Edison Benchmark Data

Total Number of Proficient Students (70% or greater)

78/705 = 11% Reading (November)	78/705 = 11% Math
85/705 = 12% Reading (November)	120/705 = 17% Math

SUPPLEMENTARY ACHIEVEMENT PLAN

Interventions

- Extended Day—297/494 average daily attendance (Goal: increase ADA to 60% students).
- Study Island—Launch 10/2006.
- Language Pilot—Grade 7 & 8 (60 students).
- Countdown to 2006 PSSA—Teacher Guide.

RECOMMENDED REFERENCES

9/11 Commission Report. (2004). *Final report of the national commission on terrorist attacks upon the U.S.* Authorized edition. New York & London: W. W. Norton & Co.

Bracey, G. (2004). *Setting the record straight.* Portsmouth, NH: Heinemann.

Burgos, F. (Ed.) (2003, March 3). High on the high school plan: Vallas strikes a blow for public education, *Philadelphia Daily News*, 17.

Chubb, J. E. & Loveless, T. (Eds.) (2002). *Bridging the achievement gap* (pp. 1–73; 131–155). Washington, DC: Brookings Institution.

Collins, J. (2004). *Good to great for educators.* New York: Harper Collins.

Delpit, L. (1995). *Other people's children* (pp. 91–104, 135–166). New York: The New Press.

Elam, S. (Ed.) (1993) *State of the nation's public schools* (pp. 194–233). Bloomington, IN: Phi Delta Kappa.

Gill, B. P., Hamilton, L. et al. (2005) *Perspiration & time: Operations and achievement in Edison Schools* (pp. 53–175). Pittsburgh, PA: Rand Corporation.

Krzyzewski, M., with Phillips, D. T. (2000). *Leading with the heart.* New York: Warner Books.

Lambert, L. (1998). *Building leadership capacity in schools* (pp. 76–125). Alexandria, VA: ASCD.

Perry, T., Steele, C., & Hilliard III, A. (2003). *Young Gifted and Black: Promoting High Achievement Among African-American Students* (pp. 40–84, 87–165). Boston: Beacon Press.

Snyder, S., & Mezzacappa, D. (2003, 28 February). Report shows progress in Edison's test scores. *Philadelphia Inquirer*, p. 83.

Socolar, P. (Ed). *Philadelphia Public School Notebook Spring 2002, 9,* No. 3; *Summer 2002, 9,* No. 4; *Fall 2002, 10,* No. 1; *Winter 2002/03, 10,* No. 2; *Winter 2004/05, 12,* No. 2; *Fall 2006, 14,* No. 1. Philadelphia, PA:

Whittle, C. (2005). *Crash course: Imagining a better future for public education.* New York: Riverhead Books, Member of Penguin Group.

CHAPTER 15

BUILDING CAPACITY AND RAISING AWARENESS

Implementing NCLB and Its Impact on World Languages

Oscar Torres, Jr.

The Federal investment in developing and maintaining foreign language and area expertise functions as a critical pipeline supporting U.S. national security.

—ED.gov (2005)

Many school districts have adopted innovative programs to enhance the skills needed for our children's future. One such program is a comprehensive foreign language experience. Most schools begin language instruction at the high school level, while others begin instruction at the middle school level. A few districts have identified the Foreign Language in the Elementary School Program (FLES) as vital, while ensuring today's students acquire the skills needed to thrive in a context where Limited English Proficient citizens will become the largest minority groups in our society.

As school districts develop innovative programs such as FLES to prepare our students for future success in a global society, we must also be aware of the regulations under the No Child Left Behind Act (NCLB). Understand-

Policy, Leadership, and Student Achievement, pages 233–242
Copyright © 2008 by Information Age Publishing
233

ing the policy and addressing the regulations are just as important as staying innovative.

The No Child Left Behind Act of 2001 provides our nation's schools with an expectation that every child will have the basic skills to achieve proficiency standards in Reading, Math, and Science by the year 2014. States across the country have submitted accountability system plans that will support the goals of NCLB. As states develop these regulations for meeting the policy requirements of No Child Left Behind, schools are finding themselves implementing new programs that address the achievement gap. Today's K–12 schools are now focused on ensuring that each school is making Adequate Yearly Progress (AYP). As the regulations are implemented by the states, schools begin to develop their own policies and regulations to prove they meet the state's proficiency standards. Programs are developed at the local level to ensure students meet the expectations and do so in order to attain local and state graduation requirements. Teachers are feeling the stress of this policy to the point where they are frustrated with the implications that can result in teachers adding or not adding value to a student's academic experience. With the fear of NCLB impacting a teacher and administrator's career, the level of frustration begins to intensify, particularly during the state assessment period.

Under the law, some districts, schools, and teachers are feeling frustrated; capacity building strategies must be in place across the system in order to address the confusion some educators experience. This is especially true when we begin to develop programs in order to meet the intended policy's goal while unintentionally abandoning programs that students genuinely enjoy and that meet the district's local goals and mission statements also embedded within NCLB policy.

Future economic success for our country is the foundation of the NCLB Act. Secretary of Education, Margaret Spellings (2006) stated that "Through the No Child Left Behind Act, we are committed to having every child in the United States learn and succeed in a global economy." Spellings continued her remarks by sharing that we are to reflect on America's place in a global environment. Because of this, we must understand what motivates other cultures. Learning other languages, cultures, and traditions are an important part of our children's education. Schools that believe in this theory are being forced to rethink their programs as well as every student's participation in World Languages programs to ensure they are providing the resources necessary to meet the accountability guidelines.

It is therefore my goal to present a Capacity Building Policy that will ensure all students have access to the same opportunities as students who achieve state proficiency levels. No student should be excluded from core programs that provide students with skills for future success even though they are having difficulties meeting the state's proficiency standards.

BUILDING CAPACITY FOR STUDENT PARTICIPATION IN WORLD LANGUAGE EXPERIENCES

Students enrolled in Support Programs designed to meet NCLB requirements must also have the opportunity to participate in innovative programs designed to provide students with the skills needed for future study and academic/economic success.

All students must be provided with the opportunities to acquire the skills that are needed to be successful in the job market and to understand their role as a member of society in a global context. It is the intent of this policy to ensure that capacity building activities are in place in order to provide our students with not only the skills they need to demonstrate proficiency in basic academic skills, but to also provide all students with the opportunities and skills necessary to function in a society where they can participate in the country's financial endeavors.

The Capacity Building Activities are as follows:

1. Identify the data on minority student involvement in world language courses.
2. Identify the data on the proficiency scores of subgroups under NCLB.
3. Develop cultural competence workshops on participating in Courageous Conversations About Race as outlined by Glen Singleton and Curtis Linton (2006).
4. Identify capacity building trainers on the discussion about race and closing the achievement gap (e.g., Belinda Williams).
5. Identify training for administrators and teachers on understanding the data identifying the gaps in achievement.
6. Identify efficiency models using current resources for meeting the needs of underachieving students.
7. Develop research-based strategies for language arts using anchors from the Language Arts Standards.
8. Work with language teachers to identify the number of second language lessons students are being "pulled out" of for support services.
9. Identify resources that can be "pushed into" the language arts classroom rather than pulling the students out of classes.
10. Request that the building achievement committees think innovatively to ensure students are minimally pulled out of core academic programs.

Thomas Friedman, author of *The World is Flat* (2005), describes to us how important countries such as China, Japan, and India are becoming in the world. China is willing to take as much outsourced positions as possible.

During my visit to China in the fall of 2005, I was able to see for myself how "Americanized" Shanghai is becoming. Learning English is a major part of getting ready for the EXPO in 2010. Friedman states that China is even willing to take outsourcing from Japan. In the northeastern city of Dalian, high school students study Japanese so they can work for companies from Japan that outsource specifically to this city. Bangalore, India is the center of outsourcing for U.S. companies. Companies such as Cisco Systems, Intel, IBM, Texas Instruments, and GE have already filed 1,000 patent applications due to their work in Bangalore. It goes without saying that, if you have been paying attention to what is happening in the world, our children will be working in a flat world. Imagine having your assistant get your presentations ready while you sleep, and available for you when you come into the office in the morning. An understanding of culture and language will be skills everyone will need.

The goal of the No Child Left Behind Act is to ensure that we do not have a two-tiered approach to educating our children in public schools, an expectation for those who "have" and a separate set of expectations for those who "have not." Pulling students from core programs designed to provide students with skills needed to be successful in the world when they leave our schools is a practice that needs to be reconsidered. Ronald H. Heck (2004) tells us that "Institutional Theory focuses on the influence of institutions" (p.150). This theory provides an understanding of the district I have focused on during my research. I have found that this district prides itself in providing students with a comprehensive and innovative academic experience. Innovative programs, like Foreign Language in the Elementary School (FLES), is one of which the district can be proud. The value of quality is evident in every school you visit in the district. The high school's profile is an example of the expectation the community has for its schools. Ninety-five percent of the high school graduates choose to further their education. In light of the success this district enjoys, NCLB also requires that the Pennsylvania System of School Assessment (PSSA) scores of the students be disaggregated by subgroups to ensure all students enjoy the success of the academic program. It became evident that more attention needed to be placed on minority students to ensure all stakeholders were doing everything possible for all students to succeed. While applying Institutional Theory to my topic, I can see how, in regard to language programs, many suburban schools or states that want to be perceived as innovative search for programs identified as looking to the future of education. That is why many schools and a few states have adopted a second language program for all students. With additional changes schools are making in order to close the achievement gap, they are developing programs that so far have not demonstrated efficiency and therefore Institutional Rational Choice may come into play when the resources of a school are redirected to fund new programs. In summary, a community's goals and values will be reflected in the policy adoption process. How will this policy make us stronger? Will we be perceived as a school or district that does not believe in the goal of NCLB? How can we help students improve their scores and still be considered a school system that is innovative and efficient in our spending? How does this policy reflect on our reputation?

Critical Theory allows us to take a look at the problem and approach it in a way that will benefit groups who, in the past have been marginalized. Once the issue of achievement has been raised, it must be addressed. In a community where excellence is the norm, understanding that resources must be made available to groups of underachieving students is a discussion that may hit the community and the staff in a manner that is unfamiliar to them. Tensions will arise. I must be able to identify the real weaknesses and obstacles that are before me. With the goal of closing the achievement gap, staff development activities may not be the only way to look at the problem and identify solutions. By adding additional support programs without talking to the students and groups affected by the interventions, we may not be addressing the real problem, but rather adding to a student's feeling of being different and not having the ability to do well on a standardized test. I recommend having the students work together and with a person who truly understands their experiences; then maybe the interventions can be more meaningful to the students and they would not have to be pulled out of experiences that will boost their self-esteem and provide them with the skills to succeed in the future.

The topic became one of interest because during the study of the achievement gap, it came to my attention that many of our minority students did not participate in the world language program until their sophomore or junior year in high school. This would only allow them to meet the basic graduation requirement. In a school where the average student completes 4.5 years of language instruction, I was astonished when I analyzed the data and realized that the African American population in the district only completed 2.5 years of language instruction. At the same time a new course was added to ensure all students were meeting adequate yearly progress and therefore were pulled out of languages classes to receive additional intensified language arts instruction.

Understanding political culture is vital to understanding the policy making process. Heck provided me with a clear understanding of the importance of grasping the national political culture as well as state culture and even how local culture plays a role in education reform. In this case, the local political culture takes hold in that there are the board members who may feel uncomfortable about the topic of race and achievement so they would ask the administration to do everything possible to "fix" the problem. Then we have the group of parents from the subgroups upset at the fact that the gap exists in this district and their children are the ones falling behind. These collective beliefs and values of policy makers and community members represent how education will be influenced. Although the policy making process can occur gradually, at times we have additional regulations that may force policies to be enacted due to outside influences. This is the case with NCLB and many school districts. Due to this law, policies that were not in line with the NCLB Act had to be revised and passed in order to meet regulatory requirements. With added attention on groups such as English Language Learners, Children with Special Needs, and minority groups, school districts began to study each of the populations and their respective scores on the PSSA.

Using the Advocacy Coalition Framework (ACF) allows me to comprehend the players in the process. Realizing that if I can identify those subsystems that may benefit from my proposed policy, it will help me to better evaluate the process and identify the steps that must be taken. This policy is grounded in the data collected during my study. I have met with the state advisor for world languages, the district coordinator of the administrative achievement committee, administrators from each of the schools, and teachers. School, district and state documents have been reviewed as well as a comprehensive look at how this topic is embedded in the NCLB Act.

My first goal was to identify the role of World Languages identified in the NCLB law. Title V of the NCLB, Part D, Subpart 9 refers to innovative programming, more specifically foreign languages in the elementary school and improved secondary foreign language study. Title IX of the NCLB informs us that foreign language is included as a core academic subject in our schools. At the federal level, both former Secretary of Education Rod Paige and Current Secretary of Education Margaret Spellings have publicly stated that the role of foreign language teaching is vital to the future of the United States and its security. Grants are currently being provided to elementary schools, middle schools, high schools, and universities to design innovative programs in the area of World Languages. In a fact sheet from the Department of Education dated January 2006, Secretary Spellings introduces the Increasing America's Competitiveness initiative.

> In 1970, half of the people in the world who held science and engineering doctorates were Americans, but by 2010 projections show that figure will have dropped to 15%. To keep America strong, we need our young people to take us to the next level of innovation. President Bush and the Congress are committed to ensuring America's high school graduates are ready for the jobs of the 21st century. (Spellings, 2006)

The National Language Security Initiative focuses on teaching languages from kindergarten through postsecondary education with the goal being increasing proficiency among all speakers. During my research I met with the Advisor for World Languages to the Pennsylvania Secretary of Education. Her goal for the last few years has been to have the World Languages standards adopted by the PA Board of Education. After meeting the requirements of the policy adoption process, the standards were quickly taken off of the agenda for adoption. In meeting with teachers and administrators from various school districts, I wondered what had happened to the process. My visit to the PA Department of Education provided me with the understanding that PA had not focused on the section of NCLB regarding foreign language instruction. At this point the focus is on making sure districts are meeting the needs of the subgroups identified in NCLB.

Mandatory presentations for administrators have been delivered across the state on the changes to the Pennsylvania System of School Assessment (PSSA), Pennsylvania Alternate System of Assessment (PASA), and the Stanford English Language Proficiency (SELP) assessments. All of these tests are designed to determine the proficiency levels of all students, including students with Individualized Education Plans, English Language Learners, and minority students. I wonder if the Advocacy Coalition Framework was a strong component of the adoption process. According to a countywide meeting with various foreign language supervisors and chairpersons, it seems as though the advisor had not rallied the language teachers effectively to ensure an overwhelming support for the adoption of the standards.

In search of the answers to my questions, my research led me to the district's chair of the Administrative Student Achievement Committee. The goal of the committee is to look at the data and begin to develop opportunities for conversations with various members of the district to determine how the district will meet the needs of the students who were falling behind. The information gathered at the meeting was very compelling. Once the data was gathered, strategies on how to have the courageous conversations with colleagues and teachers was discussed. The response of the community was also a concern. The decision to be honest with all constituents was the plan. The information was shared with all administrators, school board members, and district curriculum committees; a report to the district Diversity Committee was drafted. This would be the first time the information was shared with the public. Tensions arose along the way. This data was not evident in the day-to-day interactions with students and parents. Some people blamed the children's families for their lack of achievement. This could not be happening in an affluent community where resources are abundant. The district had decided to implement small support classes for all students who had not met the proficiency standards set by NCLB. They were pulled out of various classes when the teachers became increasingly aware of value-added initiatives across the state and how their students would determine their teaching value. This is how we ended up with the problem. In a district that values quality and innovation, why is it that in order to provide a quality support program for students who need it has to be at the cost of innovative programs such as the elementary and middle school language classes?

The policy I am proposing does not go without criticism. Policy tensions do develop some Language Arts/English teachers may begin to identify second language classes as providing skills that students who struggle do not need. Second Language teachers may look for their value in preparing students for a global society.

Community groups may want the same high-quality instruction for their children. The value of equity: the school must use as many resources as possible to support students who need a different approach. This is a social justice issue, where it is imperative that every student is provided with the opportunity to access the material and academic experience designed for all students. This is essential to the district's mission statement.

NCLB holds every school and district accountable for the education of all students attending their schools. We must identify the subsystems that will benefit from this policy change:

- Teachers having more efficient time with their students.
- Principals meeting AYP targets.
- District Administrators identifying immediate need for resources.
- Parents feeling as though their children will be prepared for the future and are academically supported when needed.
- Board members confident the schools are meeting the needs of every student.
- Strategic Planning Committee confident that all students are being prepared for the future and meeting the district missions.

Now that I have made the district and community aware of the unintentional obstacles that have been developed by implementing support programs as pull out experiences, what are the implications of my proposed policy? The cost of the support programs is currently 1.5 million dollars for the district to run. This program is an unfunded program developed by the district to meet the needs of the students who have not met proficiency guidelines. A more efficient use of the teachers hired to implement this program may in fact help more students along the way.

In fact, pushing in resources to the classroom where students are struggling may help even the students who may have just met the cutoff scores. The support teachers would also be able to show the classroom teachers the specific strategies that will assist in developing the skills needed for success on the assessment. Looking at the building schedule as a resource in scheduling and delivering the services to children may in fact allow students to participate in core programs designed to assist students with acquiring the skills for future success in the world. Additional anticipated obstacles may be that there will still be those who believe that learning a second language may hinder the development of the first language. Continued staff development opportunities and public relations, such as newsletters and segments on the district's local cable station identifying the successes of the program, will gradually address this obstacle.

The No Child Left Behind Act is a reality in today's educational system. Accountability and meeting Adequate Yearly Progress are concepts educators and school administrators must familiarize themselves with. The concept of leaving no child behind is one all educators must all agree with; identifying how we meet the needs of our students who struggle is up to the individual states, districts, and schools. It is also imperative that each school and district maintain high standards and innovation as they prepare their students for the future of our society. The policy that I am proposing will support the goals of the NCLB Act while addressing the unintentional pitfalls that may come with implementing additional support programs and experiences for our students who have not met the proficiency guidelines.

REFERENCES

Brown, H. (2001). *Teaching by principles: An interactive approach to language pedagogy.* White Plains, NY: Addison Wesley Longman.

Cunningham, W., & Cordeiro, P. (2003). *Educational leadership.* Boston: Pearson Education, Inc.

Curtain, H., & Pesola, C. (1994). *Languages and children.* White Plains, NY: Longman.

Earle, J., & Fruse, S. (1999). *Organizational literacy for educators.* Mahwah, NJ: Lawrence Erlbaum Associates.

Friedman, T. L. (2005). *The world is flat.* New York: Farrar, Straus and Giroux.

Hakuta, K., & Cancino, H. (1977, August). Trends in second language acquisition research. *Harvard Educational Review, 47*(3).

Heck, R. H. (2004). *Studying educational and social policy.* NJ: Lawrence Erlbaum Associates.

Hall, E. (1981). *Beyond culture.* New York: An Anchor Book.

Jossey-Bass. (2001). *The Jossey-Bass reader on school reform.* San Francisco: Author.

Landsman, J. (2004, November). Confronting the racism of low expectations. *Educational Leadership,* 28–32.

Lipton, G. (2004). *Practical handbook to elementary foreign language programs.* Kensington: Blueprints for Learning.

McKay, S., & Hornberger, N. (2001). *Sociolinguistics and language teaching.* New York: Cambridge University Press.

Mitchell, R., & Myles, F. (1998). *Second language learning theories.* New York: Arnold Publishers.

Moskowitz, G. (1978). *Caring and sharing in the foreign language classroom.* Cambridge: Newbury House Publishers.

New Jersey Department of Education. (1999). *World languages framework*. Trenton: Author.

Noguera, P. A., & Wing, J. Y. (2006). *Unfinished business: Closing the racial achievement gap in our schools*. San Francisco: Jossey-Bass.

Pennycook, A. (2000). Chapter 5: The social politics and the cultural politics of language classrooms. In J. Hall & H. Eggington (Eds.), *Sociopolitics of English teaching*. Bristol, UK: Multilingual Matters.

Pinker, S. (1994). *The language instinct: How the mind creates language*. New York. William Morrow and Company.

Singleton, G. E., & Linton, C. (2006). Courageous conversations about race Thousand Oaks, CA: Corwin Press.

Spellings, M. (2006, January 6). *Delivered remarks at the U.S. University Presidents Summit on International Education*. Washington, DC: United States Department of Education. Available at: http://www.ed.gov/news/speeches/2006/01/01062006. html

U.S. Department of Education. (2004). *The No Child Left Behind Act*. Washington, DC: Ed.gov

Wetherell, M., Taylor, S., & Yates, S. (2003). *Discourse theory and practice*. London: Sage.

Williams, B. (2003). *Closing the achievement gap*. Alexandria, VA: ASCD.

Wilson, J. (1988). *Foreign language articulation: Building bridges from elementary school to secondary school*. (ERIC Digest ED301069). Washington, DC.

Yaguello, M. (1981). *Language through the looking glass: Exploring language and linguistics*. New York: Oxford University Press.

CHAPTER 16

MOTIVATING STUDENTS THROUGH MEANINGFUL REPORT CARDS

Laurie Zaring

Secondary schools need to develop a better approach of motivating urban students to want to do better in school. Due to the recent influx of testing mandates, schools sometimes inaccurately label students as below basic, basic, proficient, or advanced based on their academic performances during one week of testing. This discourages low-performing students, inhibiting any motivation that they had to do well. "Underachievement is particularly problematic among the non-college-bound and non-white populations" (Meece & McColskey, 2001).

One way of improving a student's level of intrinsic motivation is to create a new report card that will accurately report student achievement and performance. Students are frustrated with typical report cards because as each of their teachers has a distinct way of determining their grade, similar grades represent different levels of student achievement. Typical report cards giving a percentage or a letter grade for each subject are not giving students effective feedback. Instead, they are giving limited, subjective information. Walter Gibson, an assistant superintendent in New Mexico pub-

Policy, Leadership, and Student Achievement, pages 243–255
Copyright © 2008 by Information Age Publishing
243

lic schools, asserts, "A student's ability to think abstractly or solve problems in creative ways, for example, can't always be quantified" (Pardini, 1997). If report cards only provide students and parents with percentage grades, they are not reporting the big picture of student performance. "Students respond to clear, measurable targets and continuous feedback about their progress toward those targets" (Wilson, 2005).

Many teachers combine academic and behavioral issues to determine a single percentage grade. Bill Page urges, "Don't confuse learning with behavior. Grades are supposed to reflect learning. If we include issues such as being late to class, not turning work in on time, not completing assignments or homework, or not using a proper heading, the grade is a misrepresentation" (Page, 2006). This does not mean that these items are not worth reporting to students and parents in some form, but it is best for teachers not to factor them into a single academic grade.

"The time has come for teachers to relinquish their old-fashioned, outdated techniques" (Ascolese, 2006). Dr. Thomas Guskey from the University of Kentucky observes that educators "do what was done to them, perpetuating some of the same, ineffective practices that have persisted in schools for years" (Delisio, 2004a,b). Most teachers combine several aspects when calculating student grades. One teacher may weight homework heavily, while another teacher may not even include it. "Some teachers base grades on as few as two or three elements, while others incorporate evidence from as many as 15 or 16" (Guskey, 2006).

"Individual teacher's grading procedures are, eh, well, individual" (Page, 2006). Students have difficulty trying to find consistency in grading practices throughout their schooling. Policy makers think that the "mismatch between grades and scores on accountability assessments stems from bias and subjectivity in teachers' grading practices" (Guskey, 2006). Currently, anyone who reads a report card has a hard time distinguishing between a student who is very intelligent but does not exert any effort versus a student who works hard but is not a good test taker. It is possible that "students with such different levels of demonstrated knowledge and skill" (Guskey, 2006) receive almost identical grades in their high school classes. The rationale for this is because teachers combine "elements of achievement, attitude, effort, and behavior" (Guskey, 2006) into a single percentage grade. Different teachers use different formulas to determine grades because their "purpose for grading is unclear" (Guskey, 2006).

The purpose of grading is hard for teachers or administrators to identify. One reason for grading is to communicate with students and parents about student performance. Another function is to classify which students are suitable for certain educational programs. Third, grading provides incentives for students to learn. Fourth, it is a way of documenting students' lack of effort or responsibility (Guskey, 2005). With so many purposes, "no one method of grading and reporting serves all purposes well" (Guskey, 2005).

"All learners, regardless of age, require feedback to efficiently improve performance" (Wilson, 2005) and schools must redesign their report cards to provide significant feedback. Current "assessment methods that teachers use are not effective in promoting good learning" (Black, Harrison, Lee, Marshall, & Williams, 2004). Teachers disclose student expectations and responsibilities for learning. In addition, "grading practices tend to emphasize competition rather than personal improvement" (Black et al., 2004). Low-achieving students "are led to believe that they 'lack ability' and so are not able to learn" (Black et al., 2004) because of the way teachers handle grading procedures.

POLICY ISSUES

Dr. Guskey states that opposition to student report cards is not new, but rather dates back to the late 1800s (Pardini, 1997). At that time, report cards included "simple lists of skills mastered as well as those that required additional practice" (Pardini, 1997), but percentage grades soon replaced these by 1910. "With larger and more diverse student populations and more complex curricula, most high schools began using percentages as a way of measuring student achievement" (Pardini, 1997), giving grades more clarity to suit the needs of society. However, percentage grades were deemed inconsistent when teachers across the country were asked to grade "the same two English and geometry papers according to their schools' standards" (Pardini, 1997). The results showed major discrepancies. Marita Moll (1998) validates, "In 1911, researchers testing the reliability of the marks entered on these cards showed that the same material could be assigned widely different marks depending on the markers." In an effort to correct these wide variations, schools switched to "rating systems such as Excellent, Good, Average, Poor and Failing, or A through F" (Pardini, 1997). Curving started in the 1930s "in an attempt to distribute grades more fairly" (Pardini, 1997) and the public accepted this because "it linked achievement to intelligence test scores, which approximated a normal probability curve" (Pardini, 1997).

Over the years, our nation and individual states have adopted subject-specific standards and changed curriculums. As school reform emerges, administrators and teachers must decide if their current system of grading matches what is happening in the classroom. Thus, the debate continues. In deciding how to best evaluate student performance and report the results, "some schools have eliminated grades altogether, others opted for pass-fail systems" (Pardini, 1997). However, the percentage grading system has remained the most popular. Teachers assign "each student a number between zero and 100, the number supposedly reflecting the percentage of the material that the student had learned" (Moll, 1998).

With the advent of NCLB and the resulting rise in student accountability, teachers and administrators have started to think differently about what and how teachers should teach. In fact, "forty-nine states have adopted standards for what all students should know and do and tests to assess their performance" (Epstein, 2004). "As curriculums are changing, so are report cards" (Delisio, 2004a,b). "Current interest in alternative grading systems can be linked to the school reform and restructuring movements of the past decade" (Pardini, 1997).

According to Dr. Guskey, most school districts are revamping report cards because they have identified "the mismatch between what they are striving to accomplish academically and what information they offer to parents regarding students' achievement in school" (Delisio, 2004a,b). "With more things to teach, assess, and track, teachers need more precise ways of assessing students than A to F" (Delisio, 2004a,b). This is a result of the national standards movement.

Recently there has been a wave of interest in standards-based report cards. In Florida, Paul W. Felsch, program manager in student assessment, states, "We have these standards that are driving instruction, so they should drive what happens on the report cards, too" (Libit, 1999). The format of these new reports matches what someone would see if they examined state standards for that particular subject and grade level. For each standard, teachers rate students as one of the following categories: Proficient, Advanced, Basic, or Below Basic. Schools that use report cards of this type must "ensure that parents can understand and make sense of the information provided" (Delisio, 2004a,b). This new approach confuses some parents because they want to know what category corresponds to what letter grade.

"Few school systems are willing to change much beyond elementary schools" (Libit, 1999). Perhaps a reason for this is that traditional letter and percentage grades at the secondary level are "the preferred way that most colleges and universities look at applicants" (Libit, 1999). Another reason for most of the changes occurring at the elementary level is that "there is less curriculum differentiation at that level" (Delisio, 2004a,b). Some elementary schools have devised a report card for which they rate students as "B" for beginning, "D" for developing, or "C" for consistently apparent. Teachers base the reports on a continuum, looking at growth over a whole period. Each subject has target areas of what the teachers expect students to master over a span of a year. An advantage of such a report is that it allows the onlooker to measure growth rather than each marking period as a separate entity. Other elementary school teachers include descriptive narratives on report cards. The narratives describe how each student is doing in school, both academically and cognitively.

In New Richmond, Ohio, school leaders feel that this alternative report card "better reflect(s) a school district's goals and gives parents more information about their children's progress" (Pardini, 1997). Principal David Riel said that because of their revised report card, "the kids' motivation is different now. I see them coming to school wanting to learn and caring less about grades" (Pardini, 1997).

Educators use a myriad of ways to determine a student's grade; however, Guskey names "three broad categories: product, process, and progress criteria" (Guskey, 2006) to which most teachers would relate. Teachers who use product criteria believe that the main purpose of grading is to "assess what students know and are able to do at a particular point in time" (Guskey, 2006), whereas teachers who use process criteria are not only interested in "the final result, but also how students got there" (Guskey, 2006). Other teachers believe that they should measure growth based on where students start and where they finish, called progress criteria (Guskey, 2006). Because of the three possible ways that a teacher could determine student grades, it is hard for everyone involved to interpret grades. It "becomes exceptionally challenging, not only for parents but also for administrators, community members, and even the students themselves" (Guskey, 2006) to compare how students are performing.

Some American schools have tried to remedy this problem by including separate grades for each set of criteria. This is a logical solution. "Marks for learning skills, effort, work habits, and learning progress are kept distinct from assessments of achievement and performance" (Guskey, 2006). For years, Canadian educators have "separated grades for product, process, and progress criteria" (Guskey, 2006). They report a single percentage grade for each subject, called an "achievement grade," but also they give separate scores "for homework, class participation, punctuality of assignment submissions, effort, learning progress, and the like" (Guskey, 2006).

In the Montgomery County Public Schools, "factors such as student behavior, attitude, attendance, and participation will not be included in the final grade" (Delisio, 2004a,b) because school officials believe that when teachers include these items, inflation occurs. Betsy Brown, the district's director of pre-K–12 curriculum development, reports, "We don't want them to get an A, B, or C [in class] and then fail a high-stakes test" (Delisio, 2004a,b). Overall, their goal is to provide students and parents with a more honest report of what is happening in their classes.

"More consistency and clarity also was the goal of the New York City Public Schools, the nation's largest school system" (Delisio, 2004a,b) when revamping report cards. The new version of their report cards uses the same scale that their state achievement tests use (Delisio, 2004a,b). In the Mohonasen Central School District, New York, "the grading key has been revised to align with the New York State system for reporting student progress"

(Mohonasen, 2005). The grading key uses E for exceeding standards, M for meeting standards, S for slightly below the state standard, W for well below the state standard, and X for "working to the best of their ability, below the expected standard" (Mohonasen, 2005).

One of the most comprehensive report cards in the nation belongs to a Texas school district, Corpus Christi (Libit, 1999). On the backside of the report cards, there is a list of the skills that students are expected to achieve. "For each subject area, there are as many as 15 standards in which teachers must report whether students have achieved the performance standard, are making progress toward the standard or failed to meet the standard" (Libit, 1999).

WHAT MOTIVATES STUDENTS

"By the time a student has reached adolescence, poor motivation has become one of the chief contributors to underachievement" (Meece & McColskey, 2001). However, newspaper headlines rarely address the topic of student motivation; instead, the public reads about standardized test results. "The focus of policy at the state level is often on district-level incentives for increased test scores and sanctions for low test scores, with little consideration of the kinds of impact such policies might have on teachers and, ultimately, student motivation" (Meece & McColskey, 2001).

Determining what factors motivate students to do well in school is not an easy task. In regards to grading procedures, it is simpler to discuss what causes a decrease in student motivation. It is upsetting to students when they receive a grade and feel they were not treated fairly. For example, students are easily frustrated by teachers who determine grades haphazardly and without reason, have favorites when grading subjective items such as art projects and essays, or give tests that do not represent material covered in class. On the other hand, students respond well to teachers using rubrics because they know exactly how their paper or project will be graded before turning it in. "Students are not as likely to perform well if they are kept in the dark about expectations and asked to work without a real understanding of how their work or performance will be assessed" (Meece & McColskey, 2001). Intrinsic motivation is increased when students know exactly what is expected of them on graded items so that they can prepare adequately. "Students' motivation to learn is greatly influenced by their teachers' expectations for student learning" (Meece & McColskey, 2001).

Unexplained grading procedures on a project or a test are harmful to students' motivation, but these feelings are compounded when the same thing happens for their report card grades. Students who really tried to do their best to receive a high grade on a report card are surprised and doubly upset when they find out that different teachers weighted graded items so differently. For example, one teacher may count homework for 10% of a report card grade, whereas another weights homework as 50% of a grade. Depending on which formula a teacher chooses, a grade may be inflated or deflated appropriately.

CONFLICTING PUBLIC VALUES

As schools revise their report cards, they must carefully balance tradition with new ideas. Parents and community members are comfortable with traditional report cards. That is what they experienced as students, and that is what they expect. They do not want their children to bring home a report card that they do not understand. They want to see growth and a clear description of how the child is performing in school. "Parents are demanding a more active role in their children's education and reporting process as a whole" (Ascolese, 2006).

History tells that Americans strive for academic excellence. As a result, parents desperately want their children to receive good grades on their report cards. When students show their parents their report card, "high grades are celebrated and rewarded: low grades are cause for serious concern" (Aidman, Gates, & Deterra Sims, 2000). Just as "equity concerns have always been a prime motivator of standards-based reforms" (Epstein, 2004), equity concerns are again motivating schools to design new report cards. It is imperative that all schools measure student performance similarly. If schools are to teach all students rigorous content, they must also report what is happening in the classroom.

Revising report cards is costly due to the time factor involved in such a process, but the cost to the district's budget would be minimal. Most districts already own computerized grading programs that allow for flexibility in the format of report cards. There are predetermined formats or schools can customize packaged items to better suit their needs.

POLITICAL DYNAMICS

Although school districts feel that they are providing information that is more meaningful to parents, many schools are finding that parents and other community members meet their efforts with a lot of resistance. This is understandable, as report cards are the most visible way—sometimes the only way—that parents can determine how well their child is doing in school. "Traditionally, the report card had been our only glimpse into the child's education process. It was also the only means of communicating student progress" (Ascolese, 2006).

Parents are not shy when it comes to voicing their opinions of new report cards. In Gloucester, Massachusetts, there was a record turnout of parents at a 1995 committee meeting that caused the school "to abandon a new reporting system that had replaced letter grades with student portfolios and narrative reports" (Pardini, 1997). Parents in Rio Rancho, New Mexico forced school leaders to reinstate letter grades. They opposed the new approach of rating "students as 'novice', 'apprentice', 'practitioner', or 'expert' on dozens of skills" (Pardini, 1997) because they felt as if teachers were labeling the students. In some cases, the battle over report card revisions became intense. In Seattle, "tensions in the Federal Way School District grew so heated this year over revising the report card used in its 23 elementary schools that a mediator ended up having to be hired" (Libit, 1999).

Parents are not the only ones complaining about new report cards. School board members in the Howard County School District near Baltimore, Maryland were upset at the district's report card committee. "They were tired of having to use a reference manual to decipher how children were performing" (Libit, 1999). Board members wanted a simple report that was easy for the public to understand.

Some stakeholders are excited that schools are changing their old-fashioned ways of reporting student performance. With a typical report card, "All of the child's labors were compressed into one neat grade and from this single grade the parent had to conjure an entire picture" (Ascolese, 2006). Several parents believe that separating grades into more than one category "provides a more comprehensive profile of their child's performance in school" (Guskey, 2006).

Standards-based report cards offer more than a single percentage grade for each subject. For each standard, teachers rate students categorically. "Such a report card actually provides more detailed, specific information than a traditional grade, though parents and students may find the change disconcerting" (Manzo, 2001). This approach is helpful to job interviewers and college admission counselors because each "can distinguish between the student who earned high grades with relatively little effort and the one who earned equally high grades through diligence and hard work" (Guskey, 2006).

In Australia, many Catholic school parents "appreciate how difficult it may be for teachers to convey bad news but they still want a fair and honest assessment of their child's abilities to determine their rate of progress" (Ferrari, 2006), while others have found the same report cards unclear and puzzling. Australia's government recently introduced report cards that have stirred controversy because they "provide information on the student's rankings according to their peers" (Ferrari, 2006).

Regarding the Canadian approach to report cards, teachers often view their grade reporting system as extra work because the items included on report cards are extremely specific. "However, most discover that by including homework assignments as part of an overall grade for students, they already face this challenge" (Guskey, 2006). Regardless of first impressions, teachers "who use the procedure claim that it actually makes grading easier and less work" (Guskey, 2006). Without reporting different marks for different categories, teachers must determine a formula for grading. It especially perplexes beginning teachers as they begin to formulate the weighting of different graded items such as projects, tests, and participation.

Members of higher education typically agree that "how you grade depends a great deal on your values, assumptions, and educational philosophy" (Davis, 1999). Barbara Gross Davis of the University of California at Berkeley recommends that professors calculate grades based only on academic performance, rather than "other considerations, such as classroom behavior, effort, classroom participation, attendance, punctuality, attitude, personality traits, or student interest in the course material" (Davis, 1999). Also, teachers should not use grading practices that limit the number of high grades. Students will have less opposition to grades if they are kept informed throughout the whole term, rather than a surprise grade at the end of a course (Davis, 1999).

SOLUTIONS

The process of providing students, parents, college admission counselors, and job interviewers with more detailed information of how a student performs in the classroom, educators must be addressed with caution. Unfortunately, I do not believe that there is a "one size fits all" solution to the problem of reporting meaningful student performance. No single report card would satisfy stakeholders in communities across the nation.

Therefore, I propose that state departments of education provide resources and necessary funding for school districts interested in revising their report cards. This would allow school districts to form committees of students, teachers, parents, administrators, and community leaders to create a meaningful report card. Stakeholders at the local level must help to create the revised report cards. A top-down approach pushed into schools across our diverse nation would equal a recipe for disaster. Larry Cuban agrees, saying today's current educational reforms "take power away from local school boards and educators, the only people who can improve what happens in classrooms, and give it to distant officials, who have little capacity to achieve results" (Epstein, 2004).

It is extremely important to involve students in this decision-making process. Especially in urban schools, "organizing urban youth to work with others to improve their schools and neighborhoods gives teenagers connections, embedding them in constructive community networks" (Anyon, 2005). Schools create new versions of report cards for students, yet sometimes they forget to include students as members of committees. "This omission is unfortunate because, as key participants in the teaching-learning initiatives, students have a profound influence on the success of those efforts" (Sergiovanni et al., 2004).

Involving community members, not just students, teachers, and administrators who are involved with schools on a daily basis, are also vital to the success of the committee's decisions. Anyon insists, "when educators work with community residents as equals and as change agents to organize for better education, movement building is taking place; and as a not inconsequential outcome, schools typically improve and student achievement increases" (Anyon, 2005).

Although I believe that each school district should have the flexibility to design their own report card, I have several suggestions for what research says will lead to a more meaningful report. To communicate effectively with non-educators, the report card needs to be free from educational jargon. Regardless of the format chosen by the committee, report cards should include more than a single grade for a six or nine-week performance. Possibilities include how much effort a student puts into the class, level of participation in class activities, the percentage of assignments completed on time, and how well the student works in a group setting. Lastly, research shows that revising report cards tends to be an emotional and complicated process (Delisio, 2004a,b). "If there's a consistency to making report card revisions, it's that such changes always lead to emotional confrontations" (Libit, 1999).

Based on his work with assessment in many schools, Grant Wiggins has 12 suggestions for success in revising report cards. Most notably, "differentiate the level of performance from the quality of the work. Little is gained by giving an A to someone who is very bright but careless and a C to someone who is behind but methodical and accurate" (Wiggins, 1997), and report cards should have a way of distinguishing this situation through comments and different grades. Wiggins also believes in the community component, saying, "The report is not designed to satisfy teachers but to inform the clients. Parents should have a say at all stages of the process, and focus groups should be used to give parents the opportunity to react to current, proposed and other systems' reporting methods" (Wiggins, 1997).

In urban schools, the percentage of students who are English language learners (ELL) is substantially high. Students "who have attended U.S. schools for at least three years must take reading assessments in English" (Epstein, 2004). These federally mandated testing practices on English language learners are unfair. However, a school district could develop a separate report card for ELL students that would accommodate their individual situation. Schools should not distribute the same exact report card, thus comparing these students to students who have been speaking English all of their lives. Instead, schools could rate their student performance on a continuum to show growth in specific areas such as English vocabulary and writing.

It is difficult, if not impossible, for anyone to quantify levels of student motivation. Over time, revising report cards to allow for a more meaningful measure of student performance will increase student motivation in wanting to do better in school. However, history shows that policymakers and the American public will want to evaluate the effectiveness of such a program. Typically, there has been only one way to complete an evaluation. Cuban asserts, "For policies intended to improve student academic achievement, effectiveness (or ineffectiveness) has been severely narrowed to gains and losses in scores on standardized tests" (Epstein, 2004). Results of statewide testing will not indicate success or lack thereof in regards to revising report cards. Instead, policymakers will have to develop trust in local school districts to make the right decisions for their students and parents.

Each school will have different struggles in the process of updating report cards, but there are some similarities among schools. Successful revisions will include student, parent, teacher, and community involvement. Schools will offer training sessions for parents and the community to understand the new report cards. The committee will choose a format that is easy to understand and free of educational jargon. Add patience and flexibility to these items for a complete picture of what it will take to implement new report cards successfully; that is, to give students and parents honest and meaningful feedback on their performance. This requires that a committee determine the best method of "accurate and understandable descriptions of student learning" "organized into a user-friendly format" (Aidman et al., 2000).

REFERENCES

Aidman, B., Gates, J., & Deterra Sims, E. (2000). Building a better report card (Report No. ED 448 499). Alexandria, VA: NAESP National Principals Resource Center. (ERIC Document Reproduction Service No. EA 030717).

Anyon, J. (2005). *Radical possibilities: Public policy, urban education & a new social movement.* New York: Routledge.

Ascolese, J. (2006) Why schools must change. Retrieved July 27, 2006, from http://www.ed.psu.edu/insys/esd/need/JA_Why.html

Black, P., Harrison, C., Lee, C., Marshall, B., & Wiliam, D. (2004, September). Working inside the black box: Assessment for learning in the classroom. *Phi Delta Kappan*, 9–21.

Black, P., & Wiliam, D. (1998). Inside the black box: Raising standards through classroom assessment. *Phi Delta Kappan*. Retrieved August 5, 2006, from www.edsource.org/edu_ass_res_black.cfm

Davis, B. (1999). Grading practices. Retrieved April 23, 2007, from http://honolulu.hawaii.edu/intranet/committees/FacDevCom/guidebk/teachtip/grading.htm

Delisio, E. (2004a). Make way for the new report cards. *Education World*. Retrieved July 20, 2006, from www.education-world.com

Delisio, E. (2004b). What will your school's next report card look like? *Education World*. Retrieved July 20, 2006, from www.educationworld.com/a_admin/admin/admin333.shtml

Epstein, N. (2004). *Who's in charge here: the tangled web of school governance and policy*. Washington, DC: Brookings Institutional Press.

Ferrari, J. (2006, June). Catholic school parents want grades. Retrieved August 5, 2006, from www.theaustralian.news.com.au

Guskey, T. (2005). Grading and reporting student learning. Presentation at Newport High School.

Guskey, T. (2006, May). Making high school grades meaningful. *Phi Delta Kappan*, 670–674.

Libit, H. (1999, November). Report card redux: the quest for better ways to communicate what students know means abandoning jargon for dots, dashes, even X's and O's. *The School Administrator*. Retrieved August 3, 2006, from http://www.aasa.org/publications/saarticledetail.cfm?ItemNumber=3717&snItemNumber=950&tnItemNumber=951

Manzo, K. M. (2001, September). Districts tinker with report cards to make better sense of standards. *Education Week*.

Meece, J., & McColskey, W. (2001). Improving student motivation: a guide for teachers and school improvement teams. Retrieved April 23, 2007, from http://www.serve.org/_downloads/publications/rdism2.pdf

Mohonasen School District. (2005). Pinewood moves to computerized report cards. Retrieved July 21, 2006, from www.mohonasen.org/03pinewood/ComputerizedReportCards.htm

Moll, M. (1998). The history of grading in three minutes. Retrieved April 27, 2007, from http://www.ctf-fce.ca/en/press/1998/PR30.HTM

Page, B. (2006). Improving classroom grading procedures. Retrieved August 5, 2006, from www.teacherteacher.com

Pardini, P. (1997, December). Alternative ways to report student progress find favor among educators but doubts among parents. *The School Administrator*. Retrieved July 19, 2006, from www.aasa.org/publications/saarticledetail.cfm?ItemNumber=4363

Sergiovanni, T., Kelleher, P., McCarthy, M., & Wirt, F. (2004). *Educational governance and administration* (5th ed). Boston: Pearson.

Wiggins, G. (1997, December). Tips on reforming student report cards. *The School Administrator*. Retrieved April 27, 2007, from http://www.aasa.org/publications/content.cfm?ItemNumber=4359

Wilson, R. (2005). Targeted growth for every student: when this district wanted an assessment program with practical applications to teaching and learning, it selected a computerized adaptive test that measures student growth over time. Retrieved July 22, 2006, from the LookSmart database.

CHAPTER 17

UNIVERSAL PRE-KINDERGARTEN AS A BASIS OF URBAN EDUCATIONAL REFORM

Greg Kratzer

This past June, a local urban school district sent out 45 furlough notices primarily to teachers and aides in the district's highly touted pre-kindergarten program. This program worked in cooperation with the Federal Head Start program, and has been regarded by district administrators as one of the success stories in the district's reform plan. The employees that received these furloughs were told that it was due to budgetary constraints. This incident is indicative of not only the district's priorities, but also the priorities of all the educational stakeholders in this country. Pre-kindergarten programs are not mandated by the federal government. Meaning that beyond the 6 billion dollars that the Federal government allocates for Head Start every fiscal year, it is the responsibility of state and local governments to raise the funds to operate these programs.

Research has shown that all manner of pre-kindergarten programs yield positive results for three-, four- and five-year-old students. These results are

Policy, Leadership, and Student Achievement, pages 257–268
Copyright © 2008 by Information Age Publishing
All rights of reproduction in any form reserved.

especially significant in Hispanic, African American, and low-income children. These programs help to significantly reduce the achievement gap of these children as they head into elementary school. The problem arises in that these programs are not universally provided, they lack funding to reach the students who truly need them, and there is a total lack of consistency between federally funded and state operated programs. To truly begin nationwide urban education reform, these problems need to be addressed. Urban education would be better served by a governmentally mandated program offering universal pre-kindergarten in urban environments ("urbanversal"), addressing the achievement gap of low-income and minority learners in these settings. This long-term plan for urban reform will require in-depth examination of the current political climate, American ideology, and evaluation of our public values.

POLICY CONTEXT

Any discussion about a drastic shift in the way we make educational policy would have to take into consideration the American political ideology. Americans look for short-term solutions to long-term problems. We need immediate, measurable results to justify creating and/or re-authorizing any policy. Also, the average American is not fully aware of the implication of most educational policy. For these two reasons, it is no wonder No Child Left Behind was originally passed and reauthorized. This legislation conveys an image of accountability for educational systems, and a 14-year plan to achieve full academic proficiency for all of America's youth. NCLB ties achievement in public schools (K–12) and meeting adequate yearly progress to both federal and state funding. Those schools that achieve shall receive. This kind of allocation system fails to address the "Achievement Gap" that research shows is clearly visible between urban minority, low income students and their white suburban peers. "On average, poor children enter school with far fewer vocabulary, literacy, math, and social skills than their middle-class peers. They start off a step behind, and never catch up; the gap in academic proficiency follows them to the end of their schooling" (Kafer, 2004). Rather than address this achievement gap, NCLB holds schools accountable for educating students who lack the necessary skills to succeed on standardized tests at very young ages, and continually ask them to build on those skills that they do not have. In short NCLB exacerbates the achievement gap in urban schools.

During Lyndon Johnson's War on Poverty, extensive research was done on the "achievement gap." As a starting point for addressing this gap, the Federal *Head Start* program was started in 1965. In its 40-year history, *Head Start* has spent 66 billion dollars on educating 21 million three- to five-year-old children (Kafer, 2004). This figures out to roughly seven thousand dollars in per-pupil expenditures. The 2005 budget allocation for *Head Start* was 6.6 billion dollars, and is expected to provide instruction for 901,851 three- to five-year-old children (www.acf.hhs.gov). In recent years more individual states have also begun funding their own pre-kindergarten (pre-K) programs to address the achievement gap. Currently 42 states offer pre-k programs, most with some type of standards for pre-k, but only 16 have the power to regulate or enforce standards (Mitchell, 2001). These programs include providing money for private schools subsidies, pre-k centers, family care centers, faith-based programs, and public school pre-k. Currently only about one-third of all public schools provide pre-k (U.S. Department of Education, 2005). Last year, 68% of kindergarteners attended some form of preschool prior to kindergarten in some type of federally or state funded program. In addition, American taxpayers spent 25 billion dollars on pre-k programs last year (U.S. Department of Education, 2005).

There are several challenges/problems for pre-k education in our current system. Considering the lack of a government mandate, programs nationwide are incredibly fragmented, inconsistent in quality, and underfunded. In a nationwide study it was found that 71% of pre-k students were served in public schools, 15% in child care centers, 7% in Head Start, less than 1% in family-care centers, less than 1% in faith-based centers, and the rest in other types of pre-k programs (Schumacher et al., 2005). This fragmentation in delivery model plays into the second problem, which is program inconsistency. Each of these types of programs operates under a very different set of standards and regulations. Pre-k service providers differ in the belief over whether or not three-year-olds benefit more from learning or play, and this belief drives the activities of the program. This causes a major problem in comparing and studying pre-k programs, for each pre-k program is drastically different. Also, teachers of pre-k tend to be the least qualified teachers of students at any grade level. The average yearly wage for an early childhood (pre-k) teacher is $19,610 compared to the average kindergarten teacher who receives $36,770 (Maeroff, 2003). Lastly is the issue of funding. As an example, Head Start has allocated by far the most money for pre-k, but their standards for teacher quality tend to be lower than the state pre-k programs; yet the states have no power to dictate how Head Start money is to be spent (Strengthening Head Start, 2003).

This fragmentation inevitably detracts from the positive effects of pre-k programs. Head Start's primary purpose is to serve the needs of the economically underprivileged, and more so than state programs they do this. Head Start serves some of the most economically distressed areas of our country. However, research shows that state-run programs have higher standards for teacher qualification and are aligned with state curriculum and therefore tend to produce better results. We need to streamline this process. We need to reach the right children, with the right staff and with adequate funding. The basis of reform exists; we simply must manage and allocate our resources in a more efficient and effective way. Any policy trying to address the achievement gap by expanding pre-k education would have to address the issue of fragmentation and inconsistency among current programs.

BALANCING PUBLIC VALUES

The repeal of our current educational policy and the implementation of a universal pre-k program for urban districts in America will raise many concerns in the public. It would be crucial to address these concerns in terms of American values before any thought of a policy change could take place. The number one concern would be that much of the public may look at a focus on pre-k as giving up on the generation of kids that are currently enrolled in urban public schools, in favor of admitting our system's failure and starting over on a new generation. People may look at this plan as "cutting losses" and giving up on our current system. Another concern is the issue of transience. Urban districts have the highest rates of students moving into and out of districts. Would this lack of consistency undermine the implementation of system like universal pre-k? Also, the repeal of our current system of appropriations would change the way that high performing schools receive funding. Would taking away the financial incentive for schools to achieve affect the level of education at already high-performing schools? Lastly, implementing a policy such as universal pre-k would require the government to convince the people that universal pre-k is an investment in our future, and it may take years to prove the overall effect of the program. In short, you would have to convince Americans to be patient, which is no small task.

The response to all of these concerns is equity. History has shown us that one of the main roles of the Federal government is to ensure the equitable treatment of all of its citizens. The Fourteenth and Nineteenth Amendments, the Civil Rights Act of 1965, Supreme Court cases such as *Brown v. Board of Education*, and many other federal statutes prove that the Federal government is responsible for promoting equity when the states and local governments are incapable of doing so. The same is true in the case of urban education. Everyone agrees that there is a problem, even a crisis, in urban education and a "one size fits all" program like NCLB cannot fix the problem. In response to the first concern of "cutting losses," the equitable thing to do in education is to address the root of the problem, which is the achievement gap that has brought us to this point in the first place. Universal pre-k will put the focus of the Federal government's role in education on breaking the cycle of consistent underachievement by urban schools, to provide an equitable learning experience for children in those schools throughout their educational career. As far as transience, that is why a "universal" pre-k program is being promoted. A universal pre-k program would target all at-risk learners in urban environments, and if they move to another urban area, the same type of program will be available. For the already successful schools, the removal of the Federal mandates of NCLB will allow them to pursue educational goals of their own, and the state, thus increasing their autonomy. Funding may not be equal, but a program like pre-k for urban environs will be targeting the areas in which there is true problem in the educational system. The last concern was the need for American patience. After the *Brown* ruling in 1954, it took more than 15 years to successfully integrate all of the nation's public schools. The American people can be patient, but it takes a pervasive and decisive movement within the Federal government to force them to be.

INTEREST GROUPS

When considering major policy overhaul such as the pre-k initiative, the coordination of many autonomous groups must be considered. The federal, state, and local governments (namely urban school districts) will have to accept and agree that a universal pre-k program is a proactive rather than a reactive answer to the crisis in urban education. Also, as is the biggest obstacle in most educational reform, is the issue of funding. All three levels of government will have to work to consolidate the fragmented basis of funding for an aggressive program such as this.

To address these interest groups it is important to start at the overall goal of a universal pre-k program, which would be to address the persistent achievement gap in urban districts to improve the quality of education nationwide. After this goal can be accepted, the work will be in how to provide this service in a cooperative fashion giving each stakeholder a meaningful role in overseeing the program. Recent history (NCLB) has shown that the bureaucratic, top-down, approach to educational reform is not well-received. For this reason, the principles of our federal system of government will have to be utilized. The Federal level, in accordance with their charge to promote the general welfare, will create a mandate for universal pre-k programs in what are considered distressed educational areas. Along with this mandate will come funding (to be discussed later). The states, which under the 10th Amendment should have the power to regulate education, will be responsible for creating regulations and standards for pre-k programs and enforcing these regulations. The states will use provided federal funding to allocate to districts in need to create the necessary facilities and hire appropriate staff to meet state regulations. This kind of cooperation will give each level legitimate and Constitutionally appropriate authority to serve the needs of education.

As stated earlier, the main obstacle is always funding. Much like the current fragmentation in terms of pre-k delivery methods and service, Federal funding is incredibly fragmented. There are six major Federal sources of funding for early childhood and pre-k education. The following is a list of each of these programs and their early childhood educational allowances:

1. Child Care and Development Fund (CCDF) – 2.1 Billion
2. Temporary Assistance to Needy Families (TANF) – 3.9 Billion
3. Head Start and Early Head Start – 6.6 Billion
4. Child and Adult Care Food Program (CACFP) – 1.7 Billion
5. Social Services Block Grant (SSBG) – 2.75 Billion (400 Million used for early childhood education)
6. Individuals with Disabilities Education Act (IDEA) – Approximately 800 million spent on early childhood education (Clothier et al., 2003).

All told, these programs provide roughly eighteen billion in early childhood education funding; including four of the programs (Head Start, CCDF, TANF, CACFP) which require some type of state matching fund to be eligible (Clothier et al., 2003). The point is this: the basis of funding is there, but it will require a streamlining of these funds into a single Federal categorical grant to be spent on universal pre-k for educationally distressed urban environments. In addition to these Federal funds, 43 states have money earmarked in their general funds for early childhood programs. States have also begun to use alternative sources of funding such as: Tobacco settlement funds, special taxes (namely "sin" taxes on cigarettes, alcohol, and gambling), family leave revenue sources, business tax credits, loans, and lotteries (Clothier et al., 2003). With appropriate cooperation, the expense of an aggressive universal pre-k program could be met.

DISINTERESTED RECOMMENDATIONS

In the interest of bringing equity to urban education, reform has to begin at the source of the problem, which has been identified as the achievement gap of minority and low-income urban learners. To address that gap, an "urbanversal" pre-k program should be established. "Urbanversal," because a true universal pre-k for the entire country is unrealistic given our fiscal situation, the lack of facility space and the fact that research shows that the economically privileged do not benefit from pre-k programs nearly as much as the underprivileged. An "urbanversal" program would identify the educationally distressed, urban areas of the country, and put into place, using Federal dollars, a pre-k program for three and four year olds. This program would be integrated with state kindergarten curriculums and be based upon state standards for academic adequacy and staffing. This type of program would bring the services necessary to close the achievement gap to the students that research shows benefit the most from such programs. This way, we can offer equitable learning experiences to all of America's youth.

Current research has shown that there is a disparity in the pre-kindergarten learning experiences between minority and nonminority children. The National Assessment of Educational Progress reported in 2003 these percentages of children who recognize the letters of the alphabet upon entering kindergarten: 80% of Asians, 71% of Whites, 59% of Blacks, and 51% of Hispanics (Maeroff, 2003). The Hispanic and Black populations make up the overwhelming majority of urban children, and are not starting out with the same set of skills in kindergarten as their White peers. This achievement gap is not being appropriately addressed by our current, fragmented pre-k providers. As an example the largest (in funding) pre-k provider, Head Start, only provided education to 901,000 three and four year olds in 2004 (www.acf.hhs.gov). This is not enough.

Georgia was the first state in the union to offer a comprehensive, universal pre-k program. Georgia created their pre-k program in 1993, and since then New York, Oklahoma, and New Jersey have started legislative initiatives to adopt similar programs (Oklahoma's program will be cited later). In 2001 Georgia conducted an in-depth evaluation of their pre-k program, and found significant results. This evaluation measured the cognitive development of 4th graders in pre-k programs offered in: their own public schools, Head Start, private schools, and private child care centers (Henry et al., 2003). 466 children that were tested before any pre-k program tested well-below national norms for language and cognitive skill development (Henry et al., 2003). These children were tested again after attending one of the various pre-k offerings in Georgia. In all of the programs students made gains of at least four points compared to national norms upon entering kindergarten (Henry et al., 2003). This study found that *Head Start* and the public school offered pre-k showed the highest gains, and the public pre-k program showed the most consistent evidence of growth (Henry et al., 2003). In examining test scores, the public pre-k students had closed the original gap in achievement when compared to the private schools and childcare centers. Georgia kindergarten teachers also reported that the public school pre-k students were better prepared than their Head Start and private school peers. (Henry et al., 2003) The researchers noted that as a part of their study, they found that the public pre-k teachers had, on average, a higher level of education than the Head Start or the private school teachers (Henry et al., 2003).

A similar study was conducted in Oklahoma in 2001 to evaluate their universal pre-k program, which was implemented in 1995. This study differed in that the researchers focused more on race and socioeconomic status of the students and how these various groups benefited from the pre-k program. Oklahoma's pre-k program was similar to Georgia's, with the exception that they offered both full- and half-day programs, which was also considered (Gormley & Phillips, 2003). Students in the study were tested both before the pre-k program and during their kindergarten year. Their major finding was that Hispanics showed the highest statistical gains in standardized test scores by attending any type of pre-k (Gormley & Phillips, 2003). Blacks also showed significant gains when enrolled in full day programs. Whites, however, did not show any statistically significant gains in any program other than the half-day pre-k (Gormley & Phillips, 2003). Of similar significance were the gains that were made by students enrolled in the pre-k programs who were receiving both free and reduced lunches. Students who qualified for free and reduced lunches benefited from both full- and half-day programs. Conversely, students who did not qualify for free and reduced lunches showed no significant improvement in test scores (Gormley, Phillips, 2003). One interpretation of this research could be that the White and nonqualifiers for free and reduced lunch students did not benefit from the pre-k program as much as the Hispanic, Black, and low-income students simply because they already possessed the skills necessary to succeed in kindergarten. This is merely more evidence of the achievement gap that exists between the economically privileged and underprivileged.

Another study conducted in 2000 by Taylor, Dearing, and McCartney sought to find a correlation between family economic resources and developmental outcomes (Taylor et al., 2004). They identified an "income gap" that affected the development of preschool children. Children from families with less economic resources developed slower than those with more. During their study they also found that students in Early Head Start were more likely to overcome this "income gap" before kindergarten (Taylor et al., 2004).

Beyond simply academic progress, various studies on the High/Scope Perry Preschool program in Chicago found that there were many other long-term social and economic effects of an effective pre-k program. These studies have found that participants in preschool are much less likely to be retained in grade or put in special education programs, thus saving tax dollars in the long run (Barnett & Hustedt, 2003). Also, participants were more likely to get jobs and earn more money after high school (Barnett & Hustedt, 2003). Lastly, participants were less likely to break laws or be incarcerated (Barnett & Hustedt, 2003).

Analysis of the research shows that a number of considerations would have to be taken into account before pursuing an "urbanversal" pre-k program. The first consideration is program quality. Research shows that not all pre-k programs produce the same results. Those that were highly successful in closing the achievement gap had high quality staff, and much more rigorous academic standards. Part of convincing the public that this approach would work to help urban education would be convincing the public that three- and four-year-old students are capable of real academic achievement and growth. Secondly, any program would have to be integrated with a state's current kindergarten curriculum. It would have to be comprehensive and focus on building a logical set of skills in a logical manner for kindergarten preparation. All of the examined research showed that there was retention loss in programs that were not comprehensive, and integrated with state curriculum. It would be the responsibility of the state to establish a pre-k curriculum and hold schools accountable for meeting these standards.

Lastly, research showed that the programs provided in public school settings were the most effective in closing the achievement gap, yet there are already Head Start and other child care facilities in existence. This could be resolved by requiring any pre-k program that operated on any state and federal funding to follow the same curriculum and maintain the same qualifications for staffing. This would help to ensure consistency across a wide variety of facilities providing the same service.

ANTICIPATED OUTCOMES

Jean Anyon made a point in her book Radical Possibilities that maybe more important than the change that you wish to make in society, is the time at which you should try to make it. She discussed the importance of gauging the "mood" and political climate of the country, and using these moods to your advantage. Regarding the proposal of an "urbanversal" education program, this is very true. The question that one would have to consider is, do people care enough about education, especially urban education, to go through with a policy initiative this aggressive? The number one criticism of this program would be the lack of equality. Suburban, predominantly White districts would be slighted, and will question the fairness of an educational program only for urban school districts. Dr. Anyon and summer institute speaker Dr. Petrosino would scoff at this proposal, claiming that White corporate America would never allow the Federal government (which they control) to fund such a program that runs counter to their interests. This is the dichotomy of urban education. Those not involved in it do not care enough about it to institute change, and those who are involved in it are so distrustful of the only institution, the Federal government, that can hope to bring about real reform to effectively petition for change. How can real reform happen given this ideological climate?

In our history, issues of equity such as segregation and voting rights have a way of working themselves out given time. The inequity in urban education may be exactly the same. Just as it took *Brown v. Board* to begin the end of segregation, a major court case may be required to bring serious reform to urban education. In 1998 the State Supreme Court of New Jersey ruled in *Abbott v. Burke* that the state's current system of educational funding was unconstitutional (http://www.state.nj.us/education/abbotts/dec/). The decision was based on the belief that New Jersey's allocation of funds did not equitably address the educational disadvantages facing children attending schools in poor urban districts. (http://www.state.nj.us/education/abbotts/dec/) As a part of this decision to make funding more equitable, the New Jersey Commissioner of Education was ordered to implement half-day pre-k programs for three- and four-year-old students as expeditiously as possible (http://www.state.nj.us/education/abbotts/dec/). As a result of this decision New Jersey now has full-day, year round pre-k programs in the 31 lowest income districts in the state (http://www.preknow.org/resource/profiles/newjersey.cfm). These programs are staffed by high quality teachers, who must have a bachelor's degree and an early childhood education certificate. These programs also follow approved state curriculum and have set class sizes of 15 students (http://www.preknow.org/resource/profiles/newjersey.cfm). In addition to these "Abbott Programs," the state of New Jersey has expanded their funding of pre-k and 100 additional pre-k programs now exist in other districts (http://www.preknow.org/resource/profiles/newjersey.cfm). These improvements have made New Jersey one of the national leaders in pre-k, and it happened in only eight years. New Jersey's addressing of the inequity in education is a microcosm of what may have to happen at the Federal level for nationwide urban educational reform to take place.

For a major political change like what happened in New Jersey to happen in the United States, people and leadership (who should be the same!) must first know the causes and nature of the problem. We must raise our awareness to the problem in urban education and the achievement gap that plagues our system. This awareness has to come from any and all stakeholders in urban education, teachers, administrators, community action groups, and most of all special interest groups. Like it or not, special interest groups wield tremendous power over our government and nearly every conceivable interest has an organization. Yet in researching, no truly prominent special interests dedicated to urban education reform could be found. Shocking, considering the magnitude of this issue. Perhaps it is up to groups like Al Sharpton's National Action Network or the NAACP to make urban education reform and the achievement gap a focus. Recent history has proven that these groups have the organization, funding, following and thus power to make people and government take notice. For true reform to happen, we as a nation must begin associating "failing" schools with the real source of the problem, which is much more than a lack of accountability or standards addressed by our current educational policy.

Governments are a reflection of the general attitude of a society. Societies that are ignorant or apathetic are ruled over by their governments, whereas those societies that care and are informed, rule themselves. America is no different, just simply caught somewhere in the middle. American people are very reactionary, and thus so are our governments. We wait until problems arise, and then usually wait longer until problems cause some type of serious, noticeable damage. Then and only then do we address the issue, typically with solutions that are based on the short term, aimed at giving immediate results. This attitude may explain why in 230 years of our existence we have been involved in 12 major military conflicts, and why we are willing to pay 9 billion dollars a month for a war, and only 18 billion dollars a year on the education of our preschool children. This reactionary attitude makes it nearly impossible to prioritize the needs of a society.

In order to truly reform urban education, we need to be proactive. We need to address the root of the problem rather than try to teach skills to students that don't have the educational basis to understand those skills. If we do not address the achievement gap that everyone can agree exists, other programs are a waste. We can collect all the data in the world to prove that an achievement gap exists, and to prove the effectiveness of pre-k programs, but until we as a society can accept the fact that urban education can not be fixed in the short term, true reform will not take place. This ideology is the real barrier to urban reform.

REFERENCES

Barnett, W. S., & Hustedt, J. T. (2003). Preschool: The most important grade. *Educational Leadership 60*, 54–57.

Clothier, S., Clemens, B., & Poppe, J. (2003). Financing early care and education: Funding and policy choices in a changing fiscal environment. *Elementary and Early Childhood Education, 12*.

Ewen, D., & Neas, K. B. (2005). *Preparing for success: How Head Start helps children with disabilities and their families.* Washington, DC: Center for Law and Social Policy.

Gold, E., Hartmann, T., & Lewis, K. (2005). *Children and families first: An evaluation of the Philadelphia Say Yes to Education program.* Philadelphia, PA: Research for Action Philadelphia.

Gormley, W. T., & Phillips, D. (2003). *The effects of universal pre-k in Oklahoma: Research highlights and policy implications* (Working Paper #2). Washington, DC: Public Policy Institute, Georgetown University.

Henry, G. T., Henderson, L.W., Ponder, B. D., Gordon, C. S., Mashburn, A. J., & Rickman, D.K. (2003). *Report of the findings from the Early Childhood Study: 2001–02.* Atlanta, GA: Andrew Young School of Policy Studies, Georgia State University.

Kafer, K. (2004).A Head Start for poor children? *Backgrounder,1755.* Issues in Education. http://www.heritage.org/Research/Education/bg1755.cfm.

Maeroff, G. (2003). *First things first: Pre-kindergarten as a starting point for education reform.* New York: Foundation for Child Development.

Mitchell, A. (2001). Prekindergarten programs in the states: Trends and issues. *Elementary and Early Childhood Education.* Climax, NY: Early Childhood Policy Research.

Office of the Assistant Secretary for Planning and Evaluation (DHHS). (2003). *Strengthening Head Start: What the evidence shows.* (BBB19057). Washington, DC: U.S. Department of Education.

Pre-K Now Resource Center. (2006). Retrieved April 10, 2007, from the Pre-K Now Web site: http://www.preknow.org/resource/profiles/newjersey.cfm

Schumacher, R., Ewen, D., Hart, K., & Lombardi, J. (2005). *All together now: State experiences in using community-based child care to provide pre-kindergarten.* Washington, DC: Center for Law and Social Policy.

State of New Jersey. (2006). Department of Education. Retrieved April 10, 2007, from the State of New Jersey Web site: http://www.state.nj.us/education/abbotts/dec/

Strengthening Head Start. (2003). Good start, grow smart: The Bush administration's early childhood initiative. Available at: http://www.whitehouse.gov/infocus/earlychildhood/sect5.html. Washington, DC: U.S. Government.

Taylor, B.A., Dearing, E., & McCartney, K. (2004). Incomes and outcomes in early childhood. *Journal of Human Resources, 39,* 980.

U.S. Department of Education. (2005). *Regional differences in kindergartners' early education experiences. Statistics in brief. NCES 2005.* Washington, DC: National Center for Education Statistics (NCES).

U.S. Department of Health and Human Services. (2005). Administration for Children and Families. Retrieved August 5, 2006, from Office of Head Start Web site: http://www.acf.hhs.gov/programs/hsb/research/factsheets.htm

U.S. Government Accountability Office. (2004). *Head Start: Better data and processes needed to monitor underenrollment. Report to Congressional requesters.* (GAO-04-17). Washington, DC: General Accounting Office.

ABOUT THE CONTRIBUTORS

Donald J. Anticoli is the Principal of Penn Treaty Middle School in Philadelphia, Pennsylvania. Penn Treaty is one 150 schools in the United States participating in the Edison Partnership.

Diane Bowen has over twenty-five years in the field of education. She is a former school principal and is currently teaching at-risk students in an "empowered" urban school district.

Roger Cadenhead is the Director of Curriculum and Instruction at Wordsworth Academy in Harrisburg, Pennsylvania. He is a doctoral student in Educational Leadership at Temple University. He has worked extensively with at-risk students in urban settings.

Bruce Campbell has taught at the post secondary level in urban settings in the United States and Latin America. He also conducts research and evaluation in K–16 learning communities, and is currently a distinguished educator with the Pennsylvania Department of Education.

David M. Gates is a former public school teacher and English department chair. David is a consultant for Pennsylvania's Classrooms for the Future initiative. In addition to assisting with the incorporation of technology into high school curricula, he also teaches graduate courses in education policy and governance.

Mark Hoff currently teaches World Cultures to eleventh grade students in Bucks County, Pennsylvania. He is a member of the National Council

Policy, Leadership, and Student Achievement, pages 269–271
Copyright © 2008 by Information Age Publishing
269

for the Social Studies and the Association for Supervision and Curriculum Development.

Vivian Ikpa is an associate professor of educational leadership and policy studies at Temple University. Her research is focused on education policy and the achievement gap.

Debra L. Johnson has held a position as an adjunct professor at Bucks County Community College. Previously, she co-owned and operated a private nursery school. She is the director of a daycare center in Philadelphia.

Greg Kratzer is a graduate student at Temple University enrolled in the Educational Administration program. He is a Social Studies teacher at the Lower Dauphin school district in Hummelstown, Pennsylvania.

Kimberly Matthews currently works as a classroom teacher in an urban school district in central Pennsylvania.

C. Kent McGuire is the Dean of the College of Education and Professor of Educational Leadership and Policy Studies at Temple University. He conducts research in the areas of education policy and school governance.

Roselyn U. Obi is professor of educational psychology in the Education Department at New Jersey City University. Her chief research areas are centered around adult learning, mentoring, teacher identity and development.

Jeannette Perez is an Academic Adviser and Recruiter for the College of Education at Temple University. She is one of the founders and coordinators of the Latino Heritage Celebration Committee for the University.

Charlyene C. Pinckney served as the operations manager of the Accountability Block Grant Program at the Pennsylvania Department of Education in Harrisburg, PA. She also worked as an administration specialist for the PA State Board of Postsecondary Private Licensed Schools, as well as an assessment advisor within the Bureau of Teacher Certification and Preparation.

Oscar Torres' teaching career has taken him to urban, suburban, private and independent schools. As a curriculum Supervisor for the Tredyffrin/ Easttown School District, he continues to impact students through his training of teachers and curriculum development.

York Williams is an Assistant Professor of Elementary and Special Education at Lincoln University, and Director of Teaching and Learning Enhancement. He conducts research primarily in gifted/special education and urban school choice reform.

Laurie Zaring received a Masters Degree in Educational Leadership from Temple University. She currently works as a classroom teacher in an urban school district in central Pennsylvania.

213 820

Breinigsville, PA USA
24 January 2010

231256BV00002B/53/P